A History of

By
George Stephen Goodspeed

PREFACE

THE preparation of this volume has occupied a much longer time than was anticipated when the invitation of the editors to contribute to this series was accepted. The new materials, constantly supplied by the indefatigable activity of excavators and by the scientific investigation of philological and historical scholars, require the unceasing adjustment, enlargement, and revision of historical conclusions, and force one quite to despair of reaching anything like finality. The historian of Babylonia and Assyria, therefore, must be satisfied to sum up fairly and fully the information at present in hand without undue appreciation of new and tentative theories. Accordingly, the present work finds its justification in the desirability of putting a compact, popular, and fairly comprehensive sketch of the history of these ancient states, as it is to-day conceived, into the hands of all who are interested in the progress of human civilization in its earliest stages, and especially in the development of the peoples who came into so close relations with the Hebrews. It is becoming increasingly evident that the Old Testament in all its elements — literary, historical, and religious — cannot be adequately understood without relating them to the history of all the peoples round about Israel, and especially to that of the Babylonians and Assyrians, who exercised so potent and permanent an influence upon the fortunes and the thoughts of the Chosen People.

A word is desirable concerning some special features of the book.

(1) The "Bibliography" does not pretend to he complete, but only to contain the outstanding works in the vast field.

(2) The "References" are intended not merely to aid the reader in widening the range of his knowledge of facts and details concerning the subject under consideration, but also to guide him in special investigation of important topics.

(3) The spelling of the proper names does not rigidly follow any body of principles. When a name has become domesticated in a popular form, that form has usually been chosen. Otherwise it has been sought to give an orthographically accurate reproduction of the original. Often, at the first use of a name, hyphens have been employed to indicate its component parts. In the index of persons and places, an attempt, doubtless quite imperfect, has been made to indicate the proper pronunciation of each name. No one can be more cognizant than the author of the inadequate results achieved in respect to the whole matter.

(4) The map has been prepared with the purpose of indicating the larger number of the places mentioned in the text. Accordingly, some localities, the positions of which with our present knowledge can be determined only tentatively, have been set down with what may seem to scholars not a little audacity. The desirability of being able to follow the description of a campaign or to fix the location of a city mentioned has induced me to run the risk of seeming to be wise above what is known.

My obligations to the scholars who for half a century have been working in the Assyriological field are manifest on every page of this work. Special mention should, however, be made where unusual service has been rendered, although I despair of making anything like complete acknowledgment. Abundant use has been made of the admirable series of translations contained in the Assyrian and Babylonian Literature, edited by Professor R. F. Harper. I am grateful to my colleague and friend, Professor Harper, for the cordial way in which he has assented to my request to employ these translations. To my colleagues, Professors Ira M. Price and Benjamin Terry, who have read the proofs of the work throughout with critical and painstaking zeal, I am indebted far more than words can express for their invaluable assistance. I am likewise under obligation to my uncle, Dr. T., W. Goodspeed, who has rendered a similar service in connection with the manuscript. I have been favored with the generous help of another colleague, Professor W. Muss-Arnolt, who has placed at my disposal his admirable bibliographical knowledge and his wide and thorough acquaintance with the Assyrian field. If the work shall be found to represent, in some approximate measure, the present standard of Assyriological science, and to be reasonably free from faults of expression, the result is due in large part to the genial and sympathetic service of these friends, although they are not to be held accountable for either its defects or its opinions. To the editors of the series to which the volume belongs I would express my thanks for their encouragement and criticism in the course of its preparation; to the publishers, Messrs. Charles Scribner's Sons, for their generous co-operation in securing its typographical excellence, and to the many friends who have shown so warm an interest in the appearance of the book. I hope that to some extent it may serve the cause of sound learning, and be worthy, both in spirit and content, to stand beside the preceding volumes of the series.

G. S. G.
THE UNIVERSITY OF CHICAGO,
August, 1902.
Since the appearance of the first edition of this book some new discoveries have been made, chief among which has been that of the Stele of Khammurabi. This important document has not, however, caused any material correction in our views of Babylonian life and history, but merely enlarged the details of our knowledge. Time has not permitted, nor has necessity required, any considerable changes in the text of this volume. Some " Additions and Corrections" to the first edition will be found on page xiv. For most of the emendations the author is indebted to reviewers, whose interest in the volume, in most cases friendly, he here acknowledges heartily, and particularly to his colleague, Dr. J. M. P. Smith, who has placed at the author's disposal the results of a careful reading of the pages of the first edition.

G. S. G. December, 1903.

INTRODUCTION

I .THE LANDS OF THE EUPHRATES AND TIGRIS

1. IN the lofty table-land of Armenia, lying some seven thousand feet above sea level, and guarded on the south by mountain walls, the rivers Tigris and Euphrates have their origin. Breaking through the southern range, the one stream on its eastern, the other on its western flank, they flow at first speedily down a steep incline from an altitude of eleven hundred feet in a general southeasterly direction, draw closer to one another as they descend, and, after traversing a region measuring as the crow flies over eight hundred miles in length, issue as one stream into the Persian gulf. This region from the northern mountains to the southern sea, dominated and nourished by the two rivers, is the scene of the historical development to be traced in this volume. A striking difference in geological structure divides it into two parts of nearly equal length. For the first four hundred miles the country falls off from the mountains in a gentle slope. The difference in elevation between the northern and southern extremities aggregates about a thousand feet. A plain of "secondary formation" is thus made, composed of limestone and selenite, through which the rivers have cut their way. From this point to the gulf succeeds a flat alluvial district, the product of the deposit of the rivers, made up of sand, pebbles, clay, and loam, upon which the rivers have built their channels and over which they spread their waters in the season of inundation.

2. The former of these two divisions was called by the Greeks Mesopotamia, a term which they probably borrowed from the Semites, to whom the district, or at least a part of it, was known in Hebrew phrase as Aram naharayim, "Aram of the two rivers," or to the Arameans as Bêth naharîn, "region (house) of the rivers." Marked out by the rivers and the northern mountains into an irregular triangle, drifting out over the Euphrates into the desert on the southwest, and rising over the Tigris to the Zagros mountains on the east and northeast, this region occupies an area of more than fifty-five thousand square miles, in size about equal to the State of Illinois. Its physical contour and characteristics separate it into two fairly well-defined districts. In the northern and higher portion, isolated ranges, thrown off from the central chains, diversify the plain, which is watered by the mountain streams gathering into rivers of considerable size, like the Balikh and the Khabur. Limestone and, in some places, volcanic rock form the basis of a fertile soil. South and southeast of the Khabur the waters cease, gypsum and marl predominate, and the plain, down to the beginning of the alluvium, becomes a veritable steppe, the home of wandering Bedouin. The northern part, at least that west and north of the Khabur, was probably the region known to the Egyptians as Nahrina, and in the Roman period constituted the province of Mesopotamia. On the other hand, Xenophon seems to call the southern portion Arabia; the term is a striking evidence of the character of the district as steppe land, hardly to be distinguished from the western desert, and Occupied by the same wandering tribes.

3. The second and southern division of the great Tigro-Euphrates valley is entirely the gift of the rivers, a shifting delta, over which they pour themselves from the higher and solider formation of Mesopotamia. The proximity of the mountains in the northeast gives the whole plain a southwestern slope with the result that the Euphrates has spread Over a portion of the southwestern desert and thereby added a considerable district to the proper alluvial region. Moreover, the process of land-making still continues in the south, the waters of the gulf being pushed back at the rate of about seventy-two feet every year. At present, this division comprises about thirty thousand square miles, but calculations, based upon the increase of the land about the Persian gulf, make it appear that in the ancient period it contained only twenty-three thousand square miles. Thus it was about equal in area to the southern half of the State of

Louisiana, which it also resembled in being largely made up of alluvial and swampy districts that are the deltas of river systems. It lay also between the same degrees of latitude (about 30-33° N.). This was the land known to the Greeks, from the name of its capital city, Babylon, as Babylonia. It is an "interminable moorland," slightly undulating in the central districts and falling away imperceptibly toward the south into swamps and marshes, where the waters of the rivers and the gulf meet and are indistinguishable. The plain also stretches away toward the east, as in Mesopotamia, beyond the Tigris for a distance of from thirty to fifty miles, until it meets the mountains; while, on the western side, across the Euphrates, it merges into the desert at a distance of twenty or thirty miles, where a line of low hills checks the river's overflow and gathers it into lakes and morasses.

4. In these regions of Mesopotamia and Babylonia, so diversified in physical characteristics, the one essential unifying element was the rivers. To them a large section of the land owed its existence; the fertility and the prosperity of the whole was dependent upon them; they were the chief means of communication, the main channels of trade, the distributors of civilization. It was in recognition of this that the ancient inhabitants called the Euphrates "the life of the land," and the Tigris "the bestower of blessing." Both are inundating rivers, nourished by mountain snows. Yet, though they lie so near together and finally become one, they exhibit many striking differences. The Euphrates is the longer. It rises on the northern side of the Taurus range and winds its way through the plateau in a southwesterly direction as though making for the Mediterranean which is only a hundred miles away. At about latitude 37° 30', it turns due south and breaks into the plain. It runs in this direction for a hundred miles, then bending around toward the east, finds at last its true southeastern course and, covering in all a distance of seventeen hundred and eighty miles, unites with the Tigris and the sea. Unlike most great rivers, its lower course is less full and majestic than its upper waters. In its passage through the Mesopotamian plain it receives but two tributaries, the Balikh and the Khabur, and these from the upper portion. Thereafter it makes its way alone between desert and steppe with waning power. From the mouth of the Khabur to the alluvium its width gradually diminishes from four hundred to two hundred and fifty yards; its velocity, from four to two and one half miles an hour. At the southern boundary of Mesopotamia it spreads out in canals and pools and swamps, some of its water reaching the Tigris; but it recovers its former greatness farther down, receiving in its turn contributions from its sister stream. The Tigris has its source on the southeastern slopes of the Taurus, and makes a much more direct and speedy journey to the sea. Its length is eleven hundred and forty-six miles; its depth, volume, and velocity much greater than those of the Euphrates. It receives numerous tributaries from the eastern mountains not far distant — in the north the Subnat, toward the middle of its course the upper and lower Zab, farther to the south the Turnat and the Radanu, — all streams of considerable size, which swell its waters as they descend The inundation of the Tigris begins earlier and is finished before that of the Euphrates. The latter, with its more northern source, rises more slowly and steadily, and its high waters continue longer. Accordingly, the whole inundation period, including that of both rivers, is spread over half the year, from March to September (Rawlinson, Five Great Monarchies, L pp. 12 f.). The water sometimes rises very high. Loftus, in the spring of 1849, found that the Tigris had risen twenty-two and one half feet, which was about five feet above the ordinary height (Chaldæa and Susiana, P. 7).

5. In consequence of the pouring down of these immense volumes of water, the rivers have dug channels through the rock of the Mesopotamian plain. The Euphrates, in particular, flows through a canyon from two to three miles wide and sunk from one hundred to three hundred feet below the surface of the steppe. On the flats at the base of the cliffs, and on the islands in mid-stream, thick groves of tamarisk alternate with patches of arable land, where usually stand the few towns which the traveller finds in his journey along the river and which constitute the stations of his pilgrimage. Likewise, the streams running into the Tigris are said to burrow

deep in the marl, forming ditches in the plateau, difficult to cross. In the alluvial region, on the other hand, the rivers raise themselves above the surrounding country, while hollowing out their beds, so that to-day the sides of the ancient canals rise like formidable ridges across the level plain and their dry beds form the most convenient roads for the caravans.

6. Mesopotamia and Babylonia, although lying between latitude 31° and 37°, do not show climatic conditions so widely diverse as might be expected. The year is divided into two seasons. From November to March the rains fall; then the drought ensues. The heat in summer is oppressive throughout the entire valley, and, when the frequent sand storms from Arabia are raging, is almost unbearable. The rainy season shows greater diversity of temperature. The northern plain, cut off from the mild airs of the Mediterranean by the western ranges, is exposed to the wintry blasts of the northern mountains. Snow and ice are not uncommon. In Babylonia, however, frost is rarely experienced. It is probable that, when the canals distributed the waters more generally over the surface of the country, the extremes of temperature were greatly reduced. Even in modern times, travellers in Babylonia speak of the remarkable dryness and regularity of the climate, the serenity of the sky and the transparency of the air, the wonderful starlight, soft and enveloping, and the coolness of the nights, even in the hot season.

7. The fertility of Babylonia was the wonder of the ancient world. The classical passage of Herodotus is still the best description: "This territory is of all that we know the best by far for producing grain; as to trees, it does not even attempt to bear them, either fig or vine or olive, but for producing grain it is so good that it returns as much as two hundred-fold for the average, and, when it bears at its best, it produces three hundred-fold. The blades of the wheat and barley there grow to be full four fingers broad; and from millet and sesame seed, how large a tree grows, I know myself, but shall not record, being well aware that even what has already been said relating to the crops produced has been enough to cause disbelief in those who have not visited Babylonia" (Herod., I. 193). This marvellous yield, however, was under the hand of man, who by a system of canals brought the water of the rivers over every foot of ground. Apart from that, the land, rich as was its soil, lay exposed to floods in the winter and to parching heat and desert sand in the summer. Thick masses of reeds, springing up in the water-courses, produced morasses. The absence of trees of any size was a serious defect. To man, also, is due the introduction of the date-palm, the fig, and the vine, the two former flourishing in splendid luxuriance along the banks of the Euphrates, the vine, indeed, cultivated so little as almost to warrant the statement of Herodotus just cited. As one advances northward upon the steppe, a treeless waste appears, stretching up to the Khabur, There are traces of former agricultural activity, but now all is barren, except in the trenches hollowed out by the great rivers. On the Euphrates side the palm has pushed northward, and groves of tamarisk and fields of grain are seen. The land east of the Tigris and that north of the Khabur, indeed, being watered, are productive. Traces of extensive forests have been found in some parts, and these regions still support an agricultural population of considerable size, by whom rice, millet, sesame, wheat, and barley are cultivated. Here, in the north, are grown a variety of small fruits, melons, peas, and cucumbers, as well as figs. Throughout the whole of Mesopotamia, indeed, the winter rains call forth a carpet of verdure "enlivened by flowers of every hue," but the heat of summer soon scorches the earth, and all cultures disappear where irrigation, natural or artificial, is not secured.

8. Over these Mesopotamian plains roamed the gazelle and the wild ass, while in the reed-thickets of the river banks the lion, the wild ox, and the wild boar were found. Once, too, the ostrich and the elephant were hunted in Mesopotamia. The rivers swarmed with fish, and in their swamps waterfowl abounded. To man is due the introduction of the domestic animals. The camel came with the Bedouin from the desert, as also his flocks of sheep and goats, The

horse is the "animal from the east." The dog was likewise imported.

9. There was neither metal nor stone to be found in all the borders of Babylonia. Northern Mesopotamia was better supplied because of neighboring mountains. From them were procured limestone and basalt, marble and alabaster. Copper and lead were obtained from the same source, as well as iron. The waters of the steppe supplied salt. In both north and south a substance was found which made the region famous in the ancient world. This was bitumen. On the northern edge of the alluvium, at the modern town of Hit on the Euphrates, were the renowned bitumen springs. A recent traveller describes them as follows: "Directly behind the town are two springs within thirty feet of one another, from one of which flows hot water, black with bitumen, while the other discharges intermittently bitumen, or, after a rainstorm, bitumen and cold water. . . . Where rocks crop out in the plain about Hit, they are full of seams of bitumen" (Peters, Nippur, I. p. 160). The less known bitumen wells of the north are on the plain east of the Tigris at the modern Karduk.

10. The present condition of these lands illustrates their primitive aspects. The alluvial deposits, indeed, have steadily pushed back the waters of the gulf which once washed the shores of Mesopotamia, but the rivers still pour their turbid floods through the gypsum canyons and overspread the lowlands in times of inundation. Traces of human occupation and activity intensify the impression of the recurrence of nature's former supremacy. Canals have silted up and at their mouths, where the water gathers in the pools, luxuriant wild growths of reeds and rushes flourish in the slime. The sand swirls unhindered over the steppe and heaps up about the mounds where once cities stood. Lions lurk in the jungles, and wandering Arabs camp over the plains. Extremes of heat and cold alternately parch and freeze the ground. Fevers hang about the marshes, and the pestilence breeds in the lagoons. The Tigris and the Euphrates, now flowing between "avenues of ruins," sweep away dykes, once reared to curb the power of these mighty streams, tear down their banks, once lined with palaces, riot at their will through channels made by their own irresistible waters, and bring with them the deposits of the mountain sides to enrich the soil of their deltas. A country of still splendid possibilities, destined sometime again to be the highway of the nations, it is a speaking testimony to the power of man. Before his advent it was uninhabitable and wild. When he had subdued it and cultivated it, it was the garden of the earth, the seat and the symbol of Paradise,

11. The valley of the Tigris and Euphrates was anything but an isolated region. Unlike Egypt, it was open on almost every side. On the south, was the Persian gulf, along whose western shore lay the rich coasts of Oman, opening into southern Arabia, and beyond them, to the far southeast, India. To the east rose the massive and complex ranges of Zagros, over which led the passes up to the eastern plateau, and from whose heights the descent was easy, by pleasant stages of hill and plain, into the fertile Babylonian bottoms. Northward was the same mountain wall, behind which stretched out the high and diversified Armenian plateau, with its lakes and fertile valleys, opened up by the upper reaches of the Tigris and its tributaries. Westward the plain melted into the Arabian desert, except at the upper extremity, where the Euphrates swung around by the slopes of the Syrian hills, and thus made the highway into the regions watered by the moist wind of the Mediterranean, — into Syria and Palestine and to the islands of the sea.

12. Such was the theatre of the activities of the peoples who made the earliest history of mankind and about whom centred the life of the ancient East. The land was admirably fitted, nay, rather, predestined, by its physical characteristics and position to produce and foster such a history. A world in itself, it lay in close touch, in unavoidable contact, with the larger world on every side, upon whose destinies its inhabitants were to exercise so impressive and so permanent an influence.

II.THE EXCAVATIONS IN BABYLONIA AND ASSYRIA

13. THE kingdoms which in the regions just described flourished during the millenniums of the world's youth, while they left a deep impression upon the imagination of later ages, were cut off suddenly and by an alien race, at a time when interest in preserving the annals of the past by means of historical narrative had not yet been born among men. Their names appeared in the records of that Jewish people which, though conquered by them, had outlived its masters, or survived in traditions which magnified and distorted the achievements of kings who had flourished during some brief years of Babylonio-Assyrian history. Soon the centre of human progress passed from the Mesopotamian valley westward to the regions of southern Europe. Assyria and Babylonia were forgotten. Their cities, too, reared upon platforms of sun-dried bricks, and raised in solid masses of the same fragile material to no great height, had been ruined by fire and sword, and gradually melted away under the disintegrating forces of nature until they became huge and shapeless mounds of earth without anything to identify them as having been once the abodes of men. The impression made by these ruins has been strikingly described by Layard:

[The observer] is now at a loss to give any form to the rude heaps upon which he is gazing. Those of whose works they are the remains, unlike the Roman and the Greek, have left no visible traces of their civilization, or of their arts: their influence has long since passed away. The more he conjectures, the more vague the results appear. The scene around is worthy of the ruin he is contemplating; desolation meets desolation; a feeling of awe succeeds to wonder; for there is nothing to relieve the mind, to lead to hope, or to tell of what has gone by. These huge mounds of Assyria made a deeper impression upon me, gave rise to more serious thought and more earnest reflection, than the temples of Balbec or the theatres of Ionia (Nineveh and its Remains, I. p. 29).

14. It is not surprising, therefore, that men came to have only vague and often fantastic notions of these ancient empires, and that the very sites of their long famous capitals were lost. For fifteen hundred years Nineveh was but a name. Babylon came to be identified with Bagdad on the Tigris, or with the ruin-heap, not far distant, at Akerkuf. Here and there was a traveller, like the Jew, Benjamin of Tudela, Who in 1160 visited Mosul and beheld on the other side of the Tigris what he thought to be the site of Nineveh, and at a three days' journey from Bagdad found, near Hillah on the Euphrates, ruins identified by him with those of Babylon and of the tower of Babel. Both of these sites afterwards were proved to be the true locations of these cities. European geographers, even at the end of the sixteenth century, were in complete uncertainty on the subject. A century and a half passed before trustworthy scientific observations were made and the Preparatory Period (1750-1820 A. D.) of Babylonio-Assyrian investigation began.

15. In 1755 the French Academy of Inscriptions received a memoir which, based primarily on a report of the Carmelite, Emmanuel de St. Albert, gathered together the various lines of evidence to prove that the true site of Babylon was near the town of Hillah on the Euphrates, and that Birs Nimrud, on the opposite side of the river, was part of the same city. Ten years later, Carsten Niebuhr, a scholar, historian, and traveller, definitely identified the ruin-mounds opposite Mosul with the ancient Nineveh, and made further observations on the site of Babylon. He also called attention to an extensive mound, called Nimrud, some fifteen miles south of Nineveh. All these travellers, and others who followed them, noted the masses of brickwork cropping out above the ground, the immense fields of débris that covered the

mounds, and the traces of strange characters found upon bricks and other objects that lay upon the surface. It could not but be evident that further progress in discovering the secrets of these cities lay, on the one hand, in going beneath the surface, in searching these mounds with the spade, and, on the other, in the study of the inscriptions With the purpose of deciphering their meaning. Both these activities henceforth Were pursued with vigor. The excavation of the cities of Babylonia and Assyria and the decipherment of their language form two brilliant pages in the scientific annals of the nineteenth century.

16. The pioneer in this new work of excavation was Claudius James Rich, who, while resident of the British East India Company in Bagdad, in 1811, visited and studied the ruins of Babylon, and, beginning in 1820, made similar investigations of the mounds of Nineveh. In these visits he made surveys, opened trenches, and prepared careful plans of the sites. He afterwards published his results in memoirs. The inscriptions, engraved gems, and other objects gathered by him in these researches were forwarded to England and deposited in the British Museum, forming at that time the most considerable collection of the kind in the world. Some years before, the British East India Company had ordered its representatives in Babylonia to gather and forward to England ancient Babylonian antiquities, and among the objects obtained was the now famous cylinder of Nebuchadrezzar II., known as the East India House inscription. Michaux, a French botanist, working in the vicinity of Ctesiphon a little before 1802, had chanced upon a marble object marked with strange signs and figures. It proved to be a fine "boundary stone" with an inscription of Mardukbaliddin I. Yet so inconsiderable were all these objects that Layard was justified in his statement, made about 1845, that four years before "a case scarcely three feet square inclosed all that remained, not only of the great city, Nineveh, but of Babylon itself!" (Nin. and its Rem., I. p. 17). Rich's results aroused wide-spread interest, not only in England, but in America. In 1849 Edward Robinson, referring to them, declared, "we can all remember the profound impression made upon the public mind, even by these cursory memorials of Nineveh and Babylon" (Preface to American ed. of Layard's Nin. and its Rem.). Twenty years were to pass before this interest was to issue in practical activity, years filled indeed with the work of scholars, seeking to solve the riddle of the language of the inscriptions, and particularly with the splendid labor of Sir Henry Rawlinson in copying and studying the Behistun inscriptions of Persia. During this time, however, the mounds of Mesopotamia were untouched.

17. In 1842, P. C. Botta was sent from France as consul to Mosul, and with his arrival begins a new period (1842-1854) which, by reason of the character both of the work and the workers, may be termed the Heroic Period of excavation. Botta began digging on the two great mounds of Nineveh, marked off by Rich, and called Nebiyunus and Kouyunjik. Failing of success here, in 1843, at the suggestion of a peasant, he removed to Khorsabad, a mound about four miles to the northeast, where his digging immediately resulted in the discovery of a series of buildings of great extent, adorned with wonderful sculptures, though in parts damaged by fire. The site proved to be Dur Sharrukin, a fortress, palace, and temple of Sargon, Assyria's greatest king. Botta and his successor, Victor Place, spent more than ten years in uncovering this palace and working upon other neighboring sites. The material was sent to Paris, and constitutes one of the chief treasures of the Louvre. In 1845, A. H. Layard, an English traveller and government official, familiar by many years of wandering in the Orient with the peoples and languages of Mesopotamia, was enabled, through the munificence of the English minister at Constantinople, to fulfil a long-cherished desire by beginning excavations in this region. He chose the mound of Nimrud, fifteen miles south of Nineveh. Here, within two years (1845-1847), he unearthed three palaces belonging, respectively, to Ashurnaçirpal, Shalmaneser II., and Esarhaddon, in one of which was found the famous black obelisk that contains the name of Jehu of Israel. The site itself was found to be the city of Kalkhi (Calah), made the capital of Assyria by Shalmaneser I. During the years 1849-1851 Layard devoted himself to the two

mounds of Nineveh, and uncovered at Kouyunjik the palace of Sennacherib, and at Nebiyunus those of Adadnirari III,, Sennacherib, and Esarhaddon. In the spring of 1852 his excavations, pursued at Kalah Sherghat, forty miles south of Nimrud, resulted in the identification of that mound as Assur, the earliest Assyrian capital, and the discovery of the cylinder inscription of Tiglathpileser I, Layard's work was continued from 1852 to 1854 by Hormuzd Rassam, his assistant, who opened the palace of Tiglathpileser I. at Assur and obtained two other copies of his cylinder inscription. At Nineveh he discovered in 1853, on the northern part of the mound Kouyunjik, the palace of Ashurbanipal, from one chamber of which he removed the famous library of over twenty thousand tablets. Nimrud yielded to him the Shamshi Adad monolith, and Nineveh, also, the two obelisks of Ashurnaçirpal. The larger part of the objects obtained by both Layard and Rassam was sent to the British Museum, and became the basis of its incomparable collection of Assyrian antiquities.

18. In Babylonia, during these years, the work done was considerable, but not so brilliant in results. Layard visited Babylonia in 1851, and experimented with diggings at Babylon and Niffer, the ancient Nippur, with little success. From 1849 to 1854, with the exception of a year spent at Susa, W, K. Loftus worked on the mounds of Senkereh and Warka, the latter of which he identified beyond doubt with Uruk, the former being the ancient Larsam. From both cities he obtained metal and clay ornaments, and some choice clay tablets, besides coffins illustrative of the ancient methods of burial. In 1854 J. E. Taylor excavated at the ruins of a temple at Mugheir which was found to be the city of Ur, and at Abu Shahrein, identified with Eridu, the southernmost and oldest city of Babylonia. The same year Sir Henry Rawlinson, directing diggings at Birs Nimrud near Babylon, opened up the great temple there, and obtained from its foundations some cylinder inscriptions of Nebuchadrezzar II. A French expedition led by Fresnel and Oppert was occupied from 1852 to 1854 in and around Babylon, the results of which, while not rich in objects obtained, were of special value for Babylonian topography. With the year 1854 the excavations halted. The twelve years had been productive of results brilliant beyond all expectation. These had been gained in large measure by men who labored for the most part alone, having usually small sums of money available, hindered and harassed on every side by fever, famine, and flood, by attacks of Arabs, by the outbreaks of fanatical populations, and by the stolid obstinacy and arrant cupidity of Turkish officials, — obstacles which would have daunted less resolute and enthusiastic workers.

19. Another gap of two decades now intervened. The vast mass of material accumulated by the excavators had satiated the appetite. A new world of ancient life had, within a short space of twelve years, been thrown open to science, — a world speaking an unknown tongue and revealing a great, but strange, literature, architecture, and art. The demand was for the study of what was already in hand, not for the search after new things; for the organization and publication of the results of excavation, not for the further heaping up of what could not be understood. These decades saw the issue of the first three volumes of "The Cuneiform Inscriptions of Western Asia," edited for the British Museum by Sir Henry Rawlinson, — an indispensable companion for all future students. During the same period, also, the secret of the language was penetrated, and Assyrian documents were being read with increasing ease and accuracy.

20. In 1873 the revival of excavation began with the expedition of George Smith to Nineveh. His purpose illustrates the new point of view reached during the intervening decades. Among the clay tablets brought back by Rassam from Ashurbanipal's library, were fragments of the Babylonian story of the Deluge. These, as translated by George Smith, aroused immense interest, which led to the desire that search be made for the missing fragments. The explorers of the Heroic Period had uncovered palaces, bas-reliefs, and statues, but had given the insignificant tablets secondary consideration. From the library chamber of Ashurbanipal's

palace Rassam had extracted only those tablets which could be conveniently reached. With the power to read attained mean while, the tablets had become fully as important as the sculptures, if not more so. George Smith's expedition indicated, therefore, that the Modern Scientific Period of excavation had begun. Its end is not yet in sight, since its goal is the investigation of all feasible localities in the Mesopotamian valley, with the purpose of throwing all available light upon the history and life of these ancient peoples. Another characteristic of this period is the careful selection of locations, and the studied organization of parties of excavators, well financed and provided with all desirable tools for investigation. The results have already been startling. George Smith's work, begun in 1873, was continued in 1874 and 1876. In that year, on his return from Nineveh, he died at Aleppo, a martyr to his self-sacrificing devotion to his task. He had obtained many more books from the Ashurbanipal library, including some of the precious Deluge fragments, and had purchased for the British Museum some valuable tablets from Babylonia. H. Rassam, the veteran of the earlier period, was sent out to take his place. From 1877 to 1882 he had great success. In Assyria his chief " finds " were the Ashurnaçirpal temple in Nimrud, the splendid cylinder of Ashurbanipal at Kouyunjik, and the unique and historically important bronze doors of the temple of Shalmaneser II., found at Balawat, fifteen miles east of Mosul. His work in Babylonia was equally brilliant. At Babylon, the problem of the location of the ancient buildings in the different mounds, a subject beset with extraordinary difficulties, was attacked by him, and he identified the famous Hanging Gardens with the mound known as Babil. A palace of Nebuchadrezzar II. at Birs Nimrud (Borsippa) was also uncovered by him. His excavations at Tell Ibrahim proved that it was the site of the ancient city of Kutha. An experimental examination of the mound at Abu Habba, in 1881, opened up to this fortunate excavator the famous temple of the sun at Sippar. There he found cylinders of Nabuna'id (Nabonidus), and the stone tablet of Nabu-apal-iddin of Babylon with its ritual bas-relief and inscription, besides some fifty thousand clay tablets containing the temple accounts.

21. Within recent years, beginning in 1877, a series of discoveries of first-rate importance has been made by the French consul at Bassorah, de Sarzec, in the Babylonian mound of Tello. He has identified this spot with the city of Shirpurla (Lagash), which had a prominent place in early Babylonian history. In the course of his several campaigns he has unearthed a truly bewildering variety of materials illustrative of these primitive ages. Palaces and statues, stelae and bas-reliefs, vases of silver, and a library containing as many as thirty thousand tablets, are among his treasures, which were purchased, or otherwise secured, by the French government for the Louvre Museum. Kings hitherto unknown, and a world of artistic achievement undreamed of for these early ages, have come into view. A similar result has followed the work of the American Expedition, under the auspices of the University of Pennsylvania, which began, in 1888, to excavate at Niffer, the site of old Nippur, a centre of early Babylonian religious life. The massive temple called Ekur has been uncovered, on which kings of all periods of Babylonian history built. During each successive year of the expedition's activity, new architectural and artistic features, and an increasing number of historical and religious records, have come to light. More than thirty thousand tablets have already been obtained, and the recent discovery of the great temple library opens up a wealth of material throwing light upon all sides of that ancient life over which hitherto there has lain almost complete darkness. The Turkish government, stimulated by the example of other nations, has begun to take steps to collect material for its museum at Constantinople, to protect its antiquities from destruction and removal, and to make excavations upon Assyrian and Babylonian soil. Work at Sippar in 1893 has resulted in the securing of a number of clay tablets; an important stele of Nabuna'id has been found at Babylon, and a bas-relief of Naram Sin, obtained at the head-waters of the Tigris, has been conveyed to the museum at Constantinople. A German expedition, excavating on the site of Babylon, has already made some important discoveries. Thus the interest in seeking for the original records of Assyrian and Babylonian civilization was never more keen and active than at the present day. Joined, as this interest is, to large resources and a scientific

temper, and enlightened by the experience of the past, it is destined to push the work of exploration and excavation in these countries to still further lengths, until, so far as lies in the power of the original records to furnish material, the history and life of these peoples become as well known as are those of Greece and Rome.

III.THE LANGUAGE AND LITERATURE

22. THE discoverers of the long-buried memorials of Assyria and Babylonia were at first and for a long time unable to read their message. But side by side with the work of the explorer and excavator went continually the investigations of the scholar. The objects sent back by European excavators and installed in museums immediately attracted the attention and enlisted the energetic activity of many students, who gave themselves to the task Of decipherment. Beginning with Georg Friedrich Grotefend, of Hannover, who, in 1815, published a translation of some brief inscriptions of the Achemænian kings of Persia, this scientific activity was immensely stimulated by the discoveries and investigations of Sir Henry Rawlinson, who, after more than fifteen years of study in the East, published, in 1851, his "Memoir on the Babylonian and Assyrian Inscriptions" containing the text, transliteration, and translation of the Babylonian part of the Behistun inscription, which records the triumph of Darius I. of Persia over his enemies. During the same period the brilliant French savant Jules Oppert, the Irish scholar Edward Hincks, and the Englishman Fox Talbot had been making their contributions to the new linguistic problem, In 1857 the accuracy and permanence of their results were established by a striking test. Copies of the inscription of Tiglathpileser I. of Assyria, recently unearthed, were placed in the hands of the four scholars, Rawlinson, Oppert, Hincks, and Fox Talbot, and they were requested to make, independently of one another, translations of the inscription in question. A comparison of these translations showed them to be substantially identical. A new language had been deciphered, and a new chapter of human history opened for investigation. Since that time these and other scholars, such as E. Schrader, Friedrich Delitzsch, Paul Haupt, A. H. Sayce, and many more in Europe and America have enlarged, corrected, and systematized the results attained, until now the stately science of Assyriology, or the organized knowledge of the language, literature, and history of Babylonia and Assyria, has a recognized place in the hierarchy of learning.

23. The Babylonio-Assyrian writing, as at first discovered in its classical forms, appears at a hasty glance like a wilderness of short lines running in every direction, each line at one end and sometimes at both ends, spreading out into a triangular mass, or wedge. From this likeness to a wedge is derived the designation, "wedge-shaped" or "cuneiform" (lat. cuneus), as applied to the characters and also to the language and literature. Closer examination reveals a system in this apparent disorder. The characters are arranged in columns usually running horizontally, and are read from left to right, the great majority of the wedges either standing upright or pointing toward the right. These wedges, arranged singly or in groups, stand either for complete ideas (called "ideograms," e. g. a single horizontal wedge represents the preposition in) or for syllables (e. g. a single horizontal crossed by a single vertical wedge represents the syllable bar). It would be natural that, in course of time, the wedges used as signs for ideas would also be used as syllables, and the same syllable be represented by different wedges, thus producing confusion. This was remedied by placing another character before the sign for a particular idea to determine its use in that sense (hence, called a "determinative;" e. g. before all names of gods a sign meaning "divine being") or, after it, a syllabic character which added the proper ending of the word to be employed there (hence, called "phonetic complement"). In spite of these devices, many signs and collocations of signs have so many possible syllabic values as to render exactness in the reading very

difficult. There are about five hundred of these different signs used to represent wOrds or syllables. Their origin is still a subject of discussion among scholars. The prevailing theory is that they can be traced back to original pictures representing the ideas to be conveyed. But, at present, only about fifty out of the entire number of signs can be thus identified, and it may be necessary to accept other sources to account for the rest.

24. The material on which this writing appears is of various sorts. The characters were incised upon stone and metal, — on the marbles of palaces, on the fine hard surfaces of gems, on silver images and on plates of bronze. There are traces, also, of the use as writing material of skins, and of a substance resembling the papyrus of ancient Egypt. But that which surpassed all other materials for this purpose was clay, a fine quality of which was most abundant in Babylonia, whence the use spread all over the ancient oriental world. This clay was very carefully prepared, sometimes ground to an exceeding fineness, moistened, and moulded into various forms, ordinarily into a tablet whose average size is about six by two and one-half inches in superficial area by one inch in thickness, its sides curving slightly outwards. On the surface thus prepared the characters were impressed with a stylus, the writing often standing in columns, and carried over upon the back and sides of the tablet. The clay was frequently moulded into cones and barrel-shaped cylinders, having from six to ten sides on which writing could be inscribed. These tablets were then dried in the sun or baked in a furnace, — a process which rendered the writing practically indestructible, unless the tablet itself was shattered.

25. This prevailing use of clay was doubtless the cause of the disappearance of the picture-writing. The details of a picture could not easily be reproduced; circles gave way to straight lines joined together; these were gradually reduced in number; the line was enlarged at the end into the wedge, for greater distinctness, until the conventional form of the signs became established.

26. This method of writing by wedges was adopted from Babylonia by other peoples, such as those of ancient Armenia, for their own languages, just as German may be written in Latin letters. A problem of serious moment and great difficulty has arisen because of a similar use of the cuneiform in Babylonia itself. Side by side with cuneiform documents of the language represented in the bulk of the literature which has come down to us, and which may be called the Babylonio-Assyrian, there are some documents, also in cuneiform, in which the wedges do not have the meanings which are connected with them in the Babylonio-Assyrian. In some cases the same document is drawn up in two forms, written side by side, in which the way of reading the characters of one will not apply to those of the other, although the meaning of the document in both forms is the same. Evidently the cuneiform signs are here employed for two languages. What the philological relations of these languages may be, has given rise to a lively controversy. On the one hand, it is claimed that the two show marked philological similarities which carry them back to a common linguistic ground, and indicate that they are two modes of expressing one language, namely, the Semitic Babylonian. The one mode, the earlier, which stood in close relation to the primitive picture-writing, and may be called the "hieratic," was superseded in course of time by the other mode, which became the "common" or "demotic," and is represented in the great mass of Babylonio-Assyrian literature. The former had its origin in the transition from the ideographic to the phonetic mode of writing, — a transition which was accompanied with "the invention of a set of explanatory terms, mainly drawn from rare and unfamiliar and obsolete words expressed by the ideograms." It was later developed into an "artificial language" by the industry of priestly grammarians (McCurdy, History Prophecy and the Monuments, I. sects, 82 f.). On the other hand, the majority of scholars maintains that the earlier so-called "hieratic" is an independent and original language whose peculiar linguistic features point decidedly to a basis essentially different from that of the Semitic Babylonian. This language they regard as hailing from a pre-Semitic population of Babylonia, the

"Sumerians," whose racial affinities are not yet satisfactorily determined. The Semitic Babylonians, coming in later, adopted from them the cuneiform writing for their own language, while permitting the older speech to continue its life for a season. Divergence of view so radical in regard to the same body of linguistic facts can have only one explanation, — the facts are not decisive and the fundamental questions must await final adjudication till a time when either new documents for philological investigation are discovered, or light is obtained from other than linguistic sources.

27. As the valley of the Tigris and Euphrates formed the common home of Babylonians and Assyrians, so the two peoples possessed a common language, and their literatures may be regarded as parts of one continuous development. Centuries before the name of Assyria appeared in history, the Babylonians possessed a written language and developed an ample literature. Both language and literature passed over to the later nation on the upper Tigris, and were cherished and continued there. Comparatively slight differences in the forms of the cuneiform signs, and a greater emphasis upon certain types of literature are all that distinguish the two peoples in these regards. Indeed, the kings of Nineveh filled their libraries in large part with copies of ancient Babylonian books, a practice which has secured to us some of the choicest specimens of Babylonian literature. In sketching their literatures, therefore, the typical forms are the same and serve as a basis for a common presentation.

28. Religion was the inspiration of the most important and the most ample division of the literature of Babylonia. Scarcely any side of the religious life is unrepresented. Worship has its collections of ritual books, ranging from magical and conjuration formulæ, the repetition of which by the proper priest exorcises the demons, delivers from sickness, and secures protection, to the prayers and hymns to the gods, often pathetic and beautiful in their expressions of penitence and praise. Mythology has been preserved in cycles which have an epic character, the chief of which is the so-called Epic of Gilgamesh, a hero whose exploits are narrated in twelve books, each corresponding to the appropriate zodiacal sign. The famous story of the Deluge has been incorporated into the eleventh book. Less extensive, but of a like character, are the stories of the Descent of Ishtar into Arallu, or Hades. Of the heroes Etana and Adapa, and the legends of the gods Dibbara (Girra) and Zu. The cosmogonic narratives are hardly to be separated from these, the best known of which is the so-called Creation Epic of which the fragments of six books have been recovered. The poetry of these epics is quite highly developed in respect to imagery and diction. Even metre has been shown to exist, at least in the poem of creation. Among the rest Of the religious texts may be mentioned fragments of "wisdom" and tables of omens for the guidance of rulers

29. If the Babylonians had a passion for religion, the Assyrians were devoted to history, and the bulk of their literature may be described as historical. The Babylonian priests, indeed, preserved lists of their kings; business documents were dated, and rulers left memorials of their doings. But the first two can hardly claim to be literature, and the royal texts, in fulness and exactness, are surpassed by those of the Assyrian kings. The series of Assyrian historical texts on the grand scale begins with the inscription of Tiglathpileser I. (about 1100 B. C.), written on an eight-sided clay cylinder, and containing eight hundred and nine lines. The inscription covers the first five years of a reign of at least fifteen years. It begins with a solemn invocation to the gods who have given the king the sovereignty. His titles are then recited, and a summary statement of his achievements given. Then, beginning with his first year, the king narrates his campaigns in detail in nearly five hundred lines. The description of his hunting exploits and his building of temples occupies the next two hundred lines. The document closes with a blessing for the one who in the future honors the king's achievements, and a curse for him who seeks to bring them to naught. This, for its day, admirable historical narrative formed a kind of model for all later royal inscriptions, many of which copy its arrangement and almost

slavishly imitate its style. Its combination of summary statement with an attempt at chronological order, somewhat unskilfully made, is dissolved in the later inscriptions. They are of two sorts, either strictly annalistic, arranged according to the years of a king's reign, or a splendid catalogue of the royal exploits organized for impressiveness of effect, and hence often called "laudatory" texts. Examples of one or both forms have been left by all the great Assyrian kings. The most important among them are the inscriptions of Ashurnaçirpal, Shalmaneser II., Sargon, Sennacherib, Esarhaddon, and Ashurbanipal.

30. Closely connected with the historical documents is the diplomatic literature. An example of this is the so-called "Synchronistic History of Assyria and Babylonia," a memorandum of the dealings, diplomatic or otherwise, of the two nations with one another, from before 1450 B. C. down to 700 B. C., in regard to the disputed territory lying between them. To the same category belong royal proclamations, tribute lists, despatches, and an immense mass of letters from officials to the court, — correspondence between royal personages or between minor officials. Such correspondence begins with the reign of Khammurabi of Babylon (about 2275 B. C.), and is especially abundant under the great Assyrian kings from Sargon to Ashurbanipal. Not belonging to the epistolary literature of Assyria and Babylonia, but written in the cuneiform character, and containing letters from kings of Assyria and Babylonia as well as to them, is the famous Tel-el-Amarna correspondence, taken from the archives of Amenhotep IV. of Egypt, — in all some three hundred letters, — which throws a wonderful light upon the life of the world of Western Asia in the fifteenth century B. C. The numerous inscriptions describing the architectural activities of the kings belong here as well as to religious literature. Among the earliest inscriptions as well as the longest which have been discovered are the pious memorials of royal temple-builders. The inscriptions of Nebuchadrezzar II. the Great deal almost entirely with his buildings.

31. The literature of law is very extensive. While no complete legal code for either Babylonia or Assyria has been discovered, some fragments of a very ancient document, containing what seem to be legal enactments, indicate that such codes were not unknown, Records of judicial decisions, of business contracts, and similar documents which are drawn up with lawyer-like precision, attested by witnesses and afterwards deposited in the state archives, come from almost all periods of the history of these peoples, and testify to their highly developed sense of justice and their love of exact legal formalities.

32. Science and religion were most closely related in oriental antiquity, and it is difficult to draw the line between their literatures. Studies of the heavens and the earth were zealously made by Babylonian priests, in the practical search after the character and will of the gods, who were thought to have their seats in these regions. In their investigations, however, the priests came upon many important facts of astronomy and physical science. These materials were collected into large works, of which some modern scholars have believed an example to exist in the so-called "Illumination of Bel," which, in seventy-two books, may go back to an age before 2000 B. C. Other similar collections are geographical lists, rudimentary maps, catalogues of animals, plants, and minerals. The ritual calendars which were carefully compiled for the priests and temple worshippers illustrate the beginnings of a scientific division of time. Education is represented also in grammatical and lexicographical works, as well as in the school books and reading exercises prepared for the training-schools of the scribes.

33. Of works in lighter vein but few examples have been found. The epics indeed may be classed as poetry, and served equally the purposes of religious edification and entertainment. Besides these, fragments of folk songs have been found. Folk tales are represented by some remains of fables. Popular legends gathered about the famous kings of the early age; an

example of which is the autobiographical fragment attributed to Sargon I. of Agade, In comparison, however, with the tales which adorn the literature of ancient Egypt, Assyria and Babylonia were singularly barren in light literature.

34. The word "literature" in the preceding paragraphs has been used with what may seem an unwarranted latitude of meaning. Neither in content, nor in form, nor in purpose could much of the writing described be strictly included in that term. But, in the study of the ancient world, every scrap of written evidence is precious to the historian, and these crude attempts are the beginnings, both in form and in thought, of true literary achievement. The form of literature was fundamentally limited by the material on which books were written. It demands simple sentences, brief and unadorned, — what might be called the lapidary style. Imitation and repetition are also characteristic. The royal inscriptions have a stereotyped order. In religious hymns and prayers, epithets of gods and forms of address tend constantly to reappear from age to age with wearisome monotony. Lack of true imaginative power, and, at the same time, a realistic sense for facts show themselves; the one in the grotesqueness of the poetical imagery, the other in the blunt straightforward statements of the historical inscriptions. Yet even in the earliest poetical composition, the principle of "parallelism," or the balancing of expressions in corresponding lines, was employed, a device which, supplying the place of rhyme, became so powerful a means of expression in the mouth of the Hebrew prophet. A progress in ease and force of utterance is traceable also in the royal inscriptions, if one compares that of Tiglathpileser I. with those of Esarhaddon or Ashurbanipal. Babylonia and Assyria, indeed, in this sphere as in so many others, were great not so much in what they actually wrought as in the example they gave and the influences they set in motion. They planted the seeds which matured after they themselves had passed away.

IV.CHRONOLOGY AND HISTORY

35. AN essential condition for adequate knowledge of an ancient people is the possession of a continuous historical tradition in the form of oral or written records. This, however, in spite of the mass of contemporaneous documents of almost every sort, which the spade of the excavator has unearthed and the skill of the scholar deciphered, is not available for scientific study of Babylonian or Assyrian antiquity. From the far-off morning of the beginnings of the two peoples to their fall, no historians appeared to gather up the memorials of their past, to narrate and preserve the annals of these empires, to hand down their achievements to later days. Consequently, where contemporaneous records fail, huge gaps occur in the course of historical development, to be bridged over only partially by the combination of a few facts with more or less ingenious inferences or conjectures. Sometimes what has been preserved from a particular age reveals clearly enough the artistic or religious elements of its life, but offers only vague hints of its political activity and progress. The true perspective of the several periods is sometimes lost, as when really critical epochs in the history of these peoples are dwarfed and distorted by a lack of sources of knowledge, while others, less significant, but plentifully stocked with a variety of available material, bulk large and assume an altogether unwarranted prominence.

36. What the Babylonians and Assyrians failed to do in supplying a continuous historical record was not accomplished for them by the later historians of antiquity. Herodotus, in the first book of his "Histories," devotes twenty-three chapters to Babylonian affairs (Bk. I. 178-200), and refers to an Assyrian history in which he will write more at length of these events (I. 184). But the latter, if written, has been utterly lost, and the chapters just mentioned, while containing information of value, especially that which he himself collected on the ground, or

drew from an earlier traveller, presumably Hecatæus of Miletus, give distorted and fantastic legends where sober history might be expected. Ctesias of Cnidos, physician at the court of Artaxerxes Mnemon (415398 B. C.), who seems to have had access to some useful Assyrian material from Persian sources, introduced his Persian History with an account of Babylonio-Assyrian affairs, in which the same semi-mythical tales were interspersed with dry lists of kings in so hopeless a jumble of truth and falsehood as to reconcile us to the disappointment of having only a few fragments of it.

37. It is, however, a cause of keen regret that the three books of Babylonian or Chaldean History, by Berosus, have come down from the past only in scanty excerpts of later historians. Berosus was a Babylonian priest of the god Bel, and wrote his work for the Macedonian ruler of Babylonia, Antiochus Soter, about 280 B. C. As the cuneiform writing was still employed, he must have been able to use the original documents, and could have supplied just the needed data for our knowledge. Still, the passages preserved indicate that he had no proper conception of his task, since he filled a large part of his book with mythical stories of creation and incredible tales of primitive history, with its prediluvian dynasties of hundreds of thousands of years. A postdiluvian dynasty of thirty-four thousand ninety-one years prepares the way for five dynasties, reaching to Nabonassar, king of Babylon (747 B. C.), from whose time the course of events seems to have been told in greater detail down to the writer's own days. Imperfect and crude as this work must have been, it was by far the most trustworthy and important compendious account of Babylonio-Assyrian history furnished by any ancient author, and for that reason would, even to-day, be highly valued. A still more useful contribution to the chronological framework of history was made by Ptolemy, a geographer and astronomer of the time of the Roman Emperor, Antoninus Pius. Ptolemy's "Canon of Kings," compiled for astronomical purposes, starts with the same Nabonassar at whose time Berosus begins to expand his history, and continues with the names and regnal years of the Babylonian kings to the fall of Babylon. Since Ptolemy proceeds with the list through the Persian, Macedonian, and Roman regnal lines in continuous succession, and connects the era of Nabonassar with those of Philip Arridæus and Augustus, a synchronism with dates of the Christian era is established, by which the reign of Nabonassar can be fixed at 747-733 B. C. and the reigns of his successors similarly stated in terms of our chronology. By this means, not only is a chronological basis of special value laid for this later age of Babylonian history, but a starting-point is given for working backward into the earlier periods, provided that adequate data can be secured from other sources.

38. Happily for historical science, the original documents of Babylonia and Assyria are unexpectedly rich in material available for this purpose. As already stated (sect. 29), the Assyrians were remarkably gifted with the historic sense, and not only do their royal annals and other similar documents contain many and exact chronological statements, but there was in vogue in the royal court a practical system which went far toward compensating for the lack of an era according to which the dates of events might be definitely fixed. From the royal officers one was appointed each year to give his name to the year. He or his official status during that period was called limu, and events or documents were dated by his name. The king usually acted as limu for the first full year of his reign. He was followed in succession by the Turtan, or commander-in-chief, the Grand Vizier, the Chief Musician, the Chief Eunuch, and the governors of the several provinces or cities. Lists of these limi were preserved in the royal archives, forming a fixed standard of the greatest practical value for the checking off of events or the dating of documents, While this system was in use in Assyria as early as the fourteenth century, the lists which have been discovered are of much later date and of varying length, the longest extending from 893 B. C. to about 650 B. C. Sometimes to the mere name of the limu was added a brief remark as to some event of his year. Such a reference to an eclipse of the sun occurring in the limu of Pur-Sagali in the reign of Ashurdan III., has been calculated to

have taken place on the fifteenth of June, 763 B. C., a fact which at once fixes the dates for the whole list and enables its data to be compared with those derived from the synchronisms of the canon of Ptolemy and other sources, The result confirms the accuracy of the Assyrian document, and affords a trustworthy chronological basis for fully three centuries of Assyrian history. For the earlier period before 900 B. C. the ground is more uncertain, but the genealogical and chronological statements of the royal inscriptions, coupled with references to contemporaneous Babylonian kings whose dates are calculable from native sources, supply a foundation which, if lacking in some parts, is yet capable of supporting the structure of historical development.

39. The Babylonians, while they possessed nothing like the well wrought out limu system of Assyria, and dated events by the regnal years of their kings, had in their kings' lists, compiled by the priests and preserved in the temples, documents of much value for historical purposes. The "Great List," which has been preserved, arranges the names in dynasties, and gives the regnal years of each king. At the end of each dynasty, the number of the kings and the sum of their regnal years are added. Though badly broken in parts, this list extends over a millennium, and contains legible names of at least seventy kings arranged in about nine dynasties. As the last division contains names of rulers appearing in the Assyrian and Ptolemaic canon, the starting-point is given for a chronological organization of the Babylonian kings, which unfortunately can be only approximately achieved, owing to the gaps in the list. The two other lists now available cover the first two dynasties only of the great list. Not only do they differ in some respects from one another, but they do not help in furnishing the missing names in the great list. These can be tentatively supplied from inscriptions of kings not mentioned on the lists, and presumably belonging to periods in which the gaps occur. Using all the means at their disposal, scholars have generally agreed in placing the beginning of the first dynasty of Babylon somewhat later than 2500 B. C.

40. For the chronology of Babylonian history before that time, the sources are exceedingly meagre, and all results, depending as they do upon calculation and inference from uncertain data, must be regarded as precarious. Numerous royal inscriptions exist, but connections between the kings mentioned are not easy to establish, and paleographic evidence, which must be invoked to determine the relative age of the documents, yields often ambiguous responses. A fixed point, indeed, in this chaos seems to be offered in a statement made by Nabuna'id, a king of the New Babylonian Empire. In searching for the foundations of the sun temple at Sippar, he came, to use his own words, upon "the foundation-stone of Naram Sin, which no king before me had found for 3200 years." As the date of the discovery is fixed at about 550 B. c., Naram Sin, king of Agade, whose name and inscriptions are known, may be placed at about 3750 B. C., and his father, Sargon, at about 3800 B. c. While much questioning has naturally been raised concerning the accuracy and trustworthiness of this date thus obtained, no valid reasons for discarding it have been presented. It affords a convenient and useful point from which to reckon backward and forward in the uncertain periods from the third to the fifth millennium B. C. By all these aids, to which are added some genealogical statements in the inscriptions, a series of dynasties has been worked out for this early age, and their chronological relations to one another tentatively determined.

41. It is possible, therefore, with a reasonable degree of accuracy, to determine chronologically not only the great turning points in Babylonio-Assyrian history, but even the majority of the dynasties and the reigns of the several kings. Founded upon this, the historical structure may be reared, and its various stages and their relations determined. A bird's-eye view of these will facilitate further progress. First in order of time comes the Rise and Development of the City-States of Old Babylonia to their unification in the City-State of Babylon. In the dawn of history different primitive centres of population in the lower Tigro-Euphrates valley appeared,

attained a vigorous and expanding life, came into contact one with another, and successively secured a limited supremacy, only to give place to others. The process was already in full course by 5000 B. C. By the middle of the third millennium, the city of Babylon pushed forward under a new dynasty; one of its kings succeeded in driving out the Elamites, who had invaded and were occupying the southern and central districts; the victory was followed by the city's supremacy, which was not only more widely extended, but, by the wisdom of its kings, was more deeply rooted, and was thus made permanent. With Babylonia united under Babylon, the first epoch closed about 2000 B. C.

42. The second period covers the Early Conflicts of Babylonia and Assyria. The peaceful course of united Babylonia was interrupted by the entrance of the Kassites from the east, who succeeded in seating a dynasty of Kassite kings upon the throne of Babylonia, and maintaining them there for nearly six hundred years, But this foreign intrusion and dominance had roused into independent life a Semitic community which had its centre at Assur on the central Tigris, and in all probability was an offshoot from Babylonia. This centre of active political life developed steadily toward the north and west, but was dominated chiefly by its hostility toward Babylonia under Kassite rule. Having become the kingdom of Assyria, it warred with the southern kingdom, the advantage on the whole remaining with the Assyrian until, toward the close of the epoch, a great ruler appeared in the north, Tiglathpileser I., under whom Assyria advanced to the first place in the Tigro-Euphrates valley; while Babylonia, its Kassite rulers yielding to a native dynasty, fell into political insignificance, The forces that controlled the age had run their course by 1000 B. C.

43. The third period is characterized by the Ascendancy of Assyria. The promise of pre-eminence given in Tiglathpileser I, was not fulfilled for two centuries, owing to the flooding of the upper Mesopotamian plain with Aramean nomads from the Arabian steppes. At last, as the ninth century began, Ashurnaçirpal led the way in an onward movement of Assyria which culminated in the extension of the kingdom over the entire region of western Asia, Shalmaneser II., Tiglathpileser III., and Sargon, great generals and administrators, turned a kingdom into an empire. The first wore out the resistance of the Syrian states, the second added Babylonia to the Assyrian Empire, and the third, as conqueror of the north, ruled from the Persian gulf to the border of Egypt and the upper sea of Ararat. The rulers that followed compelled Egypt to bow, and reduced Elam to subjection, but at the expense of the vital powers of the state. New peoples appeared upon the eastern border, revolt deprived the empire of its provinces, until, in less than two decades after the death of the brilliant monarch Ashurbanipal, Nineveh, Assyria's capital, was destroyed, and the empire disappeared suddenly and forever. Four centuries were occupied with this splendid history and its tragical catastrophe. The age closed with the passing of the seventh century (600 B. C.).

44. Of the partners in the overthrow of Assyria, the rebellious governor of the province of Babylonia received as 'his share of the spoil the Tigro-Euphrates valley and the Mediterranean provinces. He founded here the Hew Babylonian Empire. Its brief career of less than a century concluded the history of these peoples. Under his son, the famous Nebuchadrezzar II., the empire was consolidated, its resources enlarged, its power displayed. His feeble successors, however, were beset with manifold difficulties, chief of which was the rising energy of the Medes and Persians who had shared in the booty Of Assyria. United under the genius of Cyrus, they pushed westward and northward, until the hour came for advancing on Babylon. The hollow shell of the empire was speedily crushed, and the Semitic peoples, whose rulers had dominated this world of western Asia for more than four millenniums, yielded the sceptre in 538 B. C. to Cyrus the Persian.

PART I. THE CITY STATES OF BABYLONIA AND THEIR UNIFICATION UNDER BABYLON TO 2000 B. C.

I .THE DAWN OF HISTORY

45. THE earliest indications of human settlement in the Tigro-Euphrates valley come from the lower alluvial plain (sect. 3) known as Babylonia. It is not difficult to see how the physical features of this region were adapted to make it a primitive seat of civilization. A burning sun, falling upon fertile soil enriched and watered by mighty, inundating streams, — these are conditions in which man finds ready to his hand everything needed to sustain and stimulate his elemental wants. Superabounding fruitfulness of nature, plant, animal, and man, contributes to his comfort, and progress, Coming with flocks and herds from the surrounding deserts, he finds ample pasturage and inexhaustible water everywhere, an oasis inviting him to a permanent abiding-place. He cannot but abandon his nomadic life for settlement. The land, however, does not encourage inglorious ease. Wild nature must be subdued and waste tracts occupied as populations increase. The inundations are found to occur at regular intervals and to be of definite duration. They may be regulated and their fruitful waters directed upon barren soils, making them fertile. All suggests order and requires organization on the part of those settled along the river banks. From the same generous source are supplied mud and bitumen for the erection of permanent dwellings. The energies of the inhabitants of such a country would naturally be absorbed in developing its abundant resources. They would be a peaceful folk, given to agriculture. Trade, also, is facilitated by the rivers, natural highways through the land, and with trade comes industry, both stimulated by the generous gifts of nature, among which the palm-tree is easily supreme. Thus, at a time when regions less suggestive and responsive to human activity lay unoccupied and barren, this favored spot was inevitably the scene of organized progressive human activity already engaged upon the practical problems of social and political life. It furnishes for the history of mankind the most ancient authentic records at present known.

46. The position of the Babylonian plain is likewise prophetic of its history. It is an accessible land (sect. 11). Races and civilizations were to meet and mingle there. It was to behold innumerable political changes due to invasion and conquest. In turn, the union of peoples was to produce a strong and abiding social amalgam, capable of absorbing aliens and preserving their best. This civilization, because it lay thus open to all, was to contribute widely to the world's progress. It made commercial highways out of its rivers. The passes of the eastern and northern mountains were doorways, not merely for invading tribes, but also for peaceful armies of merchants marching to and from the ends of the world, and finding their common centre in its cities.

47. At the period when history begins, all these processes of development were already well advanced. Not only are the beginnings of civilization in Babylonia quite hidden from our eyes, but the various stages in the course of that first civilization, extending over thousands of years, are equally unknown, except as they may be precariously inferred from that which the beginnings of historical knowledge reveal. The earliest inscriptions which have been unearthed disclose social and political life already in full operation. Not only has mankind passed beyond the period of savage and even pastoral existence, but agriculture is the chief occupation; the irrigating canals have begun to distribute the river water to the interior of the land; the population is gathered into settled communities; cities are built; states are established, ruled over by kings; the arts of life are developed; language has already been reduced to written form, and is employed for literary purposes; religion is an essential element

of life, and has its priests and temples.

48. The seat of the most advanced and presumably the most ancient historical life appears to have been the southernmost part of the Euphrates valley. As the river reached the gulf, which then stretched more than a hundred miles northwest of its present shore line, it spread out over the surrounding country in a shallow sea. Upon the higher ground to the east and west of the lowlands made marvellously fertile by this natural irrigation, the earliest cities were planted. Farthest to the south, presumably close to the gulf and west of the river mouth, was the ancient Eridu (now Abu Shahrein or Nowawis), the seat of a temple for the worship of Ea, the god of the waters, Here, no doubt, was told the story of Oannes, the being that came up daily from the sea to converse with men, to teach them letters, arts, and sciences, everything which could tend to soften manners and humanize mankind, and at night returned to the deep, — a myth of the sun, perhaps, associated with the recollection of the beginnings of culture in this coast city which, without tradition of political importance, was hallowed as a primitive centre of civilization and religion. Some ten miles to the west lay Ur, "the city" (at present called Mugheir), now a few miles west of the river in the desert, but once, like Eridu, a commercial city on the gulf. Here was the temple of Sin, the moon god, the ruins of which rise seventy feet above the plain. Across the river, thirty miles to the northeast, stood Larsam (now Senkereh), the biblical Ellasar, where the sun god Shamash had his temple. Twelve miles away to the northwest was Uruk, the biblical Erech (now Warka), the seat of the worship of the goddess Ishtar. Mar (now perhaps Tel Ede), a little known site, lay about the same distance north. Thirty-five miles east of Mar, on the ancient canal now known as Shatt-el-Hai, connecting the Tigris with the Euphrates, was Shirpurla, or Lagash (now Tello), looking out across the eastern plain, the frontier city of the early period, although fifty miles from the Tigris. These six cities, lying at the four corners of an irregular square, form the southernmost body of primitive communities already flourishing at the dawn of history.

49. Situated almost exactly in the centre of the ancient plain between the rivers, about fifty miles north of Uruk, was the already famous city of Nippur (now Niffer). Here the patron deity was En-lil, "chief spirit," called also Bel, the "lord," god of the terrestrial world. A long period of prehistoric political prominence must be assumed to explain the religious prestige of this city and of its god. Religion is its sole distinction at the time when records begin. But how great must have been that prominence to have secured for the city a claim to stand with Eridu as one of the two earliest centres of religion ! En-lil was a father of gods, and his fame made Nippur the shrine where many kings were proud to offer their gifts.

50. North Babylonia had also its group of primitive cities, chief among which was Kutha (now Tel Ibrahim), the biblical Cuthah, more than fifty miles northwest of Nippur in the centre of the upper plain. Its god, Nergal, was lord of the world of the dead. Still further north, not far from the eastern bank of the Euphrates, was Sippar (now Abu Habba), where the sun god, Shamash, had his temple, and in its vicinity, probably, was Agade, once the famous capital of the land of Akkad. More uncertain are the sites of those northern cities which played an important part in the political activity of the earlier days, but soon disappeared, Kulunu (the biblical Calneh), Gishban(?), and Kish. It is a question whether Babylon and its sister city Borsippa should be included in this enumeration, If they were in existence, they were insignificant communities at this time, and their gods, Marduk and Nabu, do not stand high in the ranks of the earliest deities. The greatness of the two cities was to come, and to compensate by its splendor fer the lateness of their beginnings.

51. Who were the people by whose energy this region was transformed into so fair and flourishing a land, at a time when elsewhere, with hardly an exception, the upward course of humanity did not yet reveal any trace of orderly and civilized conditions? What are their

antecedents, and whence did they come to occupy the alluvial plain? These questions cannot be satisfactorily answered, because our knowledge of the facts involved is insufficient and the conclusions drawn from them are contradictory. Reference has already been made (sect. 26) to the linguistic phenomena of the early Babylonian inscriptions, and the opposite inferences drawn from them. The historical facts bearing on the question render a clearer answer, if also a more limited one. Whatever may be the conjectures based upon them as to prehistoric conditions and movements, these facts at the beginning of history testify that the civilization was that of a Semitic people. Inscriptions of an undoubtedly Semitic character are there, and the social, political, and religious phenomena presented by them have nothing that clearly demonstrates a non-Semitic character. Nor do any inscriptions, myths, or traditions testify, indubitably, either to a pre-Semitic population, or to the superimposing upon it of the Semitic stock. To the historian, therefore, the problem resolves itself into this: how and when did the Semitic people begin to occupy this Babylonian plain? As the consensus of judgment to-day seems to favor Central Arabia as the primitive home of the Semites, their advent into Babylonia must have been made from the west, by moving either upward, from the western side of the Persian gulf, or downward, along the Euphrates, — a drift from the desert as steady and continuous as the sand that creeps over the Babylonian border from the same source. When this movement began can only be conjectured from the length of time presumably required to develop the civilization which existed as early as 5000 B. C., back to which date the earliest materials must certainly be carried. The processes already indicated as having preceded this time (sects. 45, 47), suggest to what distant ages the incoming of the first settlers must be assigned.

52. The Babylonian primitive civilization did not stand alone or isolated in this dawn of history. It lay in the midst of a larger world, with some regions of which it had already entered into relations, To the northwest, along the Euphrates, nomadic tribes still wandered, although there are indications that, on the upper river, in the vicinity of the old city of Haran, a Semitic culture was already appearing. The Bedouin of the western desert hung on the frontier as a constant menace, or wandered into the cultivated land to swell the Semitic population. To the north, along the eastern banks of the upper Tigris, and on the flanks of the mountains were centres of primitive organization, as among the Guti and the Lulubi, whose kings, some centuries later, left Semitic inscriptions. But particularly active and aggressive were the people of the highlands east of Babylonia known by the collective name of Elam. The country sloped gently down to the Tigris, and was watered by streams descending from the hills. The people were hardy and warlike. They had already developed or acquired from their neighbors across the river the elements of organization and civilization. Through their borders ran the trade-routes from the east. Among the earliest memorials of history are evidences of their active interference in Babylonian affairs, in which they were to play so important a part in the future. Commerce was to bring more distant places into the circle of Babylonian life. On the borders, to the south, were the ports of southern Arabia; far to the west, the peoples of the Mediterranean coast-lands were preparing to receive the visits of traders from the Euphrates; while at the end of the then known world was the rich and progressive nation in the valley of the Nile, already, perhaps, indebted to the dwellers in Babylonia for impulses toward civilization, which they were themselves to carry to so high a point in the ages to come.

II.MOVEMENTS TOWARD EXPANSION AND UNIFICATION

53. THE cities whose existence at the dawn of history has already been noted, were, from the first, full of vigorous activity. The impulses which led to the organization of social life sought further development, Cities enlarged, came intO touch with their neighbors, and sought to

dominate them. The varying success of these movements, the rise, splendor, and decay of the several communities, their struggles with one another, and the ever-renewed activity which carried them beyond the confines of Babylonia itself, make up the first chapter in the story. It is impossible to give a connected and detailed account of the period, owing to the scantiness of the materials and the difficulty of arranging them chronologically. The excavations of the last quarter of a century have only begun to suggest the wealth of inscriptions and archæological matter which will be at the disposal ef the future student. Much new light has been gained which makes it possible to take general views, to trace tendencies, and to prepare tentative outlines which discoveries and investigations still to come will fill up and modify.

54. Some general titles borne by rulers of the period afford a striking evidence of the character of this early development. Three of these are worthy of special mention, namely, "King of Shumer and Akkad," "King of the Totality (world)," "King of the Four (world-) Regions." It is evident that two of these titles, and possibly all, refer to districts and not to cities, although great uncertainty exists as to their exact geographical position. The second and third would suggest universal empire, though they might be localized upon particular regions. The " Kingdom of the Totality" is thought by Winkler and other scholars to have its centre in northern Mesopotamia about the city of Haran. " Shumer and Akkad " are regarded as including the northern and southern parts of Babylonia. The "Four Regions," synonymous with the four points of the compass, would include the known world from the eastern mountains and the Persian gulf to the Mediterranean. Whatever may be learned in the future respecting the exact content of these titles, they illustrate the impulses and tendencies which were already potent in these primitive communities.

55. This period of expansion and unification occupies more than two millenniums (about 4500-2250 B. C.). Three stages may be distinguished in what may truly be called this wilderness of years. (1) The first is marked by the struggles of cities within Babylonia for local supremacy. The chief rivalry lay between those of the north and those of the south. (2) With the career of Sargon I. (3800 B. c.), a new era opened, characterized by the extension of authority beyond the borders of Babylonia as far as the Mediterranean and the northern mountains, while yet local supremacy shifted from city to city. (3) The third epoch, which is, at the same time, the termination of the period and the opening of a new age, saw the final consolidation of Babylonian authority at home and abroad in the city-king of Babylon, which henceforth gave its name to land and government and civilization. In each of these ages, some names of rulers stand out as fixed points in the vast void, gaps of unknown extent appear, and historic relations between individual actors upon the wide stage are painfully uncertain. Some account in the barest outline may be given of these kings, in some cases hardly more than shadows, whom the progress of investigation will in time clothe with flesh and blood, and assign the place and significance due to their achievements.

56. The struggle has already begun when the first known king, Enshagsagana (about 4500 B. C.) of Kengi, probably southwestern Babylonia, speaks of offering to the god of Nippur the spoil of Kish, "wicked of heart." Somewhat later the representative of the south in the wars with the northern cities, Kish and Gishban, was Shirpurla (sect. 48). Mesilim of Kish (about 4400 B. C.) made Shirpurla a vassal kingdom. It recovered under the dynasty of Ur Nina (about 4200 B.C.), who called himself king, while his successors were satisfied with the title of patesi, or viceroy. Two of these successors of Ur Nina, Eannatum (Edingiranagin) and Entemena, have left inscriptions of some length, describing their victories over cities of the north and south. Gishban, rivalling Kish in its hostility to the south, found a vigorous antagonist in Eannatum, whose famous "Vulture Stele" contains the terms imposed by him upon the patesi of that city. Not long after, a king of Gishban, Lugalzaggisi (about 4000 B. C.), proclaimed himself " king of Uruk, king of the Totality," brought also Ur and Larsam under

his sway, and offered his spoil at the sacred shrine of Nippur. He was practically lord of Babylonia. His inscription, moreover, goes on to declare that "from the lower sea of the Tigris and Euphrates to the upper sea (his god) made straight his path; from the rising of the sun to the setting of the same he gave him tribute." His authority extended from the Persian gulf to the Mediterranean. A later king of Kish, Alusharshid (about 3850 B. C.), wrote upon marble vases which he offered at Nippur, his boast of having subjugated Elam and Bara'se, the elevated plains to the east and northeast of Babylonia.

57. It is tempting to generalize upon these six centuries and more of history. The most obvious fact has already been mentioned, namely, that the movement toward expansion, incorporation, and unification is in full course. But more definite conclusions may be reached. There are those who see, in the arraying of north against south, the inevitable reaction of a ruder civilization against an older and higher one. The earlier culture of the south, and its more fully developed organization had pressed upon the northern communities and attempted to absorb them in the process of giving them civilization. But gradual decay sapped the strength of the southern states, and the hardier peoples of the north, having learned the arts of their conquerors, thirsted for their riches, and at last succeeded in overthrowing them, A more definite view is that which beholds in the aggressions of north upon south the steady advance of the Semitic people upon the Sumerians (sect. 26), and the process of fastening the yoke of Semitic political supremacy upon Babylonia, with the accompanying absorption of Sumerian culture by the conquerors. Another conclusion (that of Radau, Early Babylonian History) finds the Semites coming in from the south at the very beginning of the period and pushing northward beyond the confines of Babylonia. Then the Semites of the south, having become corrupted by the higher civilization of the Sumerians, were objects of attack on the part of the more virile Semites of the north who, turning back upon their former track, came down and occupied the seats of their brethren and renewed the purer Semitic element. There may be some truth in all these generalizations, but the positions are so opposed, and their foundations are as yet so precarious, that assent to their definite details must, for the present, be withheld from all of them.

58. Shargani-shar-ali, or, as he is more commonly called, Sargon I., king of the city of Agade (sect. 50), introduces the second stage in early Babylonian history. His son, Naram Sin, is said by Nabuna'id, the last king of the New Babylonian Empire, to have reigned three thousand two hundred years before his own time, that is, about 3750 B. C. Sargon lived, therefore, about 3800 B. C., the first date fixed, with reasonable certainty, in Babylonian history, and a point of departure for earlier and later chronology (sect, 40), The inscriptions coming directly from Sargon himself and his son are few and historically unimportant. Some, found at Nippur, indicate that both were patrons of the temple and worshippers of its god. A tablet of omens, written many centuries after their time, ascribes to them a wide range of activity and splendid achievement. While such a document may contain a legendary element, the truth of its testimony in general is substantiated by similar statements recorded in contract tablets of the Sargonic age. The very existence of such legends testifies to the impression made by these kings on succeeding generations. An interesting example of this type of document is the autobiographical fragment which follows:

Sargon, the powerful king, King of Agade, am I.
My mother was of low degree, my father I did not know.
The brother of my father dwelt in the mountain.
My city was Azupirani, situate on the bank of the Euphrates.
(My) humble mother conceived me; in secret she brought me forth.
She placed me in a basket-boat of rushes; with pitch she closed my door.

She gave me over to the river, which did not (rise) over me.
The river bore me along; to Akki, the irrigator, it carried me.
Akki, the irrigator, in the . . . brought me to land.
Akki, the irrigator, reared me as his own son.
Akki, the irrigator, appointed me his gardener.
While I was gardener, Ishtar looked on me with love [and]
... four years I ruled the kingdom.
(Assyrian and Babylonian Literature, p. 1.)

59. Sargon was a great conqueror. Within Babylonia, he was lord of Nippur, Shirpurla, Kish, Babylon, and Uruk. Beyond its borders, he and his son carried their arms westward to the Mediterranean, northward into Armenia, eastward into Elam and among the northeastern peoples, and southward into Arabia and the islands of the Persian gulf. To illustrate the character of these wars, reference may be made to the omen tablet, which, under the seventh omen, records a three years' campaign on the Mediterranean coast, during which Sargon organized his conquests, erected his images, and carried back the spoil to his own land. Possessed of so wide authority, Naram Sin assumed the proud title, for the first time employed by a Babylonian ruler, "King of the Four (world-) Regions."

60. The achievements of these kings were both a culmination of the activities of the earlier city-kings, and a model for those who followed. The former had from time to time gathered parts of the larger world under their own sway, as Lugalzaggisi the west, and Alusharshid the east. But the incorporation of the whole into a single empire was the work of the Sargonids, and no dynasty followed which did not strive after this ideal. The immediate descendants of Naram Sin, however, have left no monuments to indicate that they maintained their fathers' glory, and the dynasty of Agade disappeared in a darkness which stretches over nearly half a millennium. The scene shifts once more to Shirpurla. Here the patesi Ur Bau (about 3500 B. C.) ruled peacefully, and was followed by other princes, whose chief distinction in their own eyes was the building of temples and the service of the gods. Foremost among these in the number of inscriptions and works of art which commemorate his career, was Gudea (about 3100 B. C.). The only warlike deed recorded by him was his conquest of Anshan in Elam, but the wide range of countries laid under contribution for materials to build his temples and palaces has led to the conviction that he must have been an independent and vigorous ruler. The absence of any royal titles in his inscriptions, however, coupled with the slight reference to military expeditions, suggests, rather, that his building operations were made possible because his state formed part of the domains of a broad empire, like that which Sargon founded and his successors ruled.

61. Peace, however, in an oriental state is the sign of weakness, and the extensive works of Gudea may have exhausted the resources of Shirpurla so that, after a few generations, its patesis acknowledged the sway of the kings of Ur, who came forward to make a new contribution to the unification of Babylonia. Ur Gur of Ur and his son Dungi (about 3000 B. C.) were, like their predecessors of Shirpurla, chiefly proud of their temples, if the testimony of the great mass of the inscriptions from them may be accepted. But they are distinguished from Gudea in that they built their temples in all parts of the land of Babylonia, from Kutha in the north to Shirpurla, Nippur, Uruk, and Ur in the south. The title which they assumed, that of "King of Shumer and Akkad," now first employed by Babylonian kings, indicates that the end which they had attained was the union of all Babylonia, north and south, under one sceptre. The building of the various temples in the cities was the evidence both of their interest in the welfare of the whole land and of their authority over it. They realized the ideal which ruled all succeeding dynasties, namely, a united Babylonia, although it is probable that their authority over the different districts was often very slight. Patesis still maintained themselves in Shirpurla and, doubtless, elsewhere, although they acknowledged the supremacy of the king of

Ur. It is not without reason, therefore, that two dynasties ruling in other cities are assigned to the period immediately following that of the dynasty of Ur. These are a dynasty of Uruk, consisting of kings Singashid and Singamil the former of whom calls himself also king of Amnanu, and a dynasty of Isin, a city of southern Babylonia, whose site is as yet unknown. The latter group of kings claimed authority also over Nippur, Ur, Eridu, and Uruk, and called themselves "Kings of Shumer and Akkad." As such, they would be successors of the kings of Ur, in control of united Babylonia.

62. Ur came forward again after some generations and dominated the land under a dynasty whose founder was Gungunu; its members were Ine Sin, Bur Sin II., Gimil Sin, some others less known, and, probably, a second Dungi (about 2800-2500 B. C.). The various forms of titles attached to some of the kings of Ur have led some scholars to group them in several dynasties, but the evidence is not at present sufficient. The kings above mentioned, considered together, are no longer called kings of Shumer and Akkad, but bear the prouder title of "King of the Four Regions." Our knowledge of their activities fully justifies them in assuming it. Numerous contract tablets, dated from events in their reigns, testify to campaigns in Syria, Arabia, and Elam. The most vigorous of these rulers was Dungi II,, who reigned more than fifty years. He built temples in various cities, made at least nine expeditions into the west, and seems to have placed members of his own family as governors in the conquered cities, if one may trust the interpretation of inscriptions to the effect that his daughters were appointed rulers in Syria and Anshan. He was worshipped as a god after his death, and his successors named the eighth month of the year in his honor. This dynasty may, not unreasonably, be regarded as one of the most notable thus far ruling in Babylonia, uniting, as it did, authority over the homeland with vigorous movement into the surrounding regions, and control over the east and the west.

63. A period of some confusion followed the passing of this sovereignty of Ur (about 2400-2200 B. C.). A dynasty of the city of Babylon, the first recorded by the priests in the dynastic tablets, was founded by Sumu-abu (about 2400 B. C.) and contested the worldwide supremacy of Ur. Larsam was the seat of another kingdom, the first king of which was Nur Adad, who was succeeded by his son Siniddinam. The latter called himself "king of Simmer and Akkad," as though he would again bring about that unity which had disappeared with the downfall of Ur. But other movements were preparing which, apparently threatening the overthrow of Babylonian civilization and governments as a whole, were to bring about an ultimate and permanent establishment of Babylonian unity. The Elamites upon the eastern highlands, between whom and the communities of eastern Babylonia war had been frequent, and who had been more than once partially conquered, reacted under the pressure and entered the land, bent upon conquest. The southern cities suffered the most severely from this inroad, as they lay nearest the line of advance of the invading peoples. At first the Elamites raided the cities and carried off their booty to their own land, but later were able to establish themselves in Babylonian territory. How early these incursions began is quite uncertain. In the fragments of Berosus, a "Median" dynasty of eight kings is mentioned the approximate date of which is from 2450 B. C. to 2250 B. C. This statement may vaguely suggest the presence of Elamites in Babylonia during two centuries, and the culmination of their inroads in the possession of supreme authority over at least part of the land. That new dynasties appeared in Babylon and Larsam, succeeding to that of Ur about 2400 B. C., may have some connection with these inroads, and inscriptional evidence makes it certain that Elamite supremacy was felt in Babylonia by 2300 B. C. Native dynasties disappeared before the onslaught. One of these invading bodies was led by King Kudurnankhundi, whose exploits are referred to by the Assyrian king of the seventh century, Ashurbanipal. The Elamite had carried away a statue of the goddess Nana from Uruk 1635 years before, that is, about 2290 B. C. Ashurbanipal restored it to its temple. The region in which Uruk and Larsam were situated seems to have

borne the brunt of the assault. The former city was devastated and its temples sacked. The latter became a centre of Elamite power. A prince whole Semitic name is read Rim Sin, the son of a certain Kudurmabuk, ruler of Iamutbal, a district of west Elam, set up his kingdom at Larsam, apparently on the overthrow of Siniddinam, and for at least a quarter of a century (about 2275 B. C.) made himself a power in southern Babylonia. He claimed authority over Ur, Eridu, Nippur, Shirpurla, and Uruk, conquered Isin, and called himself " king of Shumer and Akkad." Evidently the Elamite element was well on the way toward absorption intro Babylonian life.

64. What the Elamites really brought to pass in Babylonia was a general levelling of the various southern city-states which had contested the supremacy with one another. Their rulers overthrown, their people enslaved, their possessions carried away, rude foreigners dominating them, they were no longer in a position to maintain the ancient rivalry with one another, or to contest the supremacy with the cities of the north. When the foreigners had weakened themselves by amalgamation with the conquered and by accepting their religion and culture, the way was opened for a purely Babylonian power, hitherto but slightly affected by these invasions, to drive out the enemy, and bring the whole land under one authority which might hope for permanence. This power was the city-state of Babylon.

65. It is tempting to seek further light on this Elamite period from two other sources. The first of these is the native religious literature. In the so-called omen tablets and the hymns, are not infrequent references to troubles from the Elamites. A hymn, associated with Uruk (RP, 2 ser. I. pp. 84 ff.), lamenting a misfortune which has fallen upon the city, is, by some scholars, connected with the expedition of Kudurnankhundi (sect. 63). In one of the episodes of the Gilgamesh epic (sect. 28), the deliverance of Uruk from a foreign enemy, Khumbaba, forms the background of the scene, It may embody a tradition of this period, and preserve the name of another Elamite invader, But the allusions are all too indefinite to serve any historical purpose other than as illustrations of the reality and severity of invasions from Elam. The Hebrew religious literature has also furnished material which is thought to bear on this epoch. In Genesis xiv. it is said, "It came to pass in the days of Amraphel king of Shinar, Arioch king of Ellasar, Chedorlaomer king of Elam, and Tidal king of Goiim; that they made war with Bera king of Sodom, and with Birsha king of Gomorrah, Shinab king of Admah, and Shemeber king of Zeboiim, and the king of Bela. . . . Twelve years they served Chedorlaomer, and in the thirteenth year they rebelled. And in the fourteenth year came Chedorlaomer, and the kings that were with him." In the situation here depicted, and the names of the kings and localities mentioned, have been found grounds for assigning the episode to the Elamite period of Babylonian history. Arioch of Ellasar would be Rim Sin (in another reading of his name, Eri-Aku) of Larsam; Amraphel of Shinar is identified with Khammurabi of Babylon; Tidal of Goiim, with Thargal of Gutium; while Chedorlaomer is a good Elamite name in the form Kudurlagamar. On this hypothesis, the latter would be the overlord of the Babylonian kings and the heir to the Babylonian authority over Syria and Palestine which had been maintained by Sargon and others of the earlier time. All this is not improbable, and adds interest to our study of this dark period, but it is not sufficiently substantiated, either by the connection in which it stands, or by the evidence of contemporaneous Babylonian material, to warrant the acceptance of it as actual historical fact. It is true that names similar to these have also been found in Babylonian tablets of various periods, but the reading of the texts is not so certain, or their relation to this epoch so clear, as to offer any substantial support to the narrative.

III.CIVILIZATION OF OLD BABYLONIA: POLITICAL AND SOCIAL

LIFE

66. WHILE the materials for sketching the historical development of the early Babylonian communities are often quite inadequate, fragmentary, and difficult to organize, those which illustrate the life of the people are not only more numerous, but they also afford a more complete picture. To present a history of the civilization in its progress is, indeed, equally impossible, but, as a compensation, it may be remembered that oriental life in antiquity passed through few changes, Kings and empires might flourish and disappear, but manners, customs, and occupations continued from century to century much as they had been in the beginning. Therefore it is possible to gather up in a single view the various aspects of the civilization of this people which, in its political career of more than two thousand years, was subject to the vicissitudes which the preceding chapters have described.

67. The earliest occupations of the inhabitants were agricultural. Great flocks of sheep and herds of cattle and goats, enumerated. in the lists of temple property, indicate that pastoral activities were not neglected. Herdsmen and shepherds formed a numerous class, recruited from the Bedouin constantly floating in from the desert. The chief grazing- grounds were to the west of the Euphrates. Here were gathered together herds belonging to different owners under the care of independent herdsmen who were paid to watch and protect their charges. But the raising of grain and fruits was by far more common, as might be expected from the nature of the country. The yield from the fertile soil was often two hundred-fold, sometimes more. All Babylonian life was affected by this predominating activity, The need of irrigation of the fields fostered an immense development of the canal system- At first, the lands nearest the rivers were watered by the primitive devices even now employed on their banks. It was a genial thought of King Urukagina to construct a canal, and wisely did he name it after the goddess Nina (Records of the Past, 2 ser. I. p. 72), for the work was worthy of divine approval. Soon the canal became the characteristic feature of the Babylonian landscape and the chief condition of agricultural prosperity. Land was named according to that which it produced, and some scholars hold that it was measured according to the amount of seed which could be sown upon it. At least three of the months had names connected with agriculture. The fruits of the fields were the chief gifts to the temples, and the king exacted his taxes in grain which was stored in royal granaries. It seems that the agricultural year began in September (the month tashritu, "beginning"). Then the farmer, usually a tenant of a rich noble, made his contract. The rent was ordinarily one-third of the farm's production, although sometimes tenant and landlord divided equally, Great care was taken that the tenant should keep everything in good order. Oxen were used for farm-work, and numerous agricultural implements were employed. Sowing and reaping, ploughing and threshing, irrigating and cultivating, — these constituted the chief events in the lives of the great mass of the Babylonian people, and made their land one of the richest and most prosperous regions in all the world.

68. The pursuits of industry appear from the beginning to have engaged the activities Of the Babylonians. Differentiation of labor has already taken place, and the names of the workers illustrate the variety of the occupations. The inscriptions mention the carpenter, the smith, the metal-worker, the weaver, the leather-worker, the dyer, the potter, the brick-maker, the vintner, and the surveyor. The abundance of wool led very early to the manufacture of woollen cloths and rugs, in which the Babylonians surpassed all others. The city of Mar (sect. 48) was famous for a kind of cloth, called after it Mairatu. Gold, silver, copper, and bronze were worked up into articles of ornament and utility. The making of bricks was a most important industry in a country where stone was practically unobtainable. The month simanu (May–June) was the "month of bricks," during which the conditions for their manufacture were most favorable; inundations had brought down the sifted alluvium which lay conveniently at hand; the sun shone mildly enough to bake the clay slowly and evenly; the reeds, used as a platform on which to lay the bricks for drying, or chopped finely and mixed with the clay, were fresh

and abundant. Innumerable quantities were used yearly. Sun-dried bricks were poor building material, and houses needed constant repairing or rebuilding after the heavy rains of the winter. The bricks baked in the kiln, of much more durable character, were used for the outer lining of temples and palaces.

69. The position of Babylonia gave it commercial importance, the evidences of which go back to the earliest times. Its central and accessible position, its wealth in natural products of an indispensable kind, its early industrial activity, all contributed to this end. Its lack of some materials of an equally indispensable character was an additional motive for exchange. Over the Persian gulf teak-wood found at Eridu was brought from India. Cotton also made its way from the same source to the southern cities. Over Arabia, by way of Ur, which stood at the foot of a natural opening from the desert, and owed its early fame and power, it may be, in no small degree, to its consequent commercial importance, were led the caravans laden with stone, spices, copper, and gold from Sinai, Yemen, and Egypt. Door-sockets of Sinaitic stone found at Nippur attest this traffic. To the north led the natural highways afforded by the rivers, and from thence, at the dawn of history, the city-kings brought cedar-wood from the Syrian mountains for the adornment of palaces and temples. From the East, down the pass of Holwan, came the marble and precious metal of the mountains. Much of this raw material was worked over by Babylonian artisans, and shipped back to the less favored lands, along with the grain, dates, and fish, the rugs and cloths, of native production. All this traffic was in the hands of Babylonian traders who fearlessly ventured into the borders of distant countries, and must have carried with them thither the knowledge of the civilization and wealth of their own home, for only thus can the wide-spread influence of Babylonian culture in the earliest periods be explained.

70. Babylonian society was well differentiated. At the basis of it lay the slave population, the necessary condition of all economic activity in antiquity. Slaves were employed upon the farms, by the manufacturers and in the temples. The sources of the supply were various. War furnished many; others had fallen from the position of free laborers; still others were purchased from abroad, or were children of native bondsmen. Rich private owners or temple corporations made a business of hiring them out as laborers. They were humanely treated; the law protected them from injury; they could earn money, hold property, and thus purchase their freedom. Laws exist which suggest that young children could not be separated from their slave-parents in case of the sale of the latter. Next in the scale stood the free laborer who hired himself out for work like that of the slave, and was his natural competitor. How he could continue to secure higher wages — as seems to be the case — is a problem which Peiser thinks explicable from the fact that his employer was not liable for damages in case of an injury, nor forced to care for him if he were sick. In both of these situations the law secured the reimbursement and protection of the slave (Mitteilungen der Vorderasiatischen Gesellschaft, 1896, 3), who could therefore safely work for less money. There are some references to wages in the contracts of the time which indicate that the free laborer received from four to six shekels ($3.00 to $4.50) a year, and food. He made a written contract with his employer in which were specified the rate and the length of time of employment. It is evident, however, that such laborers must have been few in comparison with slaves, and have steadily declined toward the lower position. The tenant-farmer must have been an important constituent of the social body, although he does not play a very prominent part. He rented the farm, hired the laborers, and superintended the agricultural operations. Great proprietors seem to have preferred the method of cultivating their estates by tenant-farmers, as many contracts of this kind attest. of the rent paid in kind mention has been made. The free peasant proprietor had by this time well-nigh disappeared before the rich and aristocratic landowner, and the tenant-farmer had taken his place. In the cities tradesmen and artisans were found in great numbers, and held in high esteem. Whether at this time they had been formed into guilds

according to their several trades, as was the case later, is uncertain. Merchants had their business organized; firms carried on their mercantile operations from generation to generation, records of which have been preserved; and this class of citizens must have been increasingly influential. At the summit of the social system was the aristocracy, headed by the king. The nobles lived on their estates and at the court of the king, alternately- The scanty evidence suggests that they held their estates from the king by a kind of feudal tenure. They owed military service and tribute. They had numerous dependants and slaves who labored for them and in turn enjoyed their protection.

71. The right of holding private property in land was already in force in Babylonia. It may be that pasture-land was still held in common, and the custom of deeding property to a son or adopted slave, on condition of the parent receiving his support during his lifetime from the property, is a relic of the transition from family to individual ownership. The king, theoretic owner by divine right of all the land, had long ago distributed it among his vassals, either in fee or perpetual possession. Careful surveys were made, and inscribed stones, set up on the limits of a property, indicated the possessor and invoked the curse of the gods on any who should interfere with property rights. Ground could be leased or handed down by will. In a community where trade was so important, wealth other than in land was common. Grain and manufactured goods, stored in warehouses in the cities, and precious metals formed no small part of the resources of the citizens. There still survived, in some transactions, payment in kind, grain or cattle; but in general the use of metals for exchange was in vogue. Naturally they became standards of value. They were weighed out and fashioned in bars. The shekel, weighing somewhat more than half an ounce avoirdupois, the mina of sixty shekels, and the talent of sixty minas were the standard weights, though there were other systems in use. Money was loaned, at first on condition of the borrower performing a certain amount of labor for it, later on an agreement to pay interest, usually at a very high rate.

72. On the whole, Babylonian life from the material point of view must have been active and agreeable. Cities were protected by high and thick walls to guard against enemies. Some sort of local organization existed for town government. Houses were simple and low, built with thick mud walls and flat roofs of reeds and mud. The streets were narrow and dirty, the receptacles of all the sweepings of the houses. When the street filled up to the level of the house doors, these were closed, the house built up another story, the floor raised to correspond, and a new door provided. Many houses were manufactories and shops at the same time, the merchant having his slaves or laborers do their work on the premises. on higher points stood the palaces of nobles and king, or the stately temples of the patron gods. In the country, the houses of the proprietors were surrounded by palm-trees and gardens. The furniture was very simple, — chair and stool to sit on by day, and a mat on which to sleep at night, flint and metal knives and a few terra-cotta bowls and jars for cooking and eating purposes, the oven for baking, and the fire-stick for kindling the fire. For food, the Babylonian had his inevitable grain and dried fish; the grain he ground and ate in round cakes seasoned with dates or other fruit; his drink was wine and beer. To wear much clothing in such a land was a superfluity. Rulers are depicted with quilted skirts reaching to the ankles, with no upper garment or headgear. others wear thick flat quilted caps. Naram Sin of Agade appears in a pointed hat with tunic thrown over his left shoulder and breast. Less important personages have hardly more than the loincloth. As for hair and beard, men of the earliest period seem to have been smoothly shaven, unless one is to suppose that the artist felt himself unequal to representing hair. Later, by the time of Sargon, the beard and hair are worn long, and the custom continued to be followed.

73. An important element of early Babylonian society was the family. It had its laws and its religion. While private property was recognized, yet often the consent of the family was

required for the sale of land belonging to one of its circle. The father was already the recognized head, Some traces of a primitive right of the mother exist, but they are survivals of what is quite antiquated. Ancient laws, preserved in late copies, illustrate family relations which long prevailed:

If a son say to his father, "Thou art not my father," he can cut off (his locks), make him a slave, and sell him for money. If a son say to his mother, "Thou art not my mother," she can cut off his locks, turn him out of town, or (at least) drive him away from home (i. e., she can have him deprived of citizenship and of inheritance, but his liberty he loses not). If a father say to his son, "Thou art not my son," the latter has to leave house and field (i. e., he loses everything). If a mother say to her son, "Thou art not my son," he shall leave house and furniture (ABL, p. 445).

Giving in marriage was an affair of the father, and was entirely on a mercantile basis. The prospective bridegroom paid a stipulated sum for his bride, varying according to his wealth, sometimes a shekel, sometimes a mina. Some religious ceremonies accompanied the marriage celebration, The wife usually brought a dowry to her husband. Polygamy and concubinage were not uncommon. The wife was completely under her husband's control. In certain circumstances she could be sold as a slave, or put to death. Divorce was very easy, since the husband had merely to bid the wife depart, giving her a writ of divorcement. The only restraint, and that probably a strong one, in the case Of a Babylonian, was that he was generally required to restore to the wife the value of her dowry. Sometimes by contract the wife had the control of her property, and was thereby in a much better position. To have children was the supreme end of marriage, and sterility was a serious misfortune. In that case adoption was a not uncommon recourse, accomplished by carefully drawn up legal forms. Children thus adopted had full rights. Adoption also was evidently an easy way of obtaining additional hands for service at home and in the fields, being really another form of hiring servants; hence often an adult was thus taken into a family.

74. The position occupied by the family in the social sphere was taken by the state in the domain of political life. It is held that the state was formed out of the union of families, indeed was a greater family with the king as father at its head (Reiser, IMAG, 1896, 3). In its first recognizable form, however, the state was a city gathered about a temple, the centre of worship. As has already been noted (sect. 48), each of the city-states of Babylonia had its god with whom its interests were identified. Religion, therefore, was fundamental in Babylonian politics, the bond of civic unity, the ground of political rights, authority, and progress. With it, no doubt, was also closely associated the economic element. The dependence of prosperity, and even of life itself, upon the proper regulation of the water supply encouraged settlement in the most favorable localities, and required organization of the activities centred there. Only by co-operation under a central authority could the canals be kept open, due regard be paid to the claims of all upon the common supply, and dangers from flood or famine be grappled with energetically and in time to safeguard the common interests, Self-protection from enemies contributed to the same end. The nomads from the desert and the mountain tribes of the east were equally eager to enjoy the fruits of the fertile Babylonian fields; their inhabitants must needs combine to ward off inroads from all sides. All these elements entered into and modified the character and course of Babylonian politics, and they gave a particular firmness and prominence to the idea of the state into which, from the earliest period, all family, clan, and tribal interests had been completely merged.

75. These Babylonian city-states have kings at their head. The earliest name given to the ruler is patesi, a term which is most satisfactorily explained as having a religious significance, and as testifying to the fundamental position and prerogative of the ruler as a priest of the city god.

It suggests that, in the primitive Babylonian community, the place of supreme importance and influence was occupied by the priest as the representative of deity, as the mediator between the clans and the gods on whom they depended. The attitude and activity of the early kings confirm this suggestion. They are, first of all, pious worshippers of the gods. They build temples and adorn them with the wealth of their kingdoms. They bestow upon the gods the richest gifts. The favor of deity is their supremest desire. Piety is their highest virtue. The duties of religion are an indispensable and interminable element of their life. Before the gods they come, as dependants and slaves, to make their offerings. They are girded about with burdensome ritual restrictions, the violation of which would entail disaster upon themselves and their people, and to which, therefore, they conform with constant alacrity and even with zeal. On the other hand, they claim before their subjects regard and reverence due to these intimate divine relations. Their inscriptions declare that they are nourished on the milk of the gods, or are their offspring, sons begotten of them; that power and sovereignty are by right of divine descent or appointment. It is not wonderful that, while these rulers placed their statues in the temples to be constantly before the eye of deity, their subjects should offer them divine homage. Indeed, from the time of Sargon of Agade, kings claim to be gods and do not hesitate to prefix the sign of divinity to their names (Radau, Early Babylonian History, pp. 307 ff.). All these prerogatives, however, do not free them from responsibility to their subjects, but rather intensify the expectations centred in them. They must obtain divine blessing for the state; they must themselves battle in defence of their people. Thus the Babylonian king is a warrior, going out to protect his dominions against wild beasts or hostile men. To kill the lion or the wild ox is an indispensable part of his duties, and he goes forth in the strength of the gods for these heroic struggles. He is as proud of the trophies of the chase as of those of the battlefield, and both alike he dedicates to the divine powers by whose aid he has conquered. He represents, also, the more peaceful interests of the state as the patron of industry; he appears like king Ur Nina, with the basket of the mason on his head, or rehearses his services in opening new canals, building granaries, and importing foreign trees to beautify and enrich the land, thus establishing his claim to be the father and shepherd of his people.

76. The constitution of a state ruled by a king with such prerogatives and position is naturally summed up in the ruler. The citizen, while he expects protection and justice, is a subject; the officials are the king's dependants; his will is law; and the strength of the state depends upon the personality of its head. Yet it is also true that, where industry and commerce were so early and so highly developed as in Babylonia, the arbitrariness of the ruler was modified by the necessity of a well-ordered and strictly administered body of constitutional principles. Trade was dependent on the admission and protection of foreigners while in the country, and they seem to have had no difficulty in securing citizenship, and even in obtaining official positions. The revenues were secured by various systems of taxation. Surveys of state property were made, on the basis of which land taxes were levied. The temples took their tithe. Customs duties were paid at the city gate. In time of war, the king rode in his chariot at the head of his troops, as illustrated in the stele of the Vultures, where Edingiranagin (sects. 56, 85) holds in his hand the curved weapon for throwing, and his warriors are armed with spears. At the close of the battle he beats out the brains of captives with his club in honor of the gods. The city of the same king seems to have possessed a coat of arms, "the lion-headed eagle with outspread wings," its claws in the backs of two lions, significant of the corporate consciousness of the state even at this early day.

77. But what shows most clearly the idea of political organization as established in Babylonia is the legal system. Fragments of law codes are still in existence governing the relations of the family (sect. 73), and, from the abundance of legal documents containing decisions, agreements, penalties, etc., might be drawn up a body of law which bore on such various topics as adoption, exchange, marriage, divorce, stealing, adultery, and other crimes, renting

and sale of property, inheritance, loans, partnership, slavery, and interest. No business arrangement seems to have been complete without a written contract, signed by the parties concerned in the presence of witnesses, who also affixed their signatures to the document. Should a difficulty or question in dispute arise, the contestants had several methods of procedure. They could choose an arbitrator by whose decision they agreed to abide; or, sometimes, the complainant appealed to the king, who with his elders heard the complaint and rendered judgment. Sometimes a court of judges was established, before which cases were brought. Whatever was the process, the decision, when rendered, was written down in all the fulness and formality of legal phraseology, duly signed and sealed with the finger-nail or the private Or official seal of all the parties. That the king himself was not above the law, at least in the ideal conception of political philosophers of the time, be concluded from an ancient bit of political

Join preserved in a copy in the library of Ashurbanipal of Assyria which begins: "If the king gives not judgment according to the law, the people perish ... if he gives not judgment according to the law of the land, (the god) Ea . . . gives his place to another, — if he gives not judgment according to the statutes, his country suffers invasion." Very suggestive is another line of the same document. "If he gives not judgment according to (the desire of) his nobles, his days are long" (IV. Rawlinson, 55). Thus gods and the king alike are regarded as pledged to the maintenance of justice. The parties to a contract swear by the god, the king, and the city that they will keep their agreements. The abundance of this legal material has led some scholars to the conclusion voiced by Professor Maspero, who declares that these records " reveal to us a people greedy of gain, exacting, litigious, and almost exclusively absorbed by material concerns " (Dawn of Civilization, p. 760). While there may be truth in this verdict, no one can deny that the spectacle of a people, in these early times, carrying on their affairs through agreements sanctioned by the state, and settling their quarrels by process of legal procedure is one which arouses surprise, if not admiration, and indicates a conception of civic order full of the promise of progress.

IV.CIVILIZATION OF OLD BABYLONIA: LITERATURE, SCIENCE, ART, AND RELIGION

78. A PEOPLE as far advanced in social and political organization as were the ancient Babylonians could not have failed to make similar progress in the higher elements of civilization. They were, indeed, pre-eminently a practical folk, and were guided in all their activities by the material ends to be gained. Their literary remains will serve as an illustration in point. Writing, in use among them from the earliest times, was primarily employed for business purposes, in contracts and other legal documents. Likewise the very practical conjuration formulæ were the most numerous of the religious texts. The art of writing was confined in great measure to priestly circles, to scribes taught in the priestly schools and associated with the temples. Documents of all kinds were written to order by these scribes, and the signature affixed by pressing the thumb-nail or a seal into the clay. The difficulty of acquiring the complicated cuneiform script cut off the majority of the people from ever using it. For teaching it, a number of text-books were employed which were copied by the students. Some of the most valuable inscriptional material, like the kings' lists, have come down to us in these students' copies. In Sippar, an inscription on a small round tablet has been found, the contents of which suggest that it may have been an ancient diploma or medal of that famous priestly school. It reads, "Whosoever has distinguished himself at the place of tablet-writing shall shine as the light" (Hilprecht, Recent Research, etc., p. 86). The scribes were, indeed, not

only an honorable, but even an indispensable element of Babylonian society; upon them depended social and political progress. The large number of letters now in our museums from officials and private persons, both men and women, shows that communication by means of writing was widespread, but all letters were probably put into writing by scribes, and it is to be presumed that scribes were employed to read them to their recipients. One cannot safely argue from these letters or from the business documents that ability to read and write belonged to the people at large.

79. Old Babylonia was, from the earliest historical period, not merely in possession of a highly conventionalized form of writing, but already had also begun to produce a literature which embraced no narrow range of subjects. The chief element in it was religious, consisting of hymns, psalms, myths, ritual prescripts, and votive inscriptions. Even where religion is not directly the subject, the documents show its influence. Thus the astronomical and astrological texts are from priestly circles, and the epic and descriptive poetry deals with the gods and heroes of mythology. Reference has already been made to the legal codes and to fragments of political wisdom, while our knowledge of the history of the age comes from the various royal inscriptions written on palace walls, cylinders, steles, and statues. The origin of this literary activity lies back of the beginning of history. Before the age of Sargon, once thought primitive, extends a long period from which important royal texts have been preserved. Sargon, indeed, is thought to have focussed the literary activity of his time in a series of religious works prepared for his royal library in Agade, and no doubt every ruler who obtained wider dominion than that over a single city-state took occasion to foster science and literature. Even Gudea of Shirpurla, whose political position is uncertain, had long narratives of his pious acts carved on his statues for the enlightenment and praise of posterity. Chief among these patrons of learning was the founder of Babylonian unity, Khammurabi, under whom the previous achievements of scholars, theologians, and poets were gathered together and edited into literary works of prime importance. In his time or shortly after, the cosmogonic narratives, the rituals, the epics, the laws, and the astronomical works were put into the form in which they are now preserved.

80. The characteristics of all Babylonio-Assyrian literature, as already enumerated (sect. 34), were stamped upon it in this early period. The material in stone and clay, upon which alone from the first men wrote, compelled simplicity of utterance. Religion, the first subject for literary effort, determined the style and dominated the content of subsequent literature. Religion is responsible for the stereotyped phraseology and the repetitiousness approaching monotony, the expressions having become fixed at an early period and employed in sacred ceremonials at a time when literature was looked upon as a gift of the gods and set apart for their service. Thus what at the beginning was a desirable repetition of holy words became at last the accepted form for all literary utterance. Poetry evidently was the earliest and most favored medium of literature, for it reached a comparatively high stage of development. The lyric appears in hymns, prayers, and psalms for use in the liturgical worship. Narrative poetry is represented in a variety of fragments which describe the adventures of early heroes who have dealings with gods and monsters of the primeval world. Even the culminating achievement of an epic has been reached in the story of Gilgamesh, preserved in twelve books, a Babylonian Odyssey. This poetry is not naïve in character; already epithets have become conventional; rhythm pervades it, rising into parallelism, the balancing of expressions in corresponding lines, phrases, or sentences, which express now antithetic ideas, now the same idea in different forms. Even metre and strophical arrangement are regarded by some scholars as discoverable in the hymns and epic fragments. How far back in the unknown past must be placed the beginnings of this literary activity which has attained such development in this early age of Babylonia!

81. The authors of these writings are unknown. A few names have come down in connection with certain poems, but it is not unlikely that they are names of scribes who copied, or of priests who recited the epics or the hymns. The fact is significant, for it indicates that the literature is the work of a class, not of individuals; that it grew into form under the shaping of many hands; that what has survived is, in its well-organized whole, the flower of uncounted generations of priestly activity. The books were made up of pages, numbered according to the number of tablets required; each tablet was marked for identification with the opening words of the book; the tablets were deposited in the temples in chambers prepared with shelves for the purpose. Editors and commentators were already busy, arranging and revising the literature of the past. Scholars have concluded that the narrative of the deluge in the Gilgamesh epic is composed of two earlier versions joined together by such a reviser. Whether these temple libraries were open to the public is questionable, and indeed one is not to conclude from this splendid outburst of early literature that the Babylonians were therefore a literary people, even as one cannot argue from the abundance of written business documents that there was a general ability to read and write. That the production of literary works and interest in them were confined primarily to the priests, and secondarily to the upper classes, is, in our present scarcity of information, the safest conclusion.

82. What has already been said will prepare the reader for a judgment upon the general character of this literature. The material on which it must needs be written, the early age in which it appears, and the priestly influence which dominates it are to be taken into account in such an estimate. It is not just to bring into comparison the literary work of later peoples, such as the Hebrews or the Greeks; the Egyptian literature of the same period may more properly be regarded as a competitor. Thus tested, the Babylonian undoubtedly comes off superior. Its imagery, while sometimes fantastic, is often bold and strong, sometimes weird, even fresh and delicate. Its form, particularly in the poetry, is highly developed, rhythmical, and flowing. Its thought is not seldom profound with the mysteries of life and death and vigorous in grappling with these problems. Especially remarkable is the fine talent for narration, as Tiele has observed in his estimate of the literature (BAG, pp. 572 f). Over against Maspero's strange dictum that "the bulk of Chaldean literature seems nothing more than a heap of pretentious trash" (Dawn of Civ., p. 771), may be placed Sayce's general remark that "even if we judge it from a merely literary point of view, we shall find much to admire" (Babylonian Literature, p. 70), and the more detailed conclusion of Baumgartner, particularly as to the Gilgamesh Epic, that, "regarded purely as poetry, it has a kind of primitive force, haunting voices that respond to the great problems of human life, suffering, death, and the future, dramatic vividness of representation and utterance, a painting of character and a depicting of nature which produce strong effects with few strokes" (Geschichte der Weltlitteratur, I. p. 84). The influence which this literature exerted upon other peoples is a proof of its power. Its mythological conceptions reappear in Hebrew imagery; its epic figures in Greek religious lore. The dependence of the Hebrew narratives of the creation and deluge upon the similar Babylonian stories may be uncertain, but the form of the hymns, their lyrical and rhythmical structure, has, in all probability, formed the model for Hebrew psalmody, while many of the expressions of religious feeling and aspiration, first wrought out in the temples of Babylonia, have entered into the sacred language of universal religion.

83. The ancient Babylonians had made some important advances in the direction of scientific knowledge and its application to life. Both the knowledge and its application, however, were inspired and dominated by religion, a fact which has its good and evil aspects. No doubt, religion acted as a powerful stimulus to the entering of the various fields of knowledge on the part of those best fitted to make discoveries, the priests; to this fact is due the remarkably early acquisitions of the Babylonians in these spheres. On the other hand, knowledge sought not for its own sake, but in the interests of religion, was conceived of under religious forms, employed

primarily for religious purposes, and subordinated to religious points of view. The notion of the universe, for example, was primarily that of a region where men and gods dwelt; its compartments were arranged to provide the proper accommodations for them. The earth was figured as an inverted basket, or bowl (the mountain of the world), its edges resting on the great watery deep. on its outer surface dwelt mankind. Within its crust was the dark abode of the dead. Above, and encompassing it, resting on the waters, was another hemisphere, the heaven, on the under side of which moved the sun, moon, and stars; on the outer side was supported another vast deep, behind which in eternal light dwelt the gods. On the east and west of heaven were gates through which the sun passed at morning and night in his movement under the heavenly dome, In a chamber just outside the eastern gate, the gods met to determine the destinies of the universe. The movements of the world, the relations of nature to man, were likewise regarded as the activities of the divine powers in making revelations to humanity or in bringing their wills to bear on mankind. Since to know their will and way was indispensable for happiness, the priest studied the stars and the plants, the winds and the rocks, and interpreted what he learned in terms of practical religion. Medicine consisted largely in the repetition of formulæ to drive out the demons of disease, a ritual of exorcism where the manipulations and the doses had little if any hygienic basis. Yet an ancient book of medical praxis and a list of medicinal herbs show that some real progress was made in the knowledge of the body and of actual curative agencies.

84. The high development of mathematical science began in the same sacred source. The forms and relations of geometry were employed for purposes of augury. The heavens were mapped out, and the courses of the heavenly bodies traced to determine the bearing of their movements upon human destinies. Astrology was born in Babylonia and became the mother of Astronomy. The world of nature in its various physical manifestations was studied for revelations of the divine will, and the resulting skill of the priests in the science of omens was unsurpassed in the ancient world. Yet, withal, they had worked out a numerical system, compounded of the decimal and the sexagesimal series. The basis was the "soss," 60; the "ner" was 600; the "sar," 3600, The metrology was accurate and elaborate, and formed the starting-point of all other systems of antiquity. All measures of length, area, capacity, and weight were derived from a single standard, the hand-breadth. The division of the circle into degrees, minutes, and seconds on the sexagesimal basis (360°, 60', 60") hails from this period and people. The ecliptic was marked off into the twelve regions, and the signs of the zodiac, as we know them, already designated. The year of three hundred sixty-five and one-fourth days was known, though the common year was reckoned according to twelve months of thirty days each, and equated with the solar year by intercalating a month at the proper times. Tables of stars and their movements, of eclipses of moon and sun, were carefully prepared. The year began with the month Nisan (March–April); the day with the rising of the sun; the month was divided into weeks of seven days; the day from sunrise to sunrise into twelve double hours of sixty minutes. The clepsydra and the sun-dial were Babylonian inventions for measuring time.

85. The materials from which are obtained a knowledge of the history of early Babylonia offer, at the same time, testimony as to the artistic development, which may be traced, therefore, through the three historic epochs. In the pre-Sargonic period almost all the available material is that in stone and metal found at Shirpurla. on a bas-relief of King Ur Nina he stands with a basket upon his head, his shoulders and bust bare, a skirt about his waist descending to his feet. Before him his children, represented as of much smaller stature, express their obeisance by the hands clasped across the breast. The heads and feet are in profile, while the bodies are presented full to the spectator, thus producing a contorted effect. The whole, while full of simplicity and vigor, is crude and rough. The long sharp noses, retreating foreheads, and large deep-set eyes give a strange bird-like appearance to the faces. The so-called "vulture stele" of Edingiranagin (sect. 76) is much more complex in its design, It is a large piece of

white stone carved on both faces. On the one side four scenes in the war are represented — the battle, the victory, the funeral rites and thank-offering, the execution of the captives. On the other side, the booty is heaped up before the gods, and the coat of arms of Shirpurla is held aloft in the king's hand. The scenes are spiritedly sketched, and artistic unity is sought in the complicated representation. The silver vase of Entemena (sect. 56) is the finest piece of metal work of the time. It rises gracefully from a bronze pedestal, rounds out to one-half its height, and ends in a wide vertical collar. Its sides are adorned with eagles, goats, lions, and other animals. The age of Sargon is introduced by the splendid bas-relief of Naram Sin, found on the upper Tigris. What remains of it is a fragment only, but it represents a royal figure, bearded, with conical cap, a tunic thrown over the breast and left shoulder, leaving bare the right arm, which grasps a weapon. The work is singularly fine and strong (Hilprecht, OBT, I. ii, pl. xxii). The height of the plastic art of the time is reached in the statues of Gudea of Shirpurla (sect, 60). They are of very hard stone, but the artist has neglected no detail. The king is represented in the attitude of submission before the gods, his hands clasped upon his breast. The head is gone from every statue, but heads of other statues have been found which illustrate the method of treatment. A thick cap or turban is worn on the head, and the tunic, as in the Naram Sin bas-relief, leaves the right arm bare and descends to the feet. Special study is given to this drapery; the very folds are somewhat timidly reproduced, In mastery of his material the artist has made much progress since the early days. The impression given is one of severe simplicity, directness, attention to detail, and concentrated power (Maspero, DC, pp. 611 ff.).

86. The works just mentioned are the highest achievements of the sculptor's and goldsmith's art. But, in a variety of smaller objects, similar artistic skill appears. The alabaster vases, dedicated by the earliest kings at Nippur, the terra-cotta vases, ornamented with rope patterns, found in the same place, the copper and bronze statuettes and vessels of various kinds, (the pottery is, in general, strange to say, rude and inartistic,) and numerous other implements and objects are testimonies to the same artistic ability. Particularly are the seal cylinders worthy of mention, Reference has already been made to the use of the seal by the Babylonians. Hard pebbles of carnelian, jasper, chalcedony, and porphyry were rounded into cylinders from two to three fifths of an inch in diameter and from three-quarters of an inch to an inch and a half in length; then upon the surface were incised scenes from mythology or figures of holy beings, such as Gilgamesh in his contest with the lion, or the sun or moon god receiving homage from his servant. Stamped upon the soft clay of a document, the seal imparted, as it were, the sanction of the gods to the agreement as well as certified to the good faith of the signer The work of the engraver of these seals is remarkable. The best of them, such as that of the scribe of Sargon of Agade (Maspero, DC, p. 601; compare B. M. Guide, pl. xxiii) show extraordinary fineness of workmanship, breadth of treatment, and realistic fidelity to fact. Indeed, of all the art of early Babylonia it may be said that it is eminently realistic; the artist has little sense of the ideal or the general. To present the fact as it is, with simplicity verging on bareness, and with a directness that is almost too abrupt, — this was at the same time the weakness and the strength of the Babylonian sculptor or engraver. This trait is specially evident in his conception of the gods. He was the first to present them as human beings. But his anthropomorphism is rude and crude. The divine beings are not greater or grander than the men who worship them. The conception, indeed, was original and epoch-making. But it was reserved for the Greeks to improve upon it by glorifying and idealizing the human forms under which they represented their Apollo and their Zeus. Another peculiarity which worked to the disadvantage of Babylonian art was the convention which demanded drapery in the representation of the human form. Here too is realism, for the changeable climate doubtless required men to wear thicker clothing, and that more constantly, than, for example, in Egypt. Hence the study of the nude body and the sense of beauty and grace which it develops were absent. The long robes give-a stiffness and sameness to the figures for which the greater skill attained in the representation of drapery hardly compensated.

87. Although the early Babylonians had little stone or wood with which to build, they used clay bricks with architectural originality and effectiveness. The palace or temple was not built upon the level of the ground, but upon a rectangular brick platform. At Shirpurla this was forty feet high; at Nippur forty-five feet above the plain. Upon it stood the palace structure of brick, one story high, with its corners usually facing the cardinal points. The walls were very thick, the chambers small and dark, the passages narrow and often vaulted. Vertical walls and flat roofs were the rule. The rooms, courts, galleries, and passages stretched away interminably, yet with a definite plan, within the rectangle. Huge buttresses of brick sustained the platform, and pilasters supported the walls of the structure built upon it. Access to the building was obtained by a staircase rising from the plain. To protect all from the tremendous rains which would tend to undermine the walls, the solid mass of the platform was threaded by terra-cotta drains which carried the water down to the plain. Ventilating shafts, likewise, were used to let in the air and drain off the moisture. The temple was sometimes, like the palace, a series of one-story buildings, but usually culminated in what was a type of temple construction peculiar to Babylonia, the ziggurat, a series of solid masses of brick, placed one above the other, each successive story smaller than the one beneath it. A staircase or an inclined plane led from the shelf of one story to the next; shrines were placed on the shelves or hollowed out of the brick; the shrine of the chief deity was at the top. At Nippur the earliest ziggurat upon the massive temple platform, built by Ur-Gur, was a rectangular oblong, about one hundred and seventy-five feet by one hundred, and composed of three stages resting one upon the other (Peters, Nippur, II. p. 124). The massiveness and monotony of these structures were relieved by the use of stucco to cover and protect the bricks both without and within. Conical nails of colored terra-cotta were embedded in this stucco, or decorative designs were painted upon it. Enamelled bricks likewise were employed for exterior coatings of walls. For supports of the roofs tree trunks were used, which were covered with metal sheathing. Thus Babylonia became the birthplace of the decorated wall and the slender column (Sayce, Babylonia and Assyria, p. 9). The earliest known keyed arch has been unearthed at Nippur. The doors of the palaces were hung in huge blocks of stone hollowed out in the centre to receive the door-posts, almost the only use of stone found in these buildings. Remembering the material at the disposal of these architects, one cannot but admire the originality and utility of the designs wrought out by them. They made up for lack of stone by the heaping together of great masses of brick. The elevation of the buildings and the thickness of the walls served, at the same time, to make the effect more imposing, to supply a surer defence against enemies, and to afford protection from heat and storms.

88. It has frequently been noted hitherto how the life of the ancient Babylonian was deeply interfused with his religion. The priests are judges, scribes, and authors. Writing is first employed in the service of the gods. Both the themes and the forms of literature are inspired by religion. Art receives its stimulus from the same source, the royal statues standing as votive offerings in the temples and the seal cylinders being engraved with figures of divine beings. Science, whether it be medicine or mathematics, has, as its ground, the activity of the heavenly powers, or, as its end, the enlarging of religious knowledge. Therefore it is fitting to close this review of early Babylonian civilization with a sketch of the religion. Already the fact has been observed that, from the beginning, the city-states possessed temples, each the centre of the worship of a particular god (sect. 48). Thus at Eridu was Ea; at Ur, Sin, the moon god; at Larsam, Shamash, the sun god; at Uruk, the goddess Ishtar; at Shirpurla, Ningirsu; at Nippur, Enlil or Bel; at Kutha, Nergal; at Sippar, Shamash; at Agade, the goddess Anunit; at Babylon, Marduk; and at Borsippa, Nabu. From this list of gods it is evident at first glance that religion was local and that the gods were in some cases powers of nature. Clearly a more than primitive stage of development had been reached, since the same god was worshipped in two different cities. Investigation has made these facts more certain by showing that Ningirsu,

Nergal, and Marduk are, probably, forms of the sun god; that Anunit is but another name for Ishtar; that Enlil was a storm god; that at each of these cities a multitude of minor deities was worshipped; and that similar local worship was carried on at less known centres of population. The religious inscriptions of Gudea of Shirpurla (sect. 60) show a well-organized pantheon consisting of a variety of male and female deities with Ningirsu in the lead. Here appears the god Anu, "the heaven," who, though not prominent in local worship, stands theoretically at the head of all the gods. The religion of early Babylonian history, then, was a local nature worship which was passing into a more or less formal organization and unification of deities as a result of political development or theological formulation.

89. Behind this advanced stage was another and very different phase of Babylonian religion testified to by a body of conjuration formulæ and hymns of similar tenor. In the great mass of this literature the names of the gods just enumerated are hardly mentioned. The world is peopled with spirits, Zi, good and evil beings, whose relations to man determine his condition and destiny. If he suffers from sickness, it is an attack of a demon who must be driven out by a formula, or by an appeal to a stronger spirit of good. These powers are summed up under various names indicative of the beginnings of organization, as, for example, "spirit of heaven" (zi ana), "spirit of earth" (zi kia); "lord of demons" (en lil); "lord of earth" (en ki). As the sense of good, of beneficent, powers got the better of the fear of harm and ruin in the minds of men, the spirit-powers passed into gods. Thus the "spirit of heaven" became Anu; the "lord of earth" or the "spirit of earth" was identified with Ea of Eridu; the "lord of demons" was found again in Bel of Nippur. A first triad of Babylonian gods was thus constituted in Anu, Bel, and Ea. As religion grew in firmness of outline and organization, the hosts of spirits retreated before the great gods, and, while not disappearing, took a subordinate place, in private or individual worship, and continued to exercise an important influence upon the faith and practice of the people. The divine beings, whether rising out of local spirits or spirits of nature or the combination of both, took the field and marked the transition to the new phase of religion in which the beneficent powers were recognized as the superior beings, and received the worship and gifts of the community.

90. The general notion of divine beings entertained by the old Babylonian is illustrated by the term for god, ilu, which conveys the root idea of power, might. It was as "strong" ones that the spirits came into contact with man from the beginning. It was the heavenly powers of sun and moon and stars and storm that of all nature-forces had most impressed him. He indicated his attitude toward them also by the favorite descriptive term "lord" (en, bel). They were above him, supreme powers whom he served and obeyed in humility and dependence. Yet mighty as were the gods, and exalted as they were above humanity, the Babylonian was profoundly conscious of the influences brought to bear by the divine world upon mankind. From the period when he felt himself surrounded by manifold spirits of the natural world, to the time when he sought to do the will of the great heavenly powers, he was ever the centre of the play of the forces of the other world. They were never far from him in purpose and action. The stars moving over the sky spoke to him of their will and emitted divine influences; the wind, the storm, the earthquake, the eclipse, the actions of animals, the flight of birds, — all conveyed the divine messages to him who could interpret them. Hence arose the immense mass of magical texts, the pseudo-science of astrology, and the doctrine of omens. The religious temper produced by such an idea of god was twofold. On the one hand the divine influence was felt as pure power, arbitrary, undefined, and not to be counted on; hence to be averted at all hazards, restrained by magical means, or rendered favorable by an elaborate ritual. Or, the worshipper felt in the divine presence a sense of ill-desert, and, in his desire for harmony with the divine ruler, flung himself in confession and appeal upon the mercy of his god in those remarkable Penitential Psalms in which fear, suffering, and a sense of guilt are so joined together as almost to defy analysis and to forbid a final judgment as to the essence of the

ethical quality. Those who first felt the emotions which these psalms reveal were certainly on the road leading to the heights of moral aspiration and renewal. The difficulty was that the element of physical power in the gods was ineradicable and, corresponding to it, the use of magic to constrain the divine beings crept into all religious activity and endeavor, thus thwarting all moral progress. Though men recognized that their world had been won from chaos to cosmos by the gods under whose authority they lived, — for this was the meaning of the victory of Marduk over Tiamat, — they conceived of the victory in terms of the natural physical universe, not as a conquest of sin by the power of holiness and truth.

91. The conduct of worship was no doubt originally the task of the priest. He afterward became king, and carried with him into his royal position many of the prerogatives and the restrictions attending the priestly office. He was the representative of the community before the gods, and therefore girt about with sanctity which often involved strict tabu. But he soon divided his powers with others, priests strictly so called, who performed the various duties connected with the priestly service and whose names and offices have in part come down to us. Rituals have been preserved for various parts of the service; many hymns have survived which were sung or recited. Sacrifices of animals were made, libations poured out, and incense burned. Priests wore special dresses, ablutions were strongly insisted upon, clean and unclean animals were carefully distinguished, special festivals were kept in harmony with the changes of the seasons and the movements of the heavenly bodies. Religious processions, in which the gods were carried about in arks, ships, or chests, were common. A calendar of lucky and unlucky days was made. A Sabbath was observed for the purpose of assuaging the wrath of the gods, that their hearts might rest (Jastrow, in Am. Jour. of Theol., II. p. 315 f.). Every indication points to the existence of a powerful priesthood whose influence was felt in all spheres of social and national life.

92. The outlook of the Babylonians upon the life beyond was sombre. Burial customs indicate that they believed in future existence, since drink and food were placed with the dead in their graves. But, in harmony with the severer conception of God, the Babylonian thought of the future had an uncertain and forbidding aspect. The poem which describes the descent of the goddess Ishtar to the abode of the dead, called Arallu, conceives of this region as dark and dusty, where the shades flit about like birds in spaces shut in by bars, whence there is no egress. There is the realm of Nergal, and of queen Allat who resents the presence of Ishtar, goddess of life and love, and inflicts dire punishments upon her. Yet in this prison-house there is a fountain of life, though sealed with seven seals; and in the Epic of Gilgamesh are heroes who have reached the home of the blessed, — indications that the higher religious aspiration was seeking after a conception of the future more in harmony with the belief in great and beneficent deities dwelling in the light and peace of the upper heaven. It was the darker view, however, that passed from Babylonia to the west and reappeared in the dusky Sheol of the Hebrews, into which all, whether good or bad, descended, there to prolong a sad and shadowy existence.

93. In concluding this presentation of early Babylonian life it is possible to sum up the dominant forces of history and progress under three heads: (1) Religion is the inspiring and regulative element of the community. In its representatives government finds its first officials. In the centre of each city is the temple with its ruling and protecting deity. Political growth is indicated by the wider worship of the local god. The citizens and their lords are servants of the god. He is the fount of justice, and his priests are guardians of culture. Industry and commerce have their sanctions in the oaths of the gods, and the temples themselves are centres of mercantile activity; they are the banks, the granaries, and the seats of exchange. All life is founded on religion and permeated by its influence. (2) The energizing element of these communities is the ruler. Already the power of personality has made itself felt. Political

organization has crystallized about the individual. He exercises supreme and unlimited power, as servant of the deity and representative of divine authority. He is the builder, the general, the judge, the high priest. All the affairs of his people are an object of solicitude to him. His name is perpetuated upon the building-stones of the temple and the palace. His figure is preserved in the image which stands before the god in his temple. He is sometimes, in literal truth, the life of his people. (3) From these two forces united, religion and the ruler, springs the third element, the impulse to expansion. Neither god nor king is satisfied with local sovereignty. The ambition of the one is sanctified and stimulated by the divine commendation, encouragement, and effectual aid of the other. The god claims universal sway. The king, his representative, goes forth to conquer under his command. The people follow their human and their divine lords whithersoever they lead. In that period circumstances were also particularly favorable to such forward movements. Communication between the different cities was made easy by the innumerable watercourses threading the plain. The mighty rivers offered themselves as avenues for wider expansion. Such was Old Babylonia in its essential characteristics. Such was the philosophy of its early history, illustrated by the details of the struggles which have already been described (Part I. chap. II.). The end was a united Babylonia, achieved by the great king Khammurabi, in whom all these forces culminated.

V .THE TIMES OF KHAMMURABI OF BABYLON.

2300-2100 B. C.

94. IT is clear that the city of Babylon did not play a prominent part in early Babylonian history (sect. 50). It was not, like Agade, Shirpurla, Uruk, or Ur, the centre of a flourishing and aggressive state, nor had it any religious pre-eminence such as was enjoyed by Nippur or Eridu. Such an assertion is not based merely on a lack of inscriptional information which future excavation may be trusted to supply. Existing inscriptions of the early time take no account of the city. This would not be the case if its importance had been recognized. The religious hymns do not mention it. Its god Marduk takes a secondary place in the later pantheon, below Bel of Nippur, Ea of Eridu, Sin of Ur, and Shamash of Sippar. In the time of the kings of Agade, Babylon is said to be a part of their dominions and Sargon built a temple there. The fact is significant, and suggests that the city was overshadowed by the greater power and fame of Sargon's capital. Only when the political and commercial pre-eminence of the more northern state passed away, was an opportunity given to Babylon. By that time, however, the southern cities had seized the leadership and had held it for a thousand years. Accordingly, not till the middle of the third millennium B. C. (sect. 63), did the first historical Babylonian king appear and the city push forward into political importance. Its progress, thereafter, was rapid and brilliant.

95. The first five kings of the first dynasty were as follows:

Sumu-abu	about	2399-2384.
Sumula-ilu	"	2384-2349.
Zabum	"	2349-2335.
Abil Sin	"	2335-2317.
Sin-muballit . . .	"	2317-2297.

Immerum (usurper?)

From none of these kings have inscriptions been recovered, but what has been called a

"Chronicle" of their doings year by year, and business documents dated in their reigns, together with references to some of them by later kings, give an insight into their affairs. The Babylonian kings' list indicates that, beginning with Zabum, son succeeded father. Immerum appears in the business documents, but without indication of his place in the dynasty. The kings' list does not name him, and he is therefore regarded as a usurper. No light has been shed on the events connected with the accession of the first king to the Babylonian throne. From the names of the kings it has been inferred that the dynasty was of Arabian origin, and that the new outburst of Babylonian might which now ensues is due to the infusion of new blood in consequence of an Arabian invasion which placed its leaders on the throne. The hypothesis is certainly plausible. The events of Sumuabu's reign are largely peaceful, temple building and the offering of crowns to the deities being the chief matters of moment. Toward the close, however, the city of Kaçallu, presumably in the vicinity of Babylon, was laid waste, — a suggestion that Babylon was already beginning to let its power be felt in the north. A later king of this dynasty, Samsu-iluna, states that he rebuilt six great walls or castles which had been built in the reign of Sumulailu, the second king, who also fortified Babylon and Sippar, overthrew Kaçallu again, and destroyed the city of Kish. He, too, was a devout worshipper of the gods. A king of New Babylonia (Nabuna'id) refers to a sun-temple in Sippar which dated back to Zabum, and the "Chronicle" speaks of other temples and shrines. The inference from these relations with cities outside Babylon suggests that by Zabum's time Babylon had extended its sway in north Babylonia and was ready to enter the south. It was, accordingly, with Sinmuballit that complications arose with southern Babylonia, then under the hegemony of Rim Sin of Larsam, an Elamite conqueror. The chronicle states that Isin was taken in the seventeenth year of the Babylonian king. If business documents which are dated by the capture of this city are properly interpreted, it appears to have been the centre of a conflict between the two powers, since it was apparently captured alternately by both. The issue of the war is unknown.

96. While so scanty an array of facts avails for the history of these early kings, with the sixth king, Khammurabi (about 2297-2254 B. C.) a much clearer and wider prospect is opened. The fact that an unusually large amount of inscriptional material comes from his reign is an indication that a change has taken place in the position and fortunes of his city. The first and most striking confirmation of the change, furnished by this material, is its testimony to the overthrow of the Elamite power (sect. 64). Knowledge of the causes which brought Khammurabi into collision with Rim Sin of Larsam, as well as of the events of the struggle, is not, indeed, furnished in the inscriptions. Sinmuballit and Rim Sin had al ready met before Isin, and the new conflict may have been merely a renewal of the war. From the narrative contained in Genesis xiv. 1, 2, it has been inferred that Khammurabi (Amraphel) had been a vassal of the Elamite king and rebelled against him (sect. 65). However that may be, the Babylonian represented the native element in a reaction against invaders and foreign overlords which resulted in their expulsion. There is probably a reference to the decisive moment of this struggle in the dating of a business document of the time "in the year in which king Khammurabi by the might of Anu and Bel established his possessions [or "good fortune"] and his hand overthrew the lord [or "land," ma-da], of Iamutbal and king Rim Sin." The Elamites seem to have retired to the east, whither the king's lieutenants, Siniddinam and Inuhsamar, pursued them, crossing the river Tigris and annexing a portion of the Elamite lowland (King, Letters and Inscriptions of Hammurabi, I. xxxvi. ff.) which was thereafter made more secure by fortifications. In the south of Babylonia the king reduced to subjection cities which opposed his progress, and destroyed their walls. His dominion extended over the whole of Babylonia and eastward across the Tigris to the mountains of Elam. He could proclaim himself in his inscriptions "the mighty king, king of Babylon, king of the Four (world-) Regions, king of Shumer and Akkad, into whose power the god Bel has given over land and people, in whose hand he has placed the reins of government (to direct them)," thus uniting in his own person

the various titles of earlier kings.

97. Though Khammurabi "was pre-eminently a conquering king" (Jastrow, Religion of Babylonia and Assyria, p. 119), he was not behind in his arrangements for the economic welfare of his kingdom. One of his favorite titles is bani matim, "builder of the land," descriptive of his measures for the recovery of the country from the devastations of the years of war and confusion. Of his canals, at least two are described in his inscriptions. One he dug at Sippar, apparently connecting the Tigris and Euphrates. In connection with it he fortified the city and surrounded it with a moat. Another and more important canal was commemorated in the following inscription which illustrates his interest in the agricultural prosperity of Babylonia:

"When Anu and Bel gave (me) the land of Shumer and Akkad to rule and entrusted their sceptre to my hands, I dug out the Khammurabi-canal (named) Nukhush-nishi, which bringeth abundance of water unto the land of Shumer and Akkad. Both the banks thereof I changed to fields for cultivation, and I garnered piles of grain, and I procured unfailing water for the land of Shumer and Akkad."

This canal was probably a great channel, passing from Babylon in a southeasterly direction parallel with the Euphrates, whose waters it received and distributed by smaller canals over the neighboring districts, while also draining the adjoining marshes. The waste lands were replanted by distribution of seed-corn to the husbandmen; depopulated districts were refilled by the return of their inhabitants or the settlement of new communities; the prosperity and permanence of the irrigating works were secured by the building of a castle, which was doubtless at the same time a regulating station for the supply of water, at the mouth of the canal. Among other building operations we hear of a palace in the vicinity of Bagdad, a great wall or fortification along the Tigris, serving as well for protection from the floods as from the Elamite invaders. Other fortifications in various parts of the land are mentioned. Yet more is known about the temple building. As the Babylonian temples were as useful to business as to religion, their restoration was a contribution to material as well as religious well-being. The king built at Larsam a temple for Shamash; at Kish one for Zamama (Ninib) and Ishtar, others at Zarilab and at Khallabi, at Borsippa and Babylon. It is not improbable that in the two latter cities he was the founder of the famous and enduring structures in honor of the gods, called respectively through all periods of Babylonian history Ezida and Esagila.

98. Five kings succeeded Khammurabi before this dynasty gave way to another. Each king seems to have been the son of his predecessor, and the long reigns which all enjoyed illustrate the condition of the times. Of inscriptions directly from them only a few are known. One from Samsuiluna (about 2254-2216), Khammurabi's son, mentions his rebuilding the walls or fortresses of his ancestor (sect. 95) and enlarging his capital city. In its proud and swelling words it reflects the consciousness of greatness and power which Kharnmurabi's achievements had begotten in his successor. "Fear of my dreaded lordship covered the face of heaven and earth. Wherefore the gods inclined their beaming countenances unto me,...to rule in peace forever over the four quarters of the world, to attain the desire of my heart like a god, daily to walk with uplifted head in exultation and joy of heart, have they granted unto me as their gift" (Keilinschriftliche Bibliothek, III. i. 130-132). The "Chronicle" tells of conflicts with the Kassites, and of rebellions in the cities of Isin and Kish which were put down by him, but by far the more numerous events there referred to relate to the digging of canals and the service of religion. From Abeshu, his successor, a few letters, and inscriptional fragments only remain. A late copy of an inscription from Ammiditana (about 2188-2151), besides stating that he was the eldest son of Abeshu, the son of Samsuiluna, proclaims him "King...of Martu," that is, presumably, "the westland," Syria. The last two kings were Ammizaduga, who reigned ten

years according to the "Chronicle," but twenty-two years according to the kings' list, and Samsuditana who reigned thirty-two years. During the one hundred and fifty years and more of the rule of these kings, everything speaks in testimony of the permanence and development of the strong political structure whose foundations had been laid by Khammurabi, and of the peace and prosperity of the several communities united into the empire.

99. Of the significance of this imperial organization and development for the social and industrial life of the land there are many illustrations. A centralized administration bound all the districts hitherto separated and antagonistic into a solid unity. Khammurabi "was not content merely to capture a city and exact tribute from its inhabitants, but he straightway organized its government, and appointed his own officers for its control" (King, Let. and Ins. of Ham., III. xx.). Communication was regularly kept up between the court and the provincial cities, which were thus brought administratively into close touch with the capital. An immensely increased commercial activity followed this new centralization, as is shown by the enormous mass of business documents from this age. Increased prosperity was followed by rising values. The price of land under Khammurabi was higher than ever before. The administration of justice was advanced through the careful oversight of the courts by the king himself, and by the creation of a royal court of appeal at Babylon, access to which was open to the humblest citizen. A calendar was established for the state and regulated by the royal officials, whose arrangements for it were approved by the king, and published throughout the country. A royal post-system, the device of an earlier age, was elaborated to make easy all this intercommunication of the various districts. Consequent upon it came greater security of life and property as well as regular and better means of transit, — blessings which were shared by all the inhabitants. It is also true, on the other hand, that this centralization involved the economic and political depression of the other cities before the capital. They gradually lost their independent significance, as the currents of trade set steadily toward Babylon, and became provincial towns, contributory to the wealth and power of the royal city. It was the statesmanship of Khammurabi that, for good or ill, laid the foundations of this mercantile and monetary supremacy of Babylon, before which the other communities passed quite out of sight. Ur, Larsam, Uruk, and Sippar are heard of no more, except as seats of local worship or of provincial administration.

100. The sphere of religion, likewise, was significantly influenced by the new imperial organization. As might be expected, Marduk, the city-god of Babylon, now became the head of the Babylonian pantheon. The change is thought to have been something more than the natural result of the new situation; it seems to have been deliberately and officially undertaken as the potent means of unifying the state. That this god's supremacy was not left to chance or to time is seen by the systematic abasement of that other god who might reasonably contest the headship with the new claimant, namely, Bel of Nippur (sect. 88). The religious pre-eminence of his temple, E-kur, in that ancient city, passed away, and it is even claimed that the shrine was sacked, the images and votive offerings destroyed, and the cult intermitted by the authority of the kings of Babylon (Peters, Nippur, II. pp. 257 f.). The proud title of Bel ("lord") passed to Marduk, and with it the power and prerogative of the older deity. It may not, however, be necessary to assume so violent an assumption of power by Marduk. The political supremacy of Babylon, the larger power and greater wealth of the priesthood of its god, the more splendid cult, and the influence of the superior literary activity of the priestly scholars of the capital may be sufficient to account for the change. However, the unifying might of a common religious centre, symbolized in the worship of the one great god of the court, was not to be despised, and Khammurabi was not the man to overlook its importance. As the provinces looked to Babylon for law and government, so they found in Marduk the supreme embodiment of the empire.

101. A striking corollary of this change in the divine world is found in the transformation of the literature. Reference has already been made to the revival of literary activity coincident with the age of Khammurabi (sect. 79). Under the fostering care of the priesthood of Babylon, the older writings were collected, edited, and arranged in the temple libraries of the capital city. A common literary culture was spread abroad, corresponding to the unity in other spheres of life. But the priests who gathered these older writings subjected them to a series of systematic literary modifications, whereby the rôle of the ancient gods, particularly that of Bel of Nippur, was transferred to Marduk of Babylon. The Creation Epic is a case in point. In the culmination of that poem — the overthrow of Tiamat, the representative of chaos — the task of representing the Babylonian gods in the struggle is assigned to Marduk, and the honors of victory are awarded to him. But it is probable that in the earlier form of the Epic both contest and victory were the part of another deity of the earlier pantheon. A careful analysis of this and other religious documents of the period has been made by Professor Jastrow, who has brilliantly demonstrated that "the legends and traditions of the past," were "reshaped and the cult in part remodelled so as to emphasize the supremacy of Marduk" (Rel. of Bab. and Assyr., chaps. vii., xxi.). In addition to this special activity on behalf of their favorite god, the priests of the time now began to build up those systems of cosmology and theology which successive generations of schoolmen elaborated into the stately structures of speculation that so mightily influenced the philosophy and religion of the ancient world.

PART II .THE RISE OF ASSYRIA AND ITS STRUGGLES WITH KASSITE BABYLONIA

I .THE KASSITE CONQUEST OF BABYLONIA AND THE APPEARANCE OF ASSYRIA. 2000-1500 B. C.

102. WITH the last king of the dynasty of Khammurabi (about 2098 B. C.) a period of darkness falls upon the history of the land between the rivers. A new dynasty of the Babylonian kings' list begins with a certain Amnanu, and continues with ten other kings whose names are anything but suggestive of Babylonian origin. The regnal years of the eleven reach the respectable number of three hundred and sixty-eight. The problem of their origin is complicated with that of deciphering the word (Uru-azagga?) descriptive of them in the kings' list. Some think that it points to a quarter of the city of Babylon. Others, reading it Uru-ku, see in it the name of the ancient city of Uruk. The length of the reigns of the several kings is above the average, and suggests peace and prosperity under their rule. It is certainly strange in that case that no memorials of them have as yet been discovered, — a fact that lends some plausibility to the theory maintained by Hommel that this dynasty was contemporaneous with that of Khammurabi and never attained significance.

103. The third dynasty, as recorded on the kings' list, consists of thirty-six kings, who reigned five hundred seventy-six years and nine months (about 1717-1140 B. C.). About these kings information, while quite extensive, is yet so fragmentary as to render exact and organized presentation of their history exceedingly difficult. The kings' list is badly broken in the middle of the dynasty, so that only the first six and the last eleven or twelve of the names are intact, leaving thirteen or fourteen to be otherwise supplied and the order of succession to be determined from imperfect and inconclusive data. Only one royal inscription of some length exists, that of a certain Agum-kakrime who does not appear on the dynastic list. The tablets found at Nippur by the University of Pennsylvania's expedition have added several names to the list and thrown new light upon the history of the dynasty. The fragments of the so-called "Synchronistic History" (sect. 30) cover, in part, the relations of the Babylonian and Assyrian kings of this age, and the recently discovered royal Egyptian archives known as the Tel-el-Amarna tablets contain letters from and to several of them. From these materials it is possible to obtain the names of all but three or four of the missing thirteen or fourteen kings, and to reach something like a general knowledge of the whole period and some details of single reigns and epochs. Yet it is evident that the absence of some royal names not only makes the order of succession in the dark period uncertain, but throws its chronology into disorder. Nor is the material sufficient to remove the whole age from the region of indefiniteness as to the aims and achievements of the dynasty, or to make possible a grouping into epochs of development which may be above criticism. With these considerations in mind it is possible roughly to divide the period into four epochs: first, the beginnings of Kassite rule; second, the appearance of Assyria as a possible rival of Kassite Babylonia; third, the culmination of the dynasty and the struggle with Assyria; fourth, the decline and disappearance of the Kassites.

104. Merely a glance at the names in the dynastic list is evidence that a majority of them are of a non-Babylonian character. The royal inscriptions prove beyond doubt that the dynasty as a whole was foreign, and its domination the result of invasion by a people called Kashhus, or, to use a more conventional name, the Kassites. They belonged to the eastern mountains, occupying the high valleys from the borders of Elam northward, living partly from the scanty products of the soil and partly by plundering travellers and making descents upon the western

plain. The few fragments of their language which survive are not sufficient to indicate its affinity either to the Elamite or the Median, and at present all that can be said is that they formed a greater or lesser division of that congeries of mountain peoples which, without unity or common name and language, surged back and forth over the mountain wall stretching from the Caspian Sea to the Persian gulf. Their home seems to have been in the vicinity of those few mountain passes which lead from the valley up to the table-land. Hence they were brought into closer relations with the trade and commerce which from time immemorial had used these passes, and thereby they were early made aware of the civilization and wealth of Babylonia.

105. Whether driven by the impulse to conquest, begotten of a growing knowledge of Babylonian weakness, or by the pressure of peoples behind and about them, the Kassites appear at an early day to have figured in the annals of the Babylonian kingdom. In the ninth year of Samsuiluna, of the first dynasty, they were invading the land. This doubtless isolated invasion was repeated in the following years until by the beginning of the seventeenth century B. C., they seem to have gained the upper hand in Babylonia. Their earlier field of operations seems to have been in the south, near the mouth of the rivers. Here was Karduniash, the home of the Kassites in Babylonia, a name subsequently extended over all the land. It is not improbable that a Kassite tribe settled here in the last days of the second dynasty, and, assimilated to the civilization of the land, was later reinforced by larger bands of the same people displaced from the original home of the Kassites by pressure from behind, and that the combined forces found it easy to overspread and gain possession of the whole country. Such a supposition is in harmony with the evident predilection of the Kassites for southern Babylonia, as well as with their maintenance of authority over the regions in which they originally had their home. It also explains how, very soon after they came to power, they were hardly to be distinguished from the Semitic Babylonians over whom they ruled. They employed the royal titles, worshipped at the ancient shrines, served the native gods, and wrote their inscriptions in the Babylonian language.

106. Of the six kings whose names appear first on the dynastic list nothing of historical importance is known. The gap that ensues in that list, covering thirteen or fourteen names, is filled up from sources to which reference has already beer made. Agumkakrime (sect. 103), whose inscription of three hundred and thirty-eight lines is the most important Kassite document as yet discovered, probably stands near the early kings, is perhaps the seventh in order (about 1600 B. C.). This inscription, preserved in an Assyrian copy, was originally deposited in the temple at Babylon, and describes the royal achievements on behalf of the god Marduk and his divine spouse Zarpanit. The king first proclaims his own glory by reciting his genealogy, his relation to the gods and his royal titles:

I am Agumkakrime, the son of Tashshigurumash; the illustrious descendant of god Shuqamuna; called by Anu and Bel, Ea and Marduk, Sin and Shamash; the powerful hero of Ishtar, the warrior among the goddesses.

I am a king of wisdom and prudence; a king who grants hearing and pardon; the son of Tashshigurumash; the descendant of Abirumash, the crafty warrior; the first son among the numerous family of the great Agum; an illustrious, royal scion who holds the reins of the nation (and is) a mighty shepherd. . . .

I am king of the country of Kashshu and of the Akkadians; king of the wide country of Babylon, who settles the numerous people in Ashnunak; the King of Padan and Alman; the King of Gutium, a foolish nation; (a king) who makes obedient to him the four regions, and has always been a favorite of the great gods (I. 1-42).

107. Agumkakrime found, on taking the throne, that the images of Marduk and Zarpanit, chief deities of the city, had been removed from the temple to the land of Khani, a region not yet definitely located, but presumably in northern Mesopotamia, and possibly on the head-waters of the Euphrates. This removal took place probably in connection with an invasion of peoples from that distant region, who were subsequently driven out; and it sheds light on the weakened and disordered condition of the land at the time of the appearance of the Kassites. These images were recovered by the king, either through an embassy or by force of arms. The inscription is indefinite on the point, but the wealth of the king as intimated in the latter part of the inscription would suggest that he was at least able to compel the surrender of them. On being recovered they were replaced in their temple, which was renovated and splendidly furnished for their reception. Gold and precious stones and woods were employed in lavish profusion for the adornment of the persons of the divine pair and the decoration of their abode. Their priesthoods were revived, the service re-established, and endowments provided for the temple.

108. In the countries enumerated by Agumkakrime as under his sway no mention is made of a people who were soon to exercise a commanding influence upon the history of the Kassite dynasty. The people of Assyria, however, although, even before that time, having a local habitation and rulers, the names of some of whom have come down in tradition, could hardly have been independent of a king who claimed authority over the land of the Kassites and the Guti, Padan, and Alman, — districts which lie in the region of the middle and upper Tigris, or on the slopes of the eastern mountains (Delitzsch, Paradies, p. 205). According to the report of the Synchronistic History, about a century and a half later Assyria was capable of treating with Babylonia on equal terms, but, even if the opening passages of that document (some eleven lines) had been preserved, they would hardly have indicated such relations at a much earlier date. The sudden rise of Assyria, therefore, is reasonably explained as connected with the greater movement which made the Kassites supreme in Babylonia.

109. The people who established the kingdom of Assyria exhibit, in language and customs and even in physical characteristics, a close likeness to the Babylonians. They were, therefore, not only a Semitic people, but, apparently, also of Semitic-Babylonian stock. The most natural explanation of this fact is that they were originally a Babylonian colony. They seem, however, to be of even purer Semitic blood than their Babylonian ancestors, and some scholars have preferred to see in them an independent offshoot from the original Semitic migration into the Mesopotamian valley (sect. 51). If that be so, they must have come very early under Babylonian influence which dominated the essential elements of their civilization and its growth down to their latest days. The earliest centre of their organization was the city of Assur on the west bank of the middle Tigris (lat. n. 35° 30'), where a line of low hills begins to run southward along the river. Perched on the outlying northern spur of these hills, and by them sheltered from the nomads of the steppe and protected by the broad river in front from the raids of mountaineers of the east, the city was an outpost of Babylonian civilization and a station on the natural road of trade with the lands of the upper Tigris. A fertile stretch of alluvial soil in the vicinity supplied the necessary agricultural basis of life, while, a few miles to the north, bitumen springs furnished, as on the Euphrates, an article of commerce and an indispensable element of building (Layard, Nineveh and its Remains, II. chap. xii.). The god of the city was Ashur, "the good one," and from him the city received its name (Jastrow, Rel. of Bab. and Assyria, p. 196).

110. The early rulers of the city of Assur were patesis (sect. 75), viceroys of Babylonian rulers. Some of their names have come down in tradition, as, for example, those of Ishme Dagan and his son, Shamshi Adad, who lived according to Tiglathpileser I. about seven hundred years before himself (that is, about 1840-1800 B. C.). Later kings of Assyria also

refer to other rulers of the early age to whom they give the royal title, but of whom nothing further is known. The first mention of Assur is in a letter of king Khammurabi of the first dynasty of Babylon, who seems to intimate that the city was a part of the Babylonian Empire (King, Let. and Inscr. of H., III. p. 3). In the darkness that covers these beginnings, the viceroys became independent of Babylonia and extended their authority up the Tigris to Kalkhi, Arbela, and Nineveh, cities to be in the future centres of the Assyrian Empire. The kingdom of Assyria took form and gathered power.

111. The physical characteristics of this region could not but shape the activities of those who lived within its borders. It is the northeastern corner of Mesopotamia. The mountains rise in the rear; the Tigris and Mesopotamia are in front. The chief cities of Assyria, with the sole exception of Assur, lie to the east of the great river and on the narrow shelf between it and the northeastern mountain ranges. They who live there must needs find nature less friendly to them than to their brethren of the south. Agriculture does not richly reward their labors. They learn, by struggling with the wild beasts of the hills and the fierce men of the mountains, the thirst for battle and the joy of victory. And as they grow too numerous for their borders, the prospect, barred to the east and north, opens invitingly towards the west and southwest. Thus the Assyrian found in his surroundings the encouragement to devote himself to war and to the chase rather than to the peaceful pursuits of agriculture; the preparation for military achievement on a scale hitherto unrealized.

112. It is not difficult to conceive how the Kassite conquest of Babylonia profoundly influenced the development of Assyria. The city of Assur, protected from the inroads of the eastern invaders by its position on the west bank of the Tigris, became, at the same time, the refuge of those Babylonians who fled before the conquerors as they overspread the land. The Assyrian community was thus enabled to throw off the yoke of allegiance to the mother country, now in possession of foreigners, and to establish itself as an independent kingdom. Its patesis became kings, and began to cherish ambitions of recovering the home-land from the grasp of the enemy, and of extending their sway over the upper Tigris and beyond. It is not unlikely that this latter endeavor was at least partially successful during the early period of the Kassite rule. It is certainly significant that Agumkakrime does not mention Assyria among the districts under his sway and if, as has been remarked (sect. 108), his sphere of influence seems to include it, his successors were soon to learn that a new power must be reckoned with, in settling the question of supremacy on the middle Tigris.

II. THE EARLY CONFLICTS OF BABYLONIA AND ASSYRIA. 1500-1150 B. C.

113. THE half millennium (2000-1500 B. C.), that saw the decline of Old Babylonia, its conquest by the Kassites and the beginnings of the kingdom of Assyria, had been also a period of transition in the rest of the ancient oriental world. In Egypt the quiet, isolated development of native life and forces which had gone on unhindered for two thousand years and had produced so remarkable a civilization, was broken into by the invasion of the Hyksos, Semitic nomads from Arabia, who held the primacy of power for three hundred years and introduced new elements and influences into the historical process. In the region lying between the Euphrates and the Nile, which in the absence of a common name may be called Syria, where Babylonian civilization, sustained from time to time by Babylonian armies, had taken deep root, similar changes, though less clearly attested by definite historical memorials, seem to have taken place. The Hyksos movement into Egypt could not but have been attended with disturbances in southern Syria, reflected perhaps in the patriarchal traditions of the Hebrews.

In the north, peoples from the mountains that rim the upper plateau began to descend and occupy the regions to the east and west of the head-waters of the Euphrates, thus threatening the security of the highways of trade, and, consequently, Babylonian authority on the Mediterranean.

114. Had the Babylonian kingdom been unhampered, it might have met and overcome these adverse influences in its western provinces and continued its hegemony over the peoples of Syria. But to the inner confusion caused by the presence of foreign rulers was added the antagonism of a young and vigorous rival, the Assyrian kingdom on the upper Tigris. Through the absorption of both powers in the complications that ensued, any vigorous movement toward the west was impossible. It was from another and quite unexpected quarter that the political situation was to be transformed. In Egypt by the beginning of the sixteenth century a desperate struggle of the native element against the ruling Hyksos began, resulting, as the century drew to a close, in the expulsion of the foreigners. Under the fresh impulses aroused by this victorious struggle the nation entered an entirely new path of conquest. The Pharaohs of the New Empire went forth to win Syria.

115. The fifteenth century B. C., therefore, marks a turning-point in the history of Western Asia. The nations that had hitherto wrought out largely by themselves their contributions tai civilization and progress came into direct political relation one with another in that middle zone between the Euphrates and the Nile, which was henceforth to be the battleground of their armies and the reward of their victories. From that time forth the politics of the kings was to be a world-politics; the balance of power was to be a burning question; international diplomacy came into being. The three great powers were Egypt, Assyria, and Babylonia. Lesser kingdoms appeared as Egypt advanced into the East, — Mitanni in northwestern Mesopotamia, whose people used the cuneiform script to express a language which cannot yet be understood, Alasia in northwestern Syria, and the Hittites just rounding into form in the highlands of northeastern Syria and destined to play so brilliant a part, if at present a puzzling one, in the history of the coming centuries. At first, Egypt carried all before her. Under the successive Pharaohs of the eighteenth dynasty, her armies passed victoriously up and down along the eastern Mediterranean and even crossed the Euphrates. All Syria became an Egyptian province, paying tribute to the empire of the Nile. Egyptian civilization was dominant throughout the whole region.

116. The effect of this Egyptian predominance in Syria upon the kingdoms of the Tigro-Euphrates valley was significant. The Egyptians obtained the monopoly of the trade of its new provinces, and the eastern kingdoms were cut off. They were crowded back as Egypt pressed forward. It is not improbable that Assyria's northern movement (sect. 112) was by this pressure forced to the east, and therefore the centre of Assyrian power shifted to the other side of the Tigris over against the eastern mountains. The image of Ishtar, goddess of Nineveh, had fallen during this time into the hands of the king of Mitanni, who sent it to Egypt (Winckler, Tel-el-Amarna Letters, 20). The pent up forces of the two peoples declined and exhausted themselves in reviving and pursuing with greater intensity and persistence the struggle for local supremacy. Assyria was numbered by Thutmose III. of Egypt (1480-1427 B. C.) among his tributaries for two years, although this may have been little more than a vainglorious boast, arising out of the endeavor of the Assyrian king to obtain the Egyptian alliance by means of gifts. That Egypt was courted by both Babylonian and Assyrian rulers is testified to by the archives of Amenhotep IV., as preserved in the Tel-el-Amarna letters, which contain communications from kings of both nations to the Pharaohs, intimating that these negotiations had been going on for half a century. The Pharaohs, having won their provinces in Syria by force of arms, were willing to maintain possession by alliances with bordering peoples whom they regarded as inferior, even while treating with them on the conventional terms imposed by

the diplomacy of the time. Thus they exchanged princesses with Mitanni, Babylon, and Assyria, and made presents of gold, the receipt of which the kings of these lands acknowledged by asking for more. Their deferential attitude toward Egypt, however, goes somewhat beyond what must have been the diplomatic courtesy of the time, and shows how Egypt stood as arbiter and head among them. A perfect illustration of the situation is given in the following paragraph from a letter of the king of Babylon to Amenhotep IV. of Egypt:

In the time of Kurigalzu, my father, the Canaanites as a body sent to him as follows: "Against the frontier of the land, let us march, and invade it. Let us make an alliance with thee." Then my father sent them this (reply), as follows: "Cease (trying) to form an alliance with me. If you cherish hostility against the king of Egypt, my brother, and bind yourselves together (with an oath), as for me, shall I not come and plunder you? — for he is in alliance with me." My father, for the sake of thy father, did not heed them. Now, (as to) the Assyrians, my own subjects, did I not send thee (word) concerning their matters? Why has (an embassy) entered thy country? If thou lovest me, let them have no good fortune. Let them secure no (advantage) whatever (ABL, p. 221).

While Egypt must needs be on friendly terms with the Mesopotamian states in order to keep them from interfering in Syria, it was with each one of them a vital matter to gain her exclusive alliance, or prevent any other of them from securing it.

117. In these conditions of world-politics, the complications between the rival states in Mesopotamia, as already remarked, were increased and intensified. The problem of a boundary line, a frequent source of trouble between nations, occasioned recurring difficulties. Kara-indash for Babylon and Ashur-bel-nisheshu for Assyria settled it (about 1450) by a treaty (Synchr. Hist., col. I. 1-4). The same procedure was followed about half a century later by the Babylonian Burnaburyas I. (?) and the Assyrian Puzur-ashur (Ibid., col. I. 5-7). Of Kadashman Bel (Kalliina Sin), who reigned at Babylon in the interval, four letters to Amenhotep III. of Egypt are preserved in the Tel-el-Amarna tablets, together with one from the Pharaoh to him, but beyond the mention of exchanging daughters as wives they contain no historical facts of importance. Kurigalzu I. (about 1380 B. C.), the son and successor of Burnaburyas (I.?), is mentioned in the same collection of documents as on good terms with Egypt, but no record remains of his relations with Assyria, where Ashur-nadin-akhi ruled. The same is true of the latter's son, Ashur-uballit and the Babylonian Burnaburyas II. (about 1350 B. C.), son of Kurigalzu I., who refers to his rival in the boastful terms already quoted (sect. 116), which, however, must be interpreted as the language of diplomacy. His six letters to the Pharaoh Amenhotep IV. are, otherwise, historically barren. Ashuruballit, "the vassal," succeeded in marrying his daughter Muballitat-sirua to the Babylonian king's son, Karakhardash, who followed his father upon the throne (about 1325 B. C.). The two kings also renewed the boundary treaty of their fathers (RP, 2 ser. V. p. 107, and Winckler, Alt. Or. Forsch. I., ii. pp. 115 f.). Here the first stage of the rivalry may be said to close. From a position of insignificance the Assyrian kingdom had been raised, by a series of able rulers, to an equality with Babylonia, and the achievement was consummated by the union of the royal houses.

118. The son of this union, Kadashman-kharbe, succeeded his father on the Babylonian throne while his grandfather, Ashuruballit, still ruled in Assyria. To him, apparently, a Babylonian chronicle fragment ascribes the clearing of the Euphrates road from the raids of the Bedouin Suti, and the building of fortresses and planting of colonies in Syria (RP, 2 scr. V., and Winckler, AOF, 1. c.). But it is not improbable that, if done by him, it was in connection with his grandfather, who, in his letter to the Pharaoh Amenhotep IV., expressly mentions the Suti as infesting the roads to the west, evidently the trade routes of the upper Mesopotamian valley (Winckler, Tel-el-Amarna Letters, pp. 30 f.). This close relation to Assyria was not pleasing to

the Kassite nobles, who rebelled against their king, killed him, and set a certain Suzigas, or Nazibugas, upon the throne. But the aged Ashuruballit hastened to avenge his grandson, marched into Babylonia, and put the usurper to death. In his stead he placed on the throne the son of Kadashman-kharbe as Kurigalzu II., who, called the "young" one, was evidently still a child. With this agrees the probable reading of the years of his reign as fifty-five upon the kings' list. He must at first have reigned under the tutelage of Ashuruballit, who, however, could not have lived long after his great-grandson's accession. The Assyrian throne was taken by his son Bel-nirari, who was followed by his son Pudi-ilu. Kurigalzu outlived both these kings, and saw Pudi-ilu's son, Adad-nirari I., succeed his father. The Babylonian king seems not to have altered his friendly attitude toward Assyria during the reigns of the first two kings. He waged a brilliantly successful war with the Elamites, captured their king Khurba-tila with his own hands, sacked Susa, his capital, and brought back great spoil. At Nippur he offered to the goddess of the shrine an agate tablet which, after having been given to Ishtar of Uruk in honor of Dungi of Ur more than a thousand years before, had been carried away to Elam in the Elamite invasion of the third millennium and was now returned to its Babylonian home. In his last years the king came into conflict with Adadnirari I. of Assyria. Was it owing to the ambition of a young and vigorous ruler who hoped to get the better of his aged rival? Or was it the Babylonian's growing distrust of the power of Assyria, which, under one of the kings of his time, Belnirari, had attacked and overthrown the Kassites in their ancestral home to the east of the Tigris? Whatever was the occasion, the two armies met, and the Assyrian was completely defeated (RP, 2 ser. V. pp. 109 ff., cf. IV. p. 28; Winckler, AOF, p. 122). A readjustment of boundaries followed. Kurigalzu II. was an industrious builder. Whether the citadel of Dur Kurigalzu, which lay as a bulwark on the northern border of the Babylonian plain, was built by him or his predecessor, the first of the name, is uncertain. The same confusion attaches to most of the Kurigalzu inscriptions, though the probabilities are in favor of ascribing the majority of them to Kurigalzu II. The temples at Ur and Nippur were rebuilt by him as well as that of Agade. A statement of the Babylonian chronicle suggests that he was the first Kassite king who favored Babylon and its god Marduk. He gives himself in his inscriptions, among other titles, that of "Viceroy of the god Bel" and may well be that Kurigalzu whom a later ruler, in claiming descent from him, proudly calls the "incomparable king" (sharru la sanaan).

119. The period of peace with the Kassite rulers of Babylonia had been improved by the Assyrian kings in extending their boundaries toward the north and east. An inscription of Adadnirari I. (KB, I. 4ff.) ascribes the beginning of this forward movement to his great-grandfather, Ashuruballit, who conquered the Subari on the upper Tigris, Belnirari and Pudi-ilu campaigned in the east and southeast in the well-watered region between the river and the mountains, where dwelt the Kuti, the Suti, the Kassi, and other peoples of the mountain and the steppe, down to the borders of Elam. Adadnirari I. continued the advance by subduing the Lulumi in the east, but his defeat by Kurigalzu II. cost him the southern conquests of his predecessors, as the boundary-line established after the battle (Syn. Hist., col. I. 21-23) and the silence of his own inscription indicate. However, he strengthened Assyria's hold on the other peoples by planting cities among them. When Kurigalzu II. was succeeded in Babylonia by his son Nazi-maruttash, the Assyrian king tried the fortune of battle with him, and this time apparently with greater success, although the new boundaries agreed upon seem very little different from those in the time of Kurigalzu II. (Syn. Hist., col. I. 24-31).

120. Under Adadnirari's son, Shalmaneser I. (about 1300?), Assyria began to push westward. The decades that had passed since the correspondence between the Amenhoteps of Egypt and the kings of Assyria and Babylonia had witnessed a great change in the political relations of Egypt and Syria. A people which in the fifteenth century was just appearing in northern Syria, the Khatti (Hittites), had pushed down and overspread the land to the borders of Palestine. The eighteenth Egyptian dynasty had disappeared, and the nineteenth, which had succeeded, found

the Khatti invincible. Ramses II., the fourth Pharaoh of that dynasty, made a treaty of peace with them, wherein he renounced all Egyptian provinces north of Palestine. With the pressure thus removed from northern Mesopotamia, Assyria was free to move in this the natural direction of her expansion. It was a turning-point in the world's history when this nation set its face toward the west. Shalmaneser followed up the Tigris, crossed its upper waters, planted Assyrian outposts among the tribes, and marched along the southern spurs of the mountains to the head-waters of the Euphrates. The chief peoples conquered by him were the Arami, by whom are to be understood the Arameans of western Mesopotamia, and the Muçri, concerning whose position little is known unless they are the people of that name living in northern Syria. In this case Shalmaneser was the first Assyrian king to carry the Assyrian arms across the Euphrates. The large additions to Assyria's territory on all sides thus made probably lay at the bottom of Shalmaneser's transfer of the seat of his administration from the ancient city of Assur to Kalkhi (Calah), forty miles to the north, and on the eastern side of the Tigris just above the point where the upper Zab empties into the great river. The strategic advantages of the site are obvious, — the protection offered by the Zab and the Tigris, the more central location and the greater accessibility from all parts of the now much enlarged state. Here the king built his city, which testified to the sagacity of its founder by remaining one of the great centres of Assyrian life down to the end of the empire. The title of Shar Kishshate, "king of the world," which he and his father Adadnirari were the first Assyrian kings to claim, is a testimony both of their greatness and of the consciousness of national enlargement which their work produced.

121. Of the Kassite kings who held Babylonia during these years little is known beyond their names and regnal years (sect. 103). An uncertain passage on the broken Ashur-naçir-pal (7) obelisk seems to refer to a hostile meeting between Kadashman-burias and Shalmaneser I. of Assyria (Hommel, GBA, p. 437). A much more important contest was that between Shalmaneser's son, Tukulti Ninib (about 1250) and the Kassite rulers. From fragments of a Babylonian chronicle (RP, 2 ser. V. p. 111), it is clear that the Assyrian king entered Babylonia, and for seven years held the throne against all comers, defeating and overthrowing, it is probable, four Babylonian kings who successively sought to maintain their rights against him. At last, owing perhaps to the dissatisfaction felt in Assyria at the king's evident preference for governing his kingdom from Babylonia, Tukulti Ninib was himself murdered by a conspiracy headed by his own son Ashurnaçirpal. Here the second stage of the struggle may be said to terminate. It had been accompanied by a remarkable development of Assyria which brought the state, though hardly yet of age, to a position of power that culminated in the humiliation and temporary subjection of her rival under Assyrian rule. During the reign of Tukulti Ninib Assyria was the mistress of the entire Tigro-Euphrates valley from the mountains to the Persian gulf.

122. During these evil years Babylonia had suffered from Elamite inroads (RP, 2 ser. V. pp. 111 f.) as well as borne the yoke of the Assyrian. But the murder of Tukulti Ninib gave the opportunity for a new and successful rebellion which placed Adad-shumuçur (Adad-nadin-akhi) upon the throne. He ruled, according to the kings' list, for thirty years. Under him and his successors, Mili-shikhu and Marduk-baliddin I. (about 1150 B. C.), a sudden and splendid uplift was given to Babylonia's fortunes. If the hints contained in the fragmentary sources are correctly understood, it appears that, toward the close of the reign of Adadshumuçur, he was attacked by the Assyrian king Bel-kudur-uçur. The battle resulted in a victory for the Babylonians, but both kings were killed. The Assyrian general, Ninib-apal-ekur, possibly a son of the king, withdrew his forces, and, pressed hard by Milishikhu, the son and successor of the Babylonian king, shut himself up in the city of Assur, apparently his capital rather than Kalkhi, where he was able to beat off the enemy. He succeeded to the Assyrian throne, but with the loss of Assyrian prestige and authority in the Mesopotamian valley. For twenty-eight

years, during the reigns of Milishikhu and his son Mardukbaliddin, Babylonia was supreme. The latter king assumed the title borne by Shalmaneser I. of Assyria, " King of the World," which implied, if Winckler's understanding of the title is to be accepted (sect. 54), authority over northern Mesopotamia between the Tigris and Euphrates. Be that as it may, this brilliant outburst of Kassite Babylonia was transient. Zamama-shum-iddin, the successor of Mardukbaliddin, was attacked and worsted by Ashurdan of Assyria, son of Ninib-apal-ekur. Within three years his successor, Bel-shum-iddin, was dethroned, and the Kassite dynasty of Babylonia came to an end after nearly six centuries of power (about 1140 B. C.).

III.CIVILIZATION AND CULTURE IN THE KASSITE PERIOD

123. THE earliest and by no means the least impressive instance of the power of civilization to dominate a rude people and mould them to its will is furnished in the relations of Babylonia to the Kassites. Tribes, vigorous and wild, hitherto possessing but slight traces of organization and culture, descended from the hills upon a region in which dwelt a nation of high social and political development, possessing a long history of achievements in culture, distinguished for the peaceful acquisitions of wealth and the enjoyment of the refinements of civilization. The outcome, it might seem, was likely to be the overthrow of the political structure, and the disappearance of the high attainment in science and the arts of life, reached by slow stages through two thousand years, to be followed by a painful rebuilding of the political and social edifice on new foundations. In reality the very opposite of this took place. The splendid work of Babylonian civilization stood intact; the conquerors entered into the inheritance of its traditions and achievements, and within a century were found laboring for its advancement and perfection. The Kassites were absorbed into the Babylonian life without a struggle. They even lost all attachment to the mountain homes whence they came and to the peoples from which they sprang, and permitted them, at last, to pass into the possession of Assyria.

124. The Kassite régime was not, however, without its influence upon Babylonian history and life. The direct contributions of purely Kassite elements were, indeed, few. Some words enriched the language; the new speech became a dialect which must be mastered by the scholars; some cults of Kassite gods were established and remained. A new racial ingredient was poured into the already varied complex which made up the Babylonian people, — an ingredient not without value in infusing fresh and vigorous elements into the doubtless somewhat enfeebled stock. For the incoming of the invaders was sufficient evidence that the native population was no longer able to defend itself against assaults, and the service of Agumkakrime, of which he boasts in his inscription (sect. 106), is an example of what the Kassites were to do for Babylonia. That such a work was not only necessary but appreciated by the nation is abundantly proved by the length of time during which the Kassite kings sat upon the throne, in spite of the difficulties which encompassed them.

125. Not as Kassite but as Babylonian kings, therefore, did these rulers contribute to the development of the land between the rivers. Entering into the heritage of preceding dynasties, they ruled like them in accordance with Babylonian precedent, and in many respects were worthy of the succession. In one thing they surpassed their predecessors; they gave to Babylonia a common name. Up to their time, the kings had been rulers of cities whose authority extended over districts round about, a state of things true even of the age of Khammurabi, when all the land was united under the sway of the city-state of Babylon. Yet these foreign conquerors were able to succeed where that great king had failed. They called themselves kings of Karduniash. This name was not that of a city, and while it was at first attached to one of the southern districts (sect. 105), soon came to be applied to the whole

country, so that, when later kings of Assyria would assert their lordship over their ancestral enemy in the south, they proudly assumed the old Kassite designation "King of Karduniash." This achievement was significant of the new unity attained under this dynasty. Reference has already been made (sect. 100) to the religious policy which guided the unifiers of Babylonia in the days of Khammurabi, It centred in the exaltation of the city-god Marduk of Babylon, and the systematic abasement of the other religious shrines, particularly that of Nippur. But in this period that very temple of Bel at Nippur seems to have returned to prominence and its god received high honor. The American explorers on that site note that one of the Kurigalzus rebuilt the ancient ziggurat, another Kassite king "built the great structure containing the Court of Columns," and the memorials of this dynasty, in the shape of votive offerings and temple archives, are the characteristic and dominating element among the objects unearthed on the site (Peters, Nippur, II. p. 259 and passim). Moreover, among the few Kassite inscriptions found elsewhere, are records of temple-building at other points. Kara-indash built at Uruk, Burnaburyash at Larsam, and Kurigalzu at Larsam and Ur. These facts have led to the inference that the Kassites represented a reaction from the systematic glorification of Marduk of Babylon as god of gods, in favor of the older deities and the provincial shrines, and that this attitude illustrates their general position in opposition to the policy of Khammurabi, whereby they favored the people of the country at large as over against the capital city, Babylon. It is true that Agumkakrime's inscription is largely occupied with his services to the temple of Marduk, and that the other kings seem to have continued to dwell at Babylon, but these facts do not deter an eminent scholar from summing up the contribution of the Kassite dynasty to the development of Babylonia in these words: "By restoring the former glory of Ekur, the ancient national sanctuary in Nippur, so deeply rooted in the hearts of the Babylonian people, and by stepping forward as the champions of the sacred rights of the 'father of the gods,' they were able to bring about a reconciliation and a final melting together of the Kassite and Semitic elements" (Hilprecht, OBT, I. i. p, 31).

126, The civilization of Karduniash — to use the name characteristic of this age — was, in the Kassite period, influenced as never before by international relations. The great nations had come into intimate communication with one another, and their intercourse demanded a code of customs for its proper regulation. Hence came the beginnings of international law. The first treaty known to history belongs to this period, — that of the Pharaoh Rameses II. with the king of the Hittites, containing the famous so-called "extradition" clause. Hints of a kind of compact between Babylonian kings and the Pharaohs are given in the Tel-el-Amarna letters. We hear now for the first time of the "brotherhood of nations." "First establish good brotherhood between us" are words contained in a letter of Amenhotep III. to Kadashman Bel (Winckler, TAL, letter 1). Ambassadors pass to and fro between the courts on the Euphrates and the Nile, They carry safe-conducts for passage through the Egyptian provinces of Syria. Their persons are sacred, and the king in whose provinces an insult has been offered to them must punish the offender. Between the royal personages who figure in these letters, it has been thought that the relations were something more than formal, and the message of a Mitannian king to Amenhotep IV. on hearing of the death of his father, has a pathetic ring: "Never did Nimmuriya, your father, break his promises — I have mourned for him deeply, and when he died, I wished to die myself! May he, whom I loved, live with God" (Tiele-Western Asia, p. 12).

127. The influence of Egypt upon the life of the Babylonians, resulting from this enlarged intercourse, cannot be followed into detail with any materials at present available. Medical science may have been improved. One might expect that religion would have been affected. The dogma of the divinity of the Pharaoh might be regarded as likely to emphasize and encourage claims of the Babylonian kings for like honors not unknown in the past (sect. 75); yet not only is no evidence presented for this, but it is even maintained that the Kassite kings

definitely set aside the remnants of the Babylonian usage in the case, and regarded themselves as delegates and representatives of the gods of whom they were the adopted sons (Sayce, BA, p. 171). In the sphere of trade and commerce the influence of Egypt was unmistakable and far reaching. No doubt, at the beginning of the advance of Egypt into Asia and throughout her domination of Syria, Babylonian commerce with the west suffered, and was at times entirely cut off. But the traders on the Euphrates directed their energies only the more toward opening and developing new markets in the north and east. According to testimony drawn from the "finds" at Nippur, they brought gypsum from Mesopotamia, marble and limestone from the Persian mountains, cedar and cypress from the Zagros, lapis lazuli from Bactria, and cobalt for coloring material, "presumably" from China (Peters, Nippur, II. p. 134). It is not impossible that the eastern affinities of the Kassite kings assisted the development of trade in this direction. On the other hand, when with some possible restrictions commerce was revived with the Egyptian provinces of Syria under royal agreements, the unification of these regions under one authority gave at that time, as often later, a substantial stimulus to trade both in its security and its extent. This fact is proved by the striking discovery at Nippur of votive offerings of magnesite, which must have been brought for the Kassite kings from the island of Eubcea (Nippur, ibid.). Egypt itself had, in its Nubian mines, the pre-eminent source of gold for the oriental world, and the letters of the eastern kings to their brethren the Pharaohs are full of requests for gifts of more of the precious metal and of better quality, for which they send in return lapis lazuli, enamel, horses and chariots, slaves, costly furniture, and works of art.

128. From the facts already stated it is clear that Karduniash flourished under its Kassite rulers. Industry was active. Manufacturing was represented not only by the objects already enumerated as gifts to the Pharaohs, but by a multitude of materials found at Nippur and mentioned in the royal inscriptions. Among the former were the ornamental axe-heads. These analysis has disclosed to be made of glass colored with cobalt and copper and resembling in character "the famous Venetian glass of the fourteenth century A. D.," moulded probably by Phoenician artists employed at the temple (Nippur, II. p. 134) Agumkakrime's description of his rehabilitation of the deities Marduk and Zarpanit of Babylon gives a picture of the superabounding wealth of the king, who clothes the images of the deities with gold-embroidered robes, heavy with jewels, and houses them in a cella of cedar and cypress woods made by cunning workmen, its doors banded with bronze, and its walls lined with strange carved animal figures. Unfortunately, no large sculptures of these kings have yet been discovered, nor do the remains of the Nippur temple ascribed to them afford any judgment as to the architecture of the time. The so-called boundary stones of Milishikhu and Mardukbaliddin I., carved with rude representations of animals and of the heavenly bodies, symbols of uncertain significance, were probably the work of provincial artists (Smith, AD, pp. 236 ff.). It is strange that these stones are the chief evidence for the legal element in the life of the time. The inscription on that Of Mardukbaliddin I. conveys a tract of land to one of his officials as a reward. The boundaries of the tract are carefully stated, the ancestry of the beneficiary is traced to the fifth generation, witnesses are named, and curses are invoked upon all who in the future may interfere with this award. Excavations yet to be made on temple sites like that of Nippur will probably reveal in sufficient abundance the deeds, contracts, and other documents which were indispensable in so active and enterprising a commercial and industrial community as was Babylonia in those days. A similar silence broods over the literature. Beyond the few royal inscriptions and letters already sufficiently described, no evidence exists to show either that the masterpieces of old were studied or that new works were being produced. This gap in our knowledge will also sometime be filled.

129. If the successful seizure of the Babylonian throne by the Kassites had given a mighty impetus to the development of Assyria as an independent kingdom (sect. 112), their continued possession of Babylonia affected deeply the history of the northern people, The Assyrians

were not thereby alienated from the civilization of the south, for this had already been wrought too deeply into the structure of their body politic. It is maintained, indeed, that the Assyrian cuneiform script of the time tends to resemble the north Mesopotamian forms rather than the Babylonian (Winckler, GBA, p. 165); but in all that may be regarded as fundamental in a people's culture Assyria remained in Babylonian leading-strings. The surprising thing is that, as time wore on, the hostility between the Kassite and Assyrian rulers did not relax, nor did it yield even when all interests were in favor of peace. The facts seem to show that the primary part in this aggressive activity was taken by Assyria. In other words, it became the settled policy of the northern state to strive for the possession of Babylonia, even when the actual Kassite element had long been absorbed into the Semitic Babylonian. The mere lust of conquest will not explain this persistence. It must have its ground in the political or economic conditions of the state. The original Assyria (sect. 111) had neither a natural frontier nor sufficient arable land to protect and sustain a nation. Hence the people, if they were not constantly to stand on guard, must expand until a natural barrier was met; they must also reach out to control the only other source of wealth in the ancient world, commerce. In the way of the attainment of both these objects stood, primarily, Babylonia. The Babylonian war was, therefore, a vital condition of Assyria's progress. Other motives may have entered in, — the feeling that the south was the home-land, the seat of religion and culture, and therefore must be recovered. Nor is it unlikely that there was in Babylonia itself a longing for union with Assyria, and consequently a pro-Assyrian party, always ready to encourage interference from the north. Yet the deeper motive is that first mentioned.

130. The fateful influence of this course into which Assyria was drawn was to intensify a military bent already sufficiently encouraged by physical surroundings. The king became the warrior, the defender of his people from wild beasts and from human enemies, the leader of au army. "He breaks in pieces the mass of his foes, he tramples down their countries," "he scatters their armies" — are phrases of Adadnirari I. in his own inscription. The gods were those representing the fierce, wild elements of nature, as Adad (Ramman), the god of the storm, the wind, and the rain, or Ishtar, the goddess of Arbela, the fierce companion in arms of the warriors, or the other Ishtar, of Nineveh, the mistress of the soldier returned from the wars, the goddess of love and lust. Above them stood Ashur, the divine king of the military state, of whom the human king was the representative and servant, — the god, who went out with the army to battle and received the spoils. The nation, thus affected and inspired, gathered close about its divine head, and followed the king his vicegerent with unquestioning obedience. The city where he had his seat, whether Assur or Kalkhi or Nineveh, became the headquarters of all activity. All other cities, Arbela excepted, were overshadowed and left to drag out a petty and insignificant existence, their names hardly known. Here the court with its aristocracy of warriors, chiefs with their clansmen, formed the centre of national life. The king usually gave his name to the first full year of his kingship; it was the limu of the king by which all events were recorded; then followed, given as official designation to year after year, the names of the warriors of the court in due succession. As king succeeded king, the limu lists were preserved, formed a chronological framework for history (sect. 38), and fostered the self-consciousness of the state as a living organism, having a past wrought out by men of might, and moving on toward the future. This system had already been adopted by the time of Adadnirari I., whose stele was set up in the year when Shalmanuasharid (Shalmaneser) was limu. It was Assyria's original contribution to historical progress, and passed over from the east to reappear in Athens, where a similar official was called the archon eponymos.

131. In this military state all spheres of life felt the impulse to realize practical results. Religion was at the service of the kings. They were devoted to the gods, indeed, since they were proud constantly to build temples. Ashuruballit and his descendant Shalmaneser I. repaired and enlarged a temple to Ishtar of Nineveh, and Adadnirari I., another to Ashur at the

capital. They were equally proud of erecting palaces. The Adadnirari stele deals more fully with the warlike achievements of the king and his ancestors than with his religious foundation. The remains of literature and art and the evidences of industry and manufacturing in this age are too scanty to warrant any judgment, the few royal inscriptions, some alabaster jars, and a bronze sword of Adadnirari I. (Maspero, SN, p, 607), chariots and horses, lapis lazuli, slaves, and precious vases mentioned as gifts sent to the Egyptian kings (Winckler, TAL, 15) being about all the available material, — enough perhaps to indicate that Assyrian scribes and merchants were following in the footsteps of their brethren on the Euphrates. Phoenician artists may have wrought in this period the ivory carvings which were found on the site of Kalkhi, the capital of Shalmaneser I. (BMG, p. 23). While it is certain from documents of later periods that the same legal forms were employed in business transactions as were in use in Babylonia, no tablets of that character belonging to this time, with possibly one exception, have been found.

132. If the power of an ancient civilization to dominate a rude people was impressively exhibited in the victory of Babylonian culture over the Kassites (sect. 123), not less significant was the spectacle of the renaissance of that culture as the Kassite domination began to wane. Contemporaneous with the splitting off of Assyria and its incessant inroads upon Karduniash was the advance of Egypt into Syria and its appearance upon the Euphrates. The reign of the Semite in Western Asia and the long era of Babylonian leadership in civilization seemed about to come to an end. But so deeply rooted and so vigorous was this culture, even in Syria, that the Egyptian conquerors were compelled to use the Babylonian speech in their diplomatic correspondence with the princes and governors of the provinces and to teach it to their officials in the Egyptian capital. And when the authority of the Pharaohs decayed and their armies disappeared from Syria, the new kingdom on the Tigris came forward and girded itself for the task of unifying under its own leadership the Semitic peoples of Western Asia, and of making that same Babylonian culture prevail from the Persian gulf to the Mediterranean.

IV.THE TIMES OF TIGLATHPILESER L1100 B. C.

133. THE splendid extension of Assyrian authority to the northwest, achieved by Shalmaneser I. and his successors (sect. 120), had not been lasting. The incursion and settlement of the Khatti in Syria proved to be merely the beginning of a series of similar migrations from the north and northwest into the regions of Western Asia. Half a century before his own time, according to the testimony of Tiglathpileser I. of Assyria, the Mushki had advanced over the boundaries of Assyria's conquests along the headwaters of the Euphrates, had conquered the Alzi and the Purukuzzi, her tributary peoples, and were sifting into the nearer region of Qummukh. The bulk of the invading peoples, indeed, poured down into Syria, and broke in pieces the loose confederation of the Khatti, but the latter in turn were thereby pushed eastward to hamper Assyrian progress. The effect of this reverse may be observed in the revival of Babylonia under the later Kassite kings (sect. 122). It was, probably, late in his long reign that Ashurdan I. of Assyria was able to make headway against his southern rivals, and inflict on the next to the last Kassite ruler a defeat which three years after seems to have cost this foreign dynasty its supremacy over Babylonia. Ashurdan died soon after, and was followed by his son Mutakkil-nusku, of whom little is known; presumably he reigned but a few years (about 1135 B. C.).

134. The dynasty which wrested the Babylonian throne from the Kassites was, as the names of its kings indicate, of native origin, and is called in the kings' list "the dynasty of Pashe." Unfortunately, that important document is imperfectly preserved at this point, and seven

names out of the whole number of eleven are quite illegible. By a strange chance the names of those kings who from other documents are known to belong to this dynasty, are among those missing from the kings' list, and it is therefore impossible to determine accurately their chronological order and the length of their reigns. Of these the greatest was Nebuchadrezzar I. A highly probable argument has been made by Hilprecht (OBT, I. i, pp. 41 ff.) to prove that he was the founder of the dynasty and its first king (about 1140-1123 B. C.), but paleographic grounds render it inconclusive, though not impossible. He was followed in turn by Belnadin-aplu (about 1122-1117 B. C.), and Marduknadin-akhi (about 1116-1105). The dynasty held the throne over one hundred and thirty-two years to about 1010 B.C.

135. The name Nebuchadrezzar, meaning "May the god Nabu protect the boundary," is significaut of the work of this energetic Babylonian ruler. Babylonia had been the tramping-ground of the nations. For centuries foreigners had ruled in the land and had warred with the Assyrians for its possession. In the last Kassite years the Elamites had renewed their inroads from the east, penetrating to the very heart of the land. The province of Namar, famous for its horses, was already occupied by them. This deep humiliation, coupled with the Assyrian success, drove the Kassite from his ascendency and opened the way for more successful defenders of the ancient state. Nebuchadrezzar undertook the task. He found the Elamites already at Der. In spite of the scorching heat of midsummer he pushed on, driving them before him. Across the Tigris, on the banks of the Ula, the final stand was made by the Elamite army, but, in the fierce battle that ensued, the king, in the words of his own inscription (ABL, p. 8), "remained the victor" and "overthrew the country of the king of Elam... carrying away its possessions." Other expeditions to the northeast into the old Kassite land and beyond it to the highlands of the Lullumi, were intended to give warning to future marauders from that region. A governor of the district was stationed at the fortress of Holwan.

136. Among the first tasks confronting such a ruler was the rewarding of his followers, — a work which at the same time meant the restoration of the Semitic-Babylonian element to its former social and political supremacy. An interesting example of his procedure in this respect is found in a document of the king, the most considerable inscription which has been preserved from his reign, containing a deed of gift. Ritti Marduk, of the house of Karziyabkhu, in the province of Namar, which had fallen into the hands of the Elamites, had valiantly supported his lord in the trying Elamite campaign. Indeed, he seems to have performed a signal personal service to Nebuchadrezzar when hail pressed by the enemy. On the return of the army the king issued a proclamation, giving back to the prince and sealing for all time former privileges by which Karziyabkhu was made a free domain, over which the royal officials were not to exercise authority, upon which they were not to levy taxes, from which no requisitions for state purposes of any sort were to be made. Of the wisdom of establishing such feudal domains in the kingdom there may be some question. It was a return to the older system of land tenure which, by weakening the force of royal authority, had made defence against invaders difficult. But, for the present at least, restoration was the order of the day, and Nebuchadrezzar proudly styles himself "the sun of his country, who makes his people to prosper, who preserves boundaries and establishes landmarks(?), the just king, who pronounces righteous judgment." According to another similar document, he rescued in his campaign a statue of the god Bel, which the Elamites may have taken from Babylon. He seized the opportunity on this occasion to re-establish, by "taking the hands of Bel," his own right to the Babylonian throne, and proceeded to renew in a yet more striking and magnificent way the ancient glories of his kingdom.

137. Centuries had passed since any Babylonian ruler either had set up the ancestral claim to possession of the "West-land," or had done anything to make that claim good. The Kassite kings had found Egypt in possession of the field, and Assyria was, from time to time, pushing

forward to cut off the road by occupying the upper waters of the Euphrates. But Nebuchadrezzar, in the spirit of a glorious past which he felt that he represented, not only called himself "conqueror of the West-land," but seems actually to have reached the Mediterranean and left his name upon the cliffs of the Nahr-el-Kelb.

138. Such an expedition was certain to bring him into contact with Assyria, and, indeed, was possible only by reason of Assyrian weakness. His activities in the northeast were equally offensive to the rival state. It is no wonder, therefore, that the Synchronistic History records a clash between the two kingdoms. Neither the time nor the details of the campaigns can be satisfactorily determined. It may be presumed that they took place toward the close of the king's reign (about 1125 B. C.). A new ruler, Ashur-rish-ishi, was king in Assyria and eager to try conclusions with the Babylonian veteran. He invaded the south, but was driven back and followed by Nebuchadrezzar, who laid siege to a border fortress. The Assyrian king succeeded in beating him off and destroying his siege-train. In a later expedition which the Babylonian sent against Assyria, another and more serious repulse was suffered; the Babylonian general Karastu was taken prisoner and forty chariots captured. Nebuchadrezzar, near the end of his career, made no further attempt to avenge this disgrace, but left the renewal of the contest to his successors (Syn. Hist., col. II.), Belnadinaplu (sect. 134), indeed, seems to have taken no steps in this direction, nor did the Assyrian king pursue his advantage, unless his campaigns in the east and southeast against the highland tribes, Ahlami, Guti, and Lullumi, are to be regarded as an intrusion into territory already claimed as the conquest ef Nebuchadrezzar (sect. 135). Evidently neither party was anxious to come to blows. Babylonia needed yet a longer period of recuperation from the exhausting struggles for deliverance from Kassite and Elamite, while the Assyrian had his task awaiting him in the restoration of Assyrian power in the north and northwest.

139. The king who was to achieve this task for Assyria and to add a brilliant page to her annals of victory was already in the field. For at least three generations the Assyrian crown had passed from father to son, when Tiglathpileser I., the fourth of the line, in the flower of his youth, mounted the throne (about 1110 B.C.).

140. To understand the significance of the career of this great king, so fully detailed in his own inscription, a glance must be given at what had come to be the traditional political policy of Assyria. Linked to Babylonia by ties of blood and culture, the state was constantly drawn into complications with the mother-land. The vicissitudes of these relations have been traced in preceding chapters. But, apart from this fundamental influence, was the problem, presented to each state, of the relation to the larger environment. For Babylonia, this problem had already been solved. Her central position on the Euphrates — the connecting link between east and west — indicated that her sphere of influence reached out through western Mesopotamia to Syria and the Mediterranean coast-lands. This predominance, realized long before Assyria was born, had been maintained, with frequent lapses, indeed, and long intervals of inactivity, down to the days of Nebuchadrezzar I. From Babylon to Haran and from Haran to the sea stretched the recognized highroad as well of Babylonia's merchants as of her armies. Assyria, newly arrived upon the scene, and once secure of her position as an independent power by the side of her more ancient rival, found the outlook for progress leading to the more rugged pathways of the highlands to the north and northwest. To this field her position in the upper corner of the Mesopotamian plain invited her. The Tigris had broken through the mountains and opened up the road thither. And when the Assyrian merchant, moving westward in the shadow of the mountain wall which formed the northern boundary of the plain, was halted at the Euphrates by Babylonian authority, he turned northward into the highlands through which the upper Euphrates poured, and thus brought to light wider regions for the extension of Assyrian commerce. In all this mountain-land the soldier had followed hard upon the heels of the trader,

so that for more than three centuries the campaigns of kings like Ashuruballit, Adadnirari, and Shalmaneser had built up the tradition that Assyria's sphere of influence was this northern highland. Though in after years, when Babylonia had yielded her supremacy of the west-land, the Assyrian kings devoted themselves to conquest in the richer lands of Syria, they never forgot the field of their earlier campaigns; they kept open the trade routes, and held in check the restless peoples of this rugged region.

141. This region, in classical times known as Armenia, containing in its fullest extent sixty thousand square miles, is an irregular rectangle, its greatest length five hundred miles, its width two hundred and fifty miles. A vast plateau, lifted some seven thousand feet above sea-level, it is girt about and traversed by mountain ranges. On its northern boundary lies the Caucasus; along the southern border, overlooking the Mesopotamian valley, runs Mt. Masius, called by the Assyrians Kashiari. Between these mountain boundaries two chains (the Armenian Taurus and the Anti-Taurus) cross this lofty region from west to east at about equal distances from one another, At its eastern border the mountains turn sharply to the southeast, and the country becomes a trackless tangle of peaks and ravines. Toward the northwest the plain runs out onto the plateau of Asia Minor, or drops to the Black Sea. To the southwest the Taurus throws out the ranges that pierce Armenia, and then itself turns off to the south in the Amanus range which forms the backbone of Syria. In this disintegration of the Taurus the entire surface of the land, like its eastern counterpart, is tossed about in a shapeless confusion of high and well-nigh impassable summits. Within Armenia, between the long ranges, lie fair and smiling plains. Between Kashiari and the Armenian Taurus the springs of the Tigris gather to form that mighty stream which breaks through the former range on the east and pours down to the sea. Behind the Armenian Taurus are the sources of the Euphrates which flows at first parallel to the Tigris, but in the opposite direction, until, turning to the southward, it tears its way through the knot of mountains in southwestern Armenia by innumerable windings, and debouches on the plain, at first to fall swiftly, then to spread out more widely on its way to the Persian gulf. The land, threaded by the head-waters of these rivers, is wild and romantic, with deep glens, lofty peaks, and barren passes. In the midst of it lies the broad, blue salt lake of Van, eighty miles long. The mountains are thickly wooded, the valleys are genial. Mineral wealth in silver, copper, and iron abounds. Inexhaustible pasturage is found for flocks and herds. All the fruits of the temperate zone grow in the valleys, and harvests of grain are reaped in the plains. The winters are cold and invigorating. It is a country of rare picturesqueness, capable of supporting a large population. The people, vigorous and hardy, till the soil of the plains, or lead flocks and herds over the hillsides. The tribal organization prevails. Villages nestle at the base of hills surmounted by rude fortresses. The larger towns, situated on the main roads which lead from Asia Minor to Mesopotamia, are centres of trade in raw materials, wool, goat's hair, and grain, or in the rude vessels of copper and silver, the spoil of the mines, or in the coarse cloths of the native weaver. The larger plains afford to the tribes opportunities for closer organization, under chiefs mustering no inconsiderable number of warriors. Border forays and the hunting of wild beasts vary the monotony of agricultural and pastoral existence, At times, under pressure of invasion, the tribes unite to defend their valleys, but fall apart again when the danger is past. A free, healthy, and abundant, if rude, life is lived under the open sky.

142. To secure control over the borders of this upland, then, Assyrian kings had girded themselves in preceding centuries. But the foothold attained by them on the upper waters of the Euphrates had been, as has been indicated (sect. 133), all but lost before Tiglathpileser became king. Scarcely had he taken his seat, when a new disaster was announced front the land of the Qummukhi. This people occupied the extensive valley between the Armenian Taurus and the Kashiari range at the sources of the Tigris, to the east of the gorge by which the Euphrates breaks through the former range to seek the Mesopotamian plain. Tribes from the

northwest, known collectively as the Mushki, not content with overpowering the Alzi and Purukuzzi (sect. 133), suddenly hurled themselves under their five kings with twenty thousand warriors upon the Qummukhi. Tiglathpileser hurried, with an army, from Assur to the scene, more than three hundred miles away. His route led him up the Tigris, half-way across the upper Mesopotamian plain, then northward over the range of Kashiari, to a point where he could overlook the valley at its centre, not far from the ancient town of Amid, the modern Diyarbekr. From here he descended with chariots and infantry upon the invaders below and crushed them in one tremendous onslaught. Surprised and overwhelmed, fourteen thousand were cut down, and the remainder captured and transported to Assur. The Qummukhi, restless and rebellious, were subdued with fire and sword; one of their clans that fled into the eastern mountains the king followed across the Tigris, and, though they were aided by the Kirkhi (Kurti), a neighboring people in the eastern plateau, he defeated them and captured their stronghold. Returning, he marched against the capital of another of their clans farther to the north. They fled at his approach; their chief submitted without fighting and was spared. The king closed the campaign by taking a detachment of infantry and thirty chariots for a dash over the northern mountains into the "haughty and unsubmissive country of Mildish," which was likewise reduced to subjection. Upon all the peoples he laid the obligation of regular tribute and, laden with booty, returned to Assyria. By one vigorous advance he had not only removed the danger from the invading peoples, but had re-established Assyrian authority over one of the largest and most important of these mountain valleys, — that one which formed the entrance into the Mesopotamian plain.

143. The second campaign, undertaken in the first full year of his reign, — the year of his accession counting as only "the beginning," — was directed chiefly against the still rebellious Qummukhi, who were made again to feel the weight of Assyrian displeasure. On their western border were settled the Shumashti (Shubarti), whose cities had been invaded by a body of tribes of the Khatti, four thousand strong in infantry and chariots. These invaders submitted on the king's advance and were transported to Assyria. Two minor events of the year were the re-establishment of authority over the Alzi and Purukuzzi, and the subjugation of the Shubari, an eastern hill-tribe.

144. In the narrative of the first year's exploits occurs a phrase which suggests that the plan subsequently followed by the king was already conceived. Not only had Ashur, the nation's god, bidden him subdue rebellious vassals, but, to use the king's own words, "now he commanded me to extend the boundaries of my country." It had become clear that, to hold the peoples of these northern valleys to their allegiance, a systematic extension of Assyrian territory there must be undertaken. The task was formidable, leading Tiglathpileser I. into far districts hitherto unheard of by Assyrian kings, and requiring a display of energy and resource that his predecessors had not approached. Three well-conceived campaigns are recorded. In the first — that of his second regnal year — the tribes to the east of Qummukhi and the sources of the Tigris, between Kashiari and the Armenian Taurus, were subdued. In the second — that of his third regnal year — the king climbed the Taurus and descended upon the sources of the Euphrates. Here were the tribes known to the Assyrians as the Nairi, living to the west of Lake Van. The army pushed steadily westward through the mountains, fighting as it advanced, crossed the Euphrates, marched along its right bank, and reached the city of Milid, the western end of the main road from Asia Minor, later called the "Royal Road," and the chief city of a district separated from the Qummukhi only by the lofty Taurus mountains. There remained only the peoples to the far west, and against these, after the interval of a year, the king proceeded in his fifth regnal year. In this region, between Qummukhi and the gulf of Issus, lived the Muçri, whom Shalmaneser I. had already encountered (sect. 120). In these mountain valleys had flourished, centuries before, one of the main branches of the wide kingdom of the Khatti, and from thence this warlike people had descended upon the Syrian

plain. Here Tiglathpileser found great fortresses, with walls and towers, blocking his advance. His reduction of the Muçri stirred up their neighbors and allies to the northwest the Qumani, and sent him still farther away into the endless confusion of rugged mountain ranges to accomplish their overthrow. One fierce battle with an army of twenty thousand warriors drove the defenders back upon Khunusa, their triple-walled fortress, which was stormed by the king with great slaughter and demolished. The way now lay open to their capital, which surrendered on his approach. Thereupon he accepted the submission of the tribes and laid the usual tribute upon them. The first stage of his stupendous task was now practically completed. The Assyrian border in this vast mountain region stretched in a huge arc from the upper Tigris and Lake Van around the head-waters of the Euphrates to the northeastern corner of the Mediterranean. Indeed it extended even farther, for, to use his own proud words:

I conquered in all, from the beginning of my reign to my fifth regnal year, forty-two countries and their princes, from the left bank of the lower Zab and the border of distant forest-clad mountains as far as the right bank of the Euphrates, the land of the Khatti, and the Upper Sea Of the setting sun (Prism Inscription, col, vi. 39-45).

145. During the strenuous years of these campaigns the king had found occasion to make at least two expeditions in other directions. The overthrow of the Shubari in the eastern hills took place in his first regnal year. In the fourth, he made a raid upon the Bedouin, who were crossing the Euphrates into western Mesopotamia, apparently for the purpose of settling in the upper plain. They were the advance guard of the Arameans. Crossing the plain due west from Assur, Tiglathpileser drove them before him along the river from the Khabur to the city of Karkhemish, followed them across into the desert, burned their villages, and carried off their goods and cattle to his capital. Necessary as such a campaign was for Aissyria's protection, it had entered territory under Babylonian influence, and could hardly have failed to stir up the Babylonian ruler to action against Assyria. Marduknadinakhi (sect. 134) was a vigorous ruler, and he seems to have responded by an invasion of Assyrian territory in the tenth year of his reign, in which may have occurred the capture of the city of Ekallati, and the removal of its gods to Babylon, an event to which a later Assyrian king, Sennacherib, refers. In the hostilities which inevitably ensued and continued for two years, possibly the seventh and eighth regnal years of Tiglathpileser, the Babylonian was severely beaten. In the first campaign Marduknadinakhi had advanced beyond the lower Zab into Assyrian territory, when he was driven back. In the second, the Assyrian king took the offensive and swept all before him. The decisive defeat was administered in northern Babylonia. Tiglathpileser captured, one after another, the chief northern cities, Upi, Dur Kurigalzu, Sippar, and Babylon, and then marched up the Euphrates to the Khabur, thereby bringing the river from Babylon to Karkhemish under Assyrian control. Satisfied with this assertion of his superiority, and the control of the chief trade routes, he did not attempt to usurp the Babylonian throne, but left Marduknadinakhi to resume his discredited authority.

146. A few more campaigns of the great Assyrian are recorded. An expedition against Elam may belong to his ninth year. Other visits to the lands of the Nairi are mentioned, in the last of which he set up, at the mouth of a grotto whence flows one of the sources of the Tigris, a stone slab upon which a full-length effigy of the conqueror is sculptured, with a proclamation of his victories over these northern peoples. It would not be surprising if he reigned little more than ten years. The numerous and fatiguing campaigns in which he led his troops, sometimes in his chariot, oftener on foot, over rugged mountains, amidst incessant fighting, must early have exhausted even his iron endurance. In the intervals of warfare he hunted with indefatigable zeal. Lists of lions slain by the king when on foot or from the chariot, of wild oxen and elephants, the trophies of his lance and bow, appear in his annals, and reveal another side of his activity. Not by himself, but by later kings, is another expedition referred to, which if, as it

seems, properly assigned to him, rounds out his career. On the broken obelisk of Ashurnaçirpal III. are some lines which describe achievements parallel to his, though the ruler's name has not been preserved. Of this unknown it is further said that he sailed in ships of Arvad, a city of Phoenicia, killed a nakhiru (sea monster of some sort) in the great sea, captured wild cattle at the foot of Lebanon, and was presented by the king of Egypt with a pagutu (hippopotamus?) and a crocodile, Shalmaneser II. speaks of the cities of Ashurutiraçbat and Mutkinu, lying over against one another on either side of the Euphrates, as once captured by Tiglathpileser. These statements imply that, in the years after his Babylonian victory, he completed his western conquests by a campaign in Syria that carried him to the Mediterranean and to the Lebanons. The fame of this exploit extorted a tribute of respect from an Egyptian ruler.

147. Enough has been said to show that the king's military activity was no purposeless series of plundering raids. His campaigns are linked together in a well-ordered system. The first item of his policy is stated in his plain but significant assertion, "The feet of the enemy I kept from my country." Even more important is his second boast, "One word united I caused them to speak." Once conquered, the peoples were organized under Assyrian rule. Of the details in the realization of this plan he himself has recorded little beyond the establishment of a regular tax and the requirement of hostages. The deportation of captured tribes is not uncommon. The conquered peoples swear solemn oaths of allegiance by the Assyrian gods. Rebels are treated with ruthless cruelty, for they have sinned against gods and men. Peoples who resist attack are exposed to slaughter and the plundering of their goods. Tribes that submit are spared, their property respected, their chiefs restored to power under Assyrian supremacy. These principles, acted upon by Tiglathpileser, formed a body of precedents for future rulers,

148. At first thought, it seems unlikely that so eager a warrior would be solicitous for the economic welfare of his country. He was statesman, however, as well as conqueror. From the conquered lands he brought back flocks and herds; he sought out useful and valuable trees for transplanting into Assyrian forests, oaks, cedars, and fruit trees of a kind unknown to Assyrian orchards. He rebuilt the crumbling walls of cities; repaired the storehouses and granaries and heaped them high with grain. Royal palaces in his various provincial cities were restored, forming citadels for defence. Most splendid of all were the temples which he built and adorned with inimitable splendor. Of the restored temple of Anu and Adad he says:

I built it from foundation to roof larger and grander than before, and erected also two great temple towers, fitting ornaments of their great divinities. The splendid temple, a brilliant and magnificent dwelling, the habitation of their joys, the house for their delight, shining as bright as the stars on heaven's firmament and richly decorated with ornaments through the skill of my artists, I planned, devised, and thought out, built, and completed. I made its interior brilliant like the dome of the heavens; decorated its walls like the splendor of the rising stars, and made it grand with resplendent brilliancy. I reared its temple towers to heaven, and completed its roof with burned brick; located therein the upper terrace containing the chamber of their great divinities; and led into the interior Anu and Adad, the great gods, and made them to dwell in their lofty house, thus gladdening the heart of their great divinities (Prism Ins., col. vii. 85-114, trans. in ABL, pp. 25 f.).

149, The height of Assyria's attainment in the arts of life may be inferred from a passage like the foregoing, which is characteristic of the inscription as a whole, written as it is in a vigorous, flowing, and some. what rhetorical style, significant of no little literary culture. The ruler who could achieve such things and find expression for them in so lofty a fashion was far from being a mere ruthless general, and his state much more than a mere military establishment. Justly could he declare that he had "enhanced the welfare of his nation," and made his people "live and dwell in peaceful homes." Well might he pray, to use his own words, that the gods

may turn to me truly and faithfully, accept graciously the lifting up of my hands, hearken unto my devout prayers, grant unto me and my kingdom abundance of rain, years of prosperity and fruitfulness in plenty (Prism. Ins,, col. viii. 24-29, trans. in ABL, p. 26).

150. Tiglathpileser was followed on the throne by his son Ashur-bel-kala, and he by his brother Shamshi Adad. The two reigns seem to have been peaceful and prosperous. The former king appears to have continued to rule over the wide domains of his father and, in addition, to have come to terms with Babylonia. There Marduk-sapik-zerim followed Marduknadinakhi, and entered into an alliance with his Assyrian neighbor. When a rebellion drove the Babylonian from his throne, the successful usurper, "son of nobody," Adad-aplu-iddin, was recognized by the son of Tiglathpileser, who took his daughter into the harem on payment of a princely dowry by her father. It has been inferred, from the finding of a statue in Nineveh hailing from the king's palace, that Ashurbelkala removed the capital from Assur to Nineveh. Such a change is quite possible, since it would place him nearer the centre of his realm. His brother, who was perhaps his successor, is known to have built on the temple of Ishtar in the latter city. The name of the son of Shamshi Adad, Ashurnaçirpal II., has been preserved, but though his striking prayer to Ishtar is in our hands (BMG, p. 68), a record of his deeds has not come down to posterity. The Assyrian kingdom goes out in darkness. The first chapter of her imperial history is finished (about 1050 B. C.).

PART III .THE ASCENDANCY OF ASSYRIA

I.HE ANCIENT WORLD AT THE BEGINNING OF THE FIRST MILLENNIUM. 1000 B. C.

151. ABOUT the year 1000 B. C. a strange and well-nigh unaccountable state of things confronts the student of the empires of the Mesopotamian valley. For a scene of vigorous activity is substituted a monotonous vacancy. Aggressive expansion yields to inertness. In place of the regal personalities whose words proclaim their achievements in sonorous detail, appear mere names, scattered here and there over the wider spaces of the years, that tell nothing of import or interest concerning the progress of the states over which these phantom rulers held feeble sway. The sources of knowledge have slowly dried up or have been cut off by the accidents to which historical memorials are always subject. Here and there a brick inscribed with a king's name, or an occasional reference in later inscriptions to some otherwise unknown rulers of the time, is all that remains of Assyrian material. The Babylonian kings' lists and chronicles are confused or discordant, and at a critical point, where they are practically the only source, are quite broken away, leaving the whole chronological structure hanging in the air. Such facts carry their own important lesson. They speak of decay or downfall, and invite inquiry into its causes.

152. The information directly gleaned from these scanty memorials may be briefly stated. Three Assyrian rulers are known to belong somewhere within the period. Ashurkirbi (?) is said by Shalmaneser II., who ruled Assyria two centuries later, to have left a memorial of himself at the Mediterranean, presumably in token of a western expedition, and also to have lost to the Arameans the two cities on opposite sides of the Euphrates, captured and probably fortified by Tiglathpileser I. to guard Assyrian ascendancy at that point (sect. 146). On the so-called broken obelisk of Ashurnaçirpal III. are mentioned kings Irba Adad and Ashurnadinakhi II,, who, probably in these days, built at the city of Assur. In Babylonia the dynasty of Pashe came to an end about 1007 B. C., and was followed by three dynasties in rapid succession, The fifth in the order of the kings' list consisted of three kings who ruled between twenty-one and twenty-three years, and was called the "Dynasty of the Sea." The sixth, the "Dynasty of Bazi," also of three kings, endured for but twenty years. An Elamite followed, reigning for six years, constituting by himself alone the seventh dynasty. The names of the kings of the eighth dynasty are quite broken away on the list, and apparently the sum of their regnal years also. How long they ruled, therefore, is quite uncertain, and, when the gap closes, the kings that begin the new series belong to the eighth century. Half a dozen names, found in other documents, occupy the vacant space over against Assyrian kings of the ninth century, from whom ampler information has come down,

153. While only a broken and baffling story of the course of these kingdoms can be drawn from such sources, it does not follow that the years gathering about the beginning of the first millennium B. C. were not of real significance to the history of Babylonia and Assyria. The kingdoms themselves pass for the time into eclipse, and the centre of interest is shifted from their capitals to the lands that hitherto have been the scene of their aggression. In those lands, however, are to be found the causes of the decline, and there a veritably new political world was forming in those years, — a world in which the leaders of the Assyrian renaissance were later to carry their arms to wider and more splendid victories.

154. It may be correct to ascribe the decline of Assyria, at least in part, to internal exhaustion, due to the tremendous strain of the numerous and costly campaigns of Tiglathpileser I.

Vigorous citizens had been drafted for the armies, many of whom perished on distant battlefields. The economic resources of the land absorbed in military campaigns were by no means compensated for by the inflowing of treasure from the conquered lands, most of which went into the royal coffers. These losses could not but disable the national strength. Yet the great king seems to have sought to guard against this danger by the statesmanlike measures already described (sect. 148), and during the reigns of his two sons some opportunity for recuperation was afforded. The prime fact was that, coincident with this period of internal decline, a series of mighty movements of peoples took place in the world without, which swept away Assyria's authority over her provincial districts, encroached upon her territory, threw Babylonia into civil war, paralyzed all foreign trade, and afforded opportunity for the consolidation of rival powers on the borders of both nations. The most important of these movements was a fresh wave of Aramean migration, which welled up in resistless volume from the Arabian peninsula. At various periods during preceding centuries, these nomads had crossed the Euphrates, and roamed through the middle Mesopotamian plain as far as the Tigris. At times they were a menace to the commerce of the rivers, but usually were held in check by the armies of the great states, driven back by systematic campaigns, or absorbed into the settled population. But in these years they came in overwhelming multitudes. Apparently by the mere force of numbers they crowded back the Assyrians and Babylonians and occupied the entire western half of the plain. They poured over into Syria as well, until stopped by the sea and the mountains. At the first they may have moved to and fro, fighting and plundering, and not without reason has it been held (Tiele, BAG, pp. 167, 178) that they carried fire and sword into the heart of Assyria itself. In course of time they yielded to the influences of civilization, and began to settle down in the rich country of upper Mesopotamia around the Euphrates, where their states are found a century after. The causes of such a movement are difficult to determine. In this case something more than the ordinary impulse to migration seems to be required. May it not he found in the rise of the kingdoms of southern Arabia which, whether Minean or Sabean, seem to have reached the acme of their prosperity just before this period? Their extension toward the north and east may have driven the Bedouin upward and precipitated the onward movement which forced the Arameans out into Mesopotamia and Syria.

155. Such a cause would account also for the other irruption from the same Arabian region, which in this period brought confusion to Babylonia. It has already been remarked (sect. 69) that Babylonian trade with southern Arabia centred about the border city of Ur near the mouth of the rivers. Along this open and attractive highway came a new horde that fell upon the coast-lands and river-bottoms, and appear henceforth in Babylonian history as the Kaldi. They pressed forward up the river, ever falling back, when defeated, into their almost inaccessible fastnesses in the swamps of the coast, and ever reappearing to contest the sovereignty of the land. The kings that followed the dynasty of Pashe were called Kings of the Sea Land; the name suggests that they may have belonged to the Kaldi. At any rate, they felt the influence of the troubles occasioned by the Arameans to the north, for an inscription of Nabu-abal-iddin of the ninth century, mentions the plundering of Akkad by the Suti, and the failure of two of the kings of the dynasty in an endeavor properly to restore the worship of the god Shamash in Sippar (KB, III. 1, p. 174), The rapid succession of dynasties in Babylonia from about 1000 to 950 B. C. is naturally explained in view of a series of incursions such as this inscription mentions and other facts suggest.

156. In the northern regions, also, the scene of the victories of Tiglathpileser, Assyrian ascendancy appears early to have been swept away. The facts are much more obscure and indecisive, but the entrance of new peoples on the scene seems fairly certain. Somewhere about or just before this time, the Phrygians entered Asia Minor from Europe, and, like a wedge, forced apart the peoples of the east and west. Vague traditions exist of a Cilician

kingdom, which rivalled that of the earlier Khatti, and united the peoples to the north and east of the gulf of Issus as far as Armenia (Maspero, SN, p. 668). It may be that the assaults of the Assyrian king, coupled with the Phrygian invasion, had resulted in welding these tribes into a semblance of unity under some powerful chieftain, before whom the authority of Assyria speedily disappeared, and the mountain passes were closed to her trade. Even more significant for the later history of Assyria was the advance from the northeast to the shores of the "Upper Sea" (Lake Van) of a new people, the Urarti, who were to exercise a predominating influence in these regions. Their advent was followed by great confusion. The northern tribes were pressed down to the south and southwest, and thereby the Assyrian ascendancy in the eastern and northern mountains was broken.

157. Behind these obstructions which effectually closed in around the Mesopotamian kingdoms, the opportunity was given for the formation of new nationalities, or the larger development of those already in existence. Especially on the Mediterranean coast was the opportunity improved. Here the warlike people known as the Philistines had established themselves as lords in the cities on the southeast coast, where the roads run up from Egypt into Syria, and were pressing up into the hill country behind. On these plateaus the Hebrews had been feeling after that national organization to which their worship of Jehovah led the way and gave the inspiration. By the impact of Philistine aggression the nation was brought into being, and sprang into full vigor under the genial leadership of David and the wise statesmanship of Solomon (about 1000-930 B. C.). Higher up along the coast the aggressive activity of the royal house of Tyre, and especially the reign of Hirom I., so strengthened and enriched that city as henceforth to make it the centre of the Phoenician communities, the commercial mart of the eastern and western worlds. In the interior of Syria, city-states, like Hamath and Khalman, Patin and Samal, grew prosperous and warred with one another and with the encroaching Arameans. The latter, while settling down in states on either side of the Euphrates, had pushed over into Syria as far as Zobah, and laid the foundations of the kingdom of Damascus, the famous trading-post and garden spot of eastern Syria. As for Egypt, she was broken by internal conflict; and though the Pharaohs of Tanis were fairly vigorous kings, and from time to time even ventured into southern Palestine, to check and dominate the Philistines (Milner, Asien and Europa, p. 389), these kings were not masters of all Egypt, and could do little to support their claims upon the Asiatic provinces possessed by the earlier dynasties. Thus the new states grew and older communities put on new life, under the impulse of the fresh masses of population, now that there was freedom from the pressure of the powers on the Tigris and the Nile. The whole face of the oriental world was changed and the centre of gravity seemed to have moved beyond the western bank of the Euphrates. By the middle of the tenth century the movement was at its height, and Syria appeared to be about to take the place of pre-eminence in the historical period that was to follow.

II. ASHURNAÇIRPAL III AND THE CONQUEST OF MESOPOTAMIA. 885-860 B. C.

158. THE year 950 B. C., by which date the confusion of the past century had spent itself and in the various districts bordering on the Mesopotamian valley was beginning to yield to order and progress, affords a convenient point from which also to observe the revival of the ancient kingdoms whose activity had been so suddenly interrupted during the preceding years, In Egypt a Libyan general, Sheshonk, high in position at the court, had usurped the throne and founded the twenty-second dynasty. His accession was soon followed by a forward movement into Palestine and an attack upon the Hebrew kingdoms. In Babylonia the eighth dynasty (sect. 152) ruled under a king of unknown name and origin, who remained on the throne for thirty-

six years and was followed by ten or eleven rulers of the same line. Assyria, however, showed most clearly the beginnings of recovery. There also a new dynasty occupied the throne, and thenceforth the crown descended in the same family, from father to son, through at least ten generations. Of Tiglathpileser II., the founder of the line, nothing is known. His son, Ashurdan II. about 930 B. C., comes forward somewhat clearly as a canal-builder, a rounder of fortresses, and a restorer of temples in Assur. With Adadnirari II. his son (911-890 B. C.), the upward movement was accelerated. The Assyrian limu list (sect. 38), that invaluable document of ancient chronology, begins with him, as though the compiler regarded his reign as a new epoch in the national history. He built upon the walls of Assur, and, according to one of his descendants, "overthrew the disobedient and conquered on every side." No record has been preserved of any of his wars except that with Babylonia. A difficulty about boundaries between the countries seems to have brought on the conflict. A forward movement by the Babylonian king Shamash-mudammiq was met by Adadnirari near Mount Yalman (Holwan) in the eastern mountains. The Babylonians were driven back, and the defeat apparently cost their king his life, for he was immediately succeeded on the throne by a usurper, Nabushumishkun. Adadnirari advanced against him, defeated his army, spoiled several cities, and brought him speedily to terms. A treaty was made in which the kings exchanged daughters, and the boundaries were adjusted, no doubt to the satisfaction of Assyria, The son of Adadnirari II. was Tukulti Ninib II,, in whose case the direct report of a campaign in the north has been preserved. At the sources of the Tigris, where Tiglathpileser I. had recorded his victories (sect. 146), his successor also inscribed his name and exploits, how with the help of his god he traversed the mighty mountains from the rising of the sun to its setting, and reduced their peoples to submission. It is evident that the work of his predecessor of two centuries before had to be done over again, He valiantly undertook the task. It is not probable that his own campaigns extended beyond the valley of the upper Tigris between the first two ranges of mountains. He reigned but six years (890-885 B. C.), giving promise of what Assyria was about to achieve and winning from his successors characteristic appreciations of his valor; his son asserted that he "laid the yoke on his adversaries and set up their bodies on stakes," and his grandson, that "he subjugated all his enemies and swept them like a tempest."

159. With Ashurnaçirpal III. (885-860 B. C.), the son and successor of Tukulti Ninib II., dawns the bright morning of the Assyrian revival. The brief reign of his father brought him to the throne at an early age, and, like Tiglathpileser I., he plunged immediately into a series of warlike activities. Of the eleven campaigns recorded in his inscriptions, out of his twenty-four full years on the throne, seven were carried through before the first quarter of his reign was over. His first concern was with the north, whither his father had already led the way. There important changes had taken place since Tiglathpileser had made his campaigns. The commotions in the far north had pushed the tribes and peoples out of their old seats, crowded them together, or brought new peoples on the scene. The Nairi (sect. 144) were now to the southwest of Lake Van, and partly within the southern valley to the east of the sources of the Tigris. The Kirkhi had been pressed together and lay toward the south of the same valley. On the western side Aramean tribes had crowded up on the east of the Qummukhi, and formed several communities about Amid and to the west of the upper Tigris, pushing the Qummukhi back towards the mountains through which the Euphrates flows. Several tribes about the upper Tigris had retired into Kashiari, and there occupied the passes and valleys on the border of the Mesopotamian plain. On the east and northeast the mountain peoples had been thrown forward to the ridges overlooking the valley, and constituted a new problem for the Assyrian rulers. Ashurnaçirpal marched into the very centre of the disturbed region to check the advance of the Nairi, found their easternmost tribe (the Nimme) already to the couth of Lake Van, and crushed them, A dash over the mountains to the east brought the Kirruri to terms, and secured the homage of peoples to the far east in the upper valleys of the greater Zab (Gilzan and Khubushkia).

160. The western plateau south of the Armenian Taurus was then entered. Back and forth and up and down from the Bitlis to Qummukh and from Tauru to Kashiari, he marched and fought in the four campaigns of the years 885, 884, 883, and 880 B. C. The upper Tigris was first cleared by the overthrow of the Kirkhi, and the tribute of Qummukh was gathered. At this time apparently the Aramean communities of that valley submitted. Then followed the recovery of the southwestern part of the plateau, where vigorous opposition had developed under the leadership of a city which had once been an Assyrian outpost. The trouble was spreading northward among the Aramean cities. Reaching the sources of the Tigris, where he set up his image by the side of those of his predecessors, Ashurnaçirpal marched southward along the ridge overlooking Qummukh to Kashiari, on whose southwestern flanks were the strongholds of the enemy. Here the cities of the Nirbi were destroyed, and a fortified post on the right bank of the Tigris was established in the city of Tushkha, as the centre of Assyrian influence in the southwestern plateau. The reduction of the Nairi in the northern valleys was undertaken in the campaign of 880 B. C., and their tribute brought to Tushkha. With this the conquest of the various peoples of these districts was completed. A governor was appointed for the whole region, with his seat in that city.

161. The king's movement into the north, in the beginning of his reign, seems to have been regarded by the hill peoples of the eastern border as a menace, against which it behooved them to prepare. That they were growing into a sort of confederacy is shown in the common name attached to the region — Zamua. A chieftain whose tribe occupied the outermost fringe of mountains at the head of the pass of Babite, succeeded after two years in uniting all Zamua in an alliance. The united tribes presented an independent front to Assyria and proceeded to fortify the pass. To Ashurnaçirpal this move was equivalent to rebellion. Besides, it threatened the security of his eastern border as well as the control of the trade with the hinterland. He withdrew, therefore, from active operations in the northwest, and for two years (882-881 B. C.) campaigned among these eastern mountains. His first attack had for its purpose the opening of the pass. The struggle was a severe one, and the summer was gone before the first line of defences was pierced. The king then withdrew to the Assyrian border. Winter came on early in the high mountain valleys, and the inhabitants must have felt secure for the time, but in September the Assyrian army appeared again within the mountain barrier. A fortified camp was established, and expeditions sallied out in all directions into the heart of the enemy's country, striking hard blows, and retiring swiftly on their base of operations. All Zamua was terrified and hastened to do homage. The next year's campaign was in the southeast, where some Zamuan chiefs continued in rebellion. A rapid march to the sources of the Turnat brought the king into the centre of the disaffected region, which was laid waste; thence the army turned northward, burning and plundering through the upper valleys, and descended to the fortified camp of the previous winter. A second time all the chieftains of Zamua came and kissed the king's feet. While the leading rebels had escaped the vengeance of the king, the confederacy had been broken up, and the country severely punished. From the northern border were brought down the gifts of Gilzan and Khubushkia, lands which had tendered their submission in his opening year. Fortified posts were established in Zamua, and a governor was appointed with his seat at Kalkhi.

162. These six years of campaigning (885-880 B. C.) make up a cycle of vigorous achievement of which any warrior might be proud. From the head-waters of the river Turnat on the southeast, to the northwestern mountains through which the Euphrates flowed, the long arc of mountain borderland had been brought under Assyrian authority. The advancing tribes had been repressed and Assyria's borders relieved. A change of capital followed, possibly was occasioned by this extension of territory. In connection with his eastern wars the attention of Ashurnaçirpal had been directed to Kalkhi. Its favorable situation, in the angle where the

greater Zab falls into the Tigris, and equidistant from the eastern and northern mountain borders, may have been the ground which induced him to remove the seat of government thither. His first work was piously to rebuild the temple of his patron god, Ninib, and place in it a colossal statue of that divinity, to set up his shrine and appoint his festal seasons, Building went forward from this time upon the various edifices which were to adorn the site, while the king himself turned to a new field of warfare, and undertook a series of expeditions that occupied him for at least four years.

163. While in Quinmukh, on the expedition of 884 B. C., word was brought to Ashurnaçirpal that the communities on the Khabur River were in commotion. The Arameans had already established petty principalities in the rich plains bordering on the Euphrates from the Khabur to the mountains (sect. 154). One of these states was aspiring to something more than local supremacy. This community, to the north of the Balikh, and situated in a fertile region, the seat of an ancient civilization, and an immemorial centre of trade, was called by the Assyrians Bit Adini from a certain Adinu, probably the founder of a dynasty of ambitious chiefs. How far it had extended its influence by this time cannot be determined, but its interference in the affairs of Suru on the Khabur had brought about a revolution there, whereby a chief from Bit Adini was raised to the throne. When the king heard of it, he at once recognized the gravity of the situation. A union of these communities was a serious danger to Assyria, and, as in the case of the tribes of the eastern mountains, he regarded it as an act of "rebellion," warranting immediate action on his part. Marching southward to the upper waters of the Khabur, he descended along the river bank to the scene of disturbance. A portion of the inhabitants of Suru submitted. The remainder, showing resistance, were cruelly punished, and their new chief carried off to be flayed alive at Nineveh. The neighboring tribes up and down the Euphrates brought tribute.

164. The four years following saw the completion of the work undertaken in the north and east (sects. 160, 161). Not till 879 B. C. did the king undertake another western expedition. Unfortunately, the three expeditions that follow 879 B. C. are left undated in his inscriptions, and it is uncertain whether these occupied the years immediately following (i. e. 878-876 B. C.), though it is usually assumed that they did. In the first two campaigns (879-878) he took Suru on the Khabur as a base of operations, and chastised the tribes north and south on either bank of the Euphrates. The southern tribes, the Sukhi, were supported by Babylonian troops under the command of Zabdanu, the brother of Nabupaliddin, king of Babylonia, and Ashurnaçirpal proudly claims to have stricken with terror "the land of Babylonia and the Kaldi, by taking prisoner the Babylonian general and three thousand of his troops. He obtained boats, and, sailing across and down the Euphrates, plundered the villages, burned the grain-fields, and marched into the desert. Somewhere in the region between the Khabur and the Balikh he built two fortresses on either side of the Euphrates, called Kar Ashurnaçirpal and Nibarti Ashur. The third expedition (877?) was aimed directly at Bit Adini, and the resistance offered by Akhuni, its king, collapsed with the storming of his citadel of Kaprabi. With the submission of this Aramean kingdom Ashurnaçirpal was in control of all upper Mesopotamia.

165. The last western campaign (876?) had the Mediterranean for its objective point. From Bit Adini the Euphrates was crossed, and Karkhemish, the capital of Sangara, king of the Khatti, surrendered without fighting. Ashurnaçirpal now had before him the plateau of upper Syria, which, lying behind the Euphrates hills, stretched away westward to the mountains and the seacoast in a series of fruitful plains, filled with inhabitants. Petty city-states divided the land between them and occupied themselves in perpetual warfare. At this time the leading state was that of Patin, which, under its king Lubarna, controlled the country about the lower Orontes and its northern affluents. Ashurnaçirpal marched directly on Patin. Lubarna offered no resistance, and was left in possession of his kingdom as an Assyrian vassal. The march led

across the orontes southward through the mountains. The city of Aribua was selected as an Assyrian outpost and base of supplies. From thence the march may be told in the king's own words:

Then I approached the slopes of Lebanon. To the great sea of Akharri [i. e. the Mediterranean] I ascended. In the great sea I purified my weapons and offered sacrifices to the gods. Tribute of the kings on the shores of the sea, of Tyre, Sidon, Byblos, Makhallata, Maiça, Kaiça, Akharri, and Aramada [Arvad] in the midst of the sea, silver, gold, lead, copper, copper vessels, variegated and linen garments, a large and small pagutu, ushu and ukarinu wood, tusks of the nakhiri, the sea monster, I received in tribute, They embraced my feet (Standard Inscr., col. iii. 84-88).

Returning northward, he went up into the Amanus mountains to cut choice timber for his palaces and temples, and, after setting up the usual image of himself with a memorial of his deeds, made his way back to Assyria.

166. The chronicle of these conquests naturally suggests comparison with those of Tiglathpileser I, That warrior undoubtedly extended Assyria's fame and influence more widely than did Ashurnaçirpal, whose campaigns did not carry him beyond the upper Euphrates, or the boundaries of Babylonia. In many of his measures the later king imitated the earlier, — in the personal leadership of his troops, in the imposition of tribute upon conquered countries and the requirement of hostages, in the deportation of subdued populations, and in the treatment of enemies. On the other hand, in some respects, Ashurnaçirpal shows himself in advance of his predecessor. His army was improved by the addition of a cavalry squadron, supplementing the infantry and chariots. This first appears in the Zamuan campaigns, and is developed in the western wars, where it may have been modelled after the Aramean cavalry. It was certainly useful in following up the Bedouin when foot-soldiers and chariots would have been useless; it formed thenceforth a constantly enlarging division of the Assyrian force. Another measure of the king was the incorporation of the troops of subject peoples in his army. This appears on the largest scale in his Syrian expedition, in which he added, successively, the soldiers of the Aramean communities on the Euphrates, of Karkhemish, and of Patin. While the desire to leave no enemies in his rear may have been a partial ground of this action, it is probable that these detachments continued to remain under his control and were carried with him to Kalkhi. There he seems to have established a great military centre, where these and other troops were maintained and drilled. In this procedure he solved a standing problem of Assyrian politics, namely, how to continue the wars without drawing too heavily on Assyria's citizens. While thereby introducing elements of serious danger into the state, he was, nevertheless, enabled thus to hand down to his successor an undiminished power, and make it possible for him to undertake an even greater series of military operations.

167. In organizing his conquered territory the king made a distinct advance. A line of Assyrian outposts was established. Some of these guardeal exposed districts; others formed the central points of regions more or less geographically compacted. Of the former class were Atlila, called Dur Assur, in Zamua on the Elamite-Babylonian border, the fortified post of Tukulti-ashur-açbat among the eastern mountains, the city of Ashurnaçirpal at the sources of the Tigris, the "royal cities" Damdamusa in the northwest and Uda in Kashiari, the two fortresses on opposite sides of the Euphrates (sect. 164), and Aribua in Patin, apparently guarding the Orontes valley. To the latter type belonged Kakzi, in the eastern Assyrian plain, the starting-point of the Zamuan campaigns, and Tushkha in Kirkhi, where the king built a palace and granaries. Various officials represented Assyria in these districts. Their names and jurisdiction are not altogether clear. Sometimes the former rulers were confirmed in their dignities on submission to the conqueror, or native nobles were chosen, whose exaltation to posts of honor

and influence would be expected to insure their fidelity. Thus, the zabil kuduri, stationed among the northern peoples, had charge of the collection and delivery of tribute to the king. The exact duties of a qipu, the honorable title given to local chiefs, are not defined. An office of higher and wider jurisdiction is that of shaknu, which may be held by a native chief or, in some cases apparently, by an Assyrian noble who, in important territories like those of the Kirkhi and Nairi, is responsible directly to the king. The position of the urasi, another personage mentioned in the inscriptions, may have been hardly more than that of "resident" in cities under Assyrian control. The placing of Assyrian colonists in some of the cities, though not a new measure, is with all the rest a significant indication of the new beginning of systematic endeavors toward close supervision and control of the subjugated lands.

168. The method of Ashurnaçirpal in reducing many of these regions to subjection was so severe as potently to aid in holding them to Assyrian allegiance,

One illustration, drawn from the conqueror's own account of the overthrow of Tela on the slopes of Kashiari, is sufficient:

I drew near to the city of Tela, The city was very strong; three walls surrounded it. The inhabitants trusted to their strong walls and numerous soldiers; they did not come down or embrace my feet. With battle and slaughter I assaulted and took the city. Three thousand warriors I slew in battle. Their booty and possessions, cattle, sheep, I carried away; many captives I burned with fire. Many of their soldiers I took alive; of some I cut off hands and limbs; of others the noses, ears, and arms; of many soldiers I put out the eyes. I reared a column of the living and a column of heads, I hung up on high their heads on trees in the vicinity of their city. Their boys and girls I burned up in the flame. I devastated the city, dug it up, in fire burned it; I annihilated it (Standard Inscr., col. i. 113-118).

Such punishment was reserved for those communities which once under Assyrian authority now offered opposition. This was regarded as rebellion and punished by extermination, or by penalties which rendered the unhappy survivors a warning to their neighbors. Native officials, once trusted by their Assyrian masters, but afterwards rebellious, were, when captured, flayed alive and their skins hung upon the city walls. Communities for the first time summoned to submit to Assyria, if they resisted, were subject to the ordinary fate of the conquered, but not otherwise treated with special cruelty. The opposition encountered by Ashurnaçirpal was usually not very strong; the cities were beaten in detail; they had not yet learned how to unite against the common enemy. The numbers definitely mentioned in the inscriptions indicate a total of less than thirty thousand soldiers slain by the Assyrians in all these campaigns, but this estimate does not probably include more than a third of the persons who perished in the storming of the cities. Without doubt the stress of suffering fell upon the northern mountaineers, for more than half of the slain recorded by the king belong to this region, which evidently had caused the chief trouble and required the most strenuous efforts to keep under control. In fact, the last campaign of Ashurnaçirpal, in his eighteenth year (867 B. C.), directed against the districts to the northwest, was something of a failure. The city of Amid seems to have held out, and further trouble was promised for the future.

169. The importance of the conquests is shown in the long lists of the spoil and tribute obtained, beside which the booty of Tiglathpileser I. seems insignificant. Least productive were the lands of Zamua, yet they had one important and indispensable product, the splendid horses raised on their plateaus and famed throughout the Orient. From all the mountain regions came cattle and sheep in countless numbers, besides wine and corn. Of precious metals, these districts produced copper, which was manufactured in various forms, and gold and silver. The Aramean communities of the western Mesopotamian plain were the most remunerative, and

their spoil reveals the wealth and civilization of that region. Even the Aramean states to the west of the sources of the Tigris contributed, besides horses, cattle, and sheep, chariots and harness, armor, silver, gold, lead, copper, variegated garments and linen cloths, wood and metal work, and furniture in ivory and gold. To these the chief of Bit Adini added ivory plates, couches and thrones, gold beads and pendants and weapons of gold; the king of Karkhemish, cloths of purple light and dark, marvellous furniture, silver baskets, precious woods and stones, elephant tusks and female slaves; and Syria, her fragrant cedars and the other woods of her mountain-forests.

170. Abundant opportunity for the use and bestowment of these spoils of war was given in the king's building enterprises at his capital of Kalkhi. Besides the temple already referred to (sect. 162), his crowning work was his magnificent palace. This stood on the western side of a rectangular platform which was reared along the east bank of the Tigris from north to south. Around its base to the north and east lay the city. The palace itself was about three hundred and fifty feet square; its entrances looked northward upon the great temple structure that occupied the northwestern corner of the platform and overhung the city and the river. A series of long narrow galleries, lined with sculptured alabaster slabs, surrounded a court in size one hundred and twenty-five by one hundred feet. The chief of these rooms, probably a throne chamber, one hundred and fifty-four by thirty-three feet, still contains at its eastern end the remains of a dais which once may have supported the throne. On the slabs were wrought, in low relief, scenes from the life and experiences of the king. Now he offers thanksgiving for the slaying of a wild ox or a lion; now he pursues the fleeing enemy in his chariots; now his army besieges a city, or advances to the attack across a river, or, led by the king, marches through the mountains. Everywhere inscriptions commemorate his achievements and recite his titles. At the doorways stood the monstrous man-headed bulls, or lions, only head and shoulders completely wrought out, as if leaping forth from the wall, the rest still half sculptured in the stone, — divine spirits guarding the entrances. Scenes of religious worship abound, gods, spirits, and heroes engaged in exercises of which the meaning is not yet clear. Everywhere is the combination of energy with repose, of massive strength with dignity; though crude and imperfect in the technique of the sculptor, the reliefs are the most vivid and lifelike achievements of Assyrian art, the counterpart in stone of the grandiose story of the king's campaigns, which is written above and on either side of them. The narrow galleries were spanned with cedar beams and decorated with silver and gold and bronze. The priceless ivories of the west, showing by subject and style the unmistakable influence of Egypt, have been picked up from the palace floors by modern explorers. All was a wonderful commentary upon Ashurnaçirpal's own words:

"A palace for my royal dwelling-place, for the glorious seat of my royalty, I founded for ever and splendidly planned it. I surrounded it with a cornice (?) of copper. Sculptures of the creatures of land and sea carved in alabaster," I made and placed them at the doors. Lofty door-posts of... wood I made, and sheathed them with copper and set them up in the gates. Thrones of "costly" woods, dishes of ivory containing silver, gold, lead, copper, and iron, the spoil of my hand, taken from conquered lands I deposited therein. (Monolith Inscr., concl. 12-24).

The king had a palace in Nineveh also, and built temples there and elsewhere. The evidence of his having contributed to the inner development of his country is not abundant. An aqueduct to supply Kalkhi with water drawn from the upper Zab was referred to; it brought fruitfulness to the surrounding country, as its name "producer of fertility" proves. The rebuilding of Kalkhi, and the wealth in cattle and sheep, as well as other property, brought in by the successful wars, must be regarded as most important contributions to Assyrian economic resources.

171. Varying judgments have been passed on the character of Ashurnaçirpal. Of his energy there can be no question. As hunter and warrior he was untiring and resistless. But to some he is chiefly a monster of remorseless cruelty, whose joy it was to maim, flay, burn, or impale his conquered enemies. If this verdict is finally to be rendered, he will be convicted out of his own mouth, for the evidence is derived solely from his frank, unsoftened narrative of his own ruthless barbarities. But while they are not to be palliated, it must be remembered that war has since engendered even more hideous crimes, of which his narrative shows him to be guiltless; that in an iron age, when Assyria was recovering from a century of dishonor and collapse, fierce and bloody vengeance had come to be the rule; and that in almost every instance these last penalties were inflicted upon communities which, from the Assyrian point of view, had violated their pledges to God and man. It is evident, moreover, that the statements of the king are not inspired by the lust of cruelty and blood, but have been inscribed with the same purpose as that with which the punishments were inflicted, — to strike terror into the heart of the opposer and to warn the intending rebel of his fate. That this verdict is more reasonable is strengthened by the probability that, with the sole exception of the campaign of 867 B. C., the king's wars ceased before his reign was half over. The lesson had been learned, and the king, having taught it in this savage fashion, was well content to turn his energies to the pursuits of. peace. Of these latter years there is but scanty record. Wisely to govern a peaceful empire had not yet come to stand among the glories of monarchs. Nevertheless in the remarkable statue of Ashurnaçirpal found in the temple of Ninib, not far from his palace, "the only extant perfect Assyrian royal statue in the round," a suggestion is given of the statesman as well as the warrior. A rude heroic figure, he stands upright before tle god, looking straight forward, his brawny arms bare, the left hand holding to his breast the mace, weapon of the soldier, but the right dropped by his side, grasping the sceptre, emblematic of the shepherd of his people.

III.HE ADVANCE INTO SYRIA AND THE RISE OF URARTU: FROM SHALMANESER II TO THE FALL OF HIS HOUSE. 860-745 B. C.

172. FOR more than a century after the death of Ashurnaçirpal (860 B. C.) his descendants occupied the throne of Assyria. The period is one of great variety in details; new peoples come upon the scene as the empire widens; new political problems appear for solution in the increasing complexity of the field and the factors involved; inner difficulties arise the presence of which is not easily to be accounted for, though of obvious significance; the dynasty at last gives way to a successful revolution. But, in the main features, the historical development of Assyria continues as before, with the same lines of policy, the same unwearied military activity, the same unceasing effort after expansion, the same methods of government, the same relations to peoples without. Accordingly, to trace in repetitious detail the campaigns of the several kings in turn, would be wearisome and unprofitable. Their work may be considered as a whole, its general features described, and its results summarized, while the special achievements of each ruler are properly appreciated. Ashurnaçirpal was succeeded by his son Shalmaneser II., whose thirty-five years of reigning (860-825 B. C.) were one long military campaign. Either under his own leadership, or that of his commanding general, the Turtan, his armies marched in all directions, coercing rebellious vassals, and collecting their tribute, or seeking new peoples to conquer. An obelisk of black basalt records in brief sentences, year by year, thirty-two of these expeditions, and its testimony is supplemented on the other monuments of the king by fuller accounts of particular achievements. His son, Shamshi Adad IV., reigned less than half as long as his father (825-812 B. C.), and has left, as his memorial, a monolith, the inscription of which covers only half of his years. Adadnirari III. followed (812-783 B. C.), ascending the throne of his father, apparently, in early youth, but ruling with great energy and splendor for nearly thirty years. Unfortunately, no satisfactory annals of his reign

have been preserved. Royal inscriptions from the next three kings utterly fail. Shalmaneser III. (783-773 B. C.), Ashurdan III. (773-755 B. C.), and Ashurnirari II. (755-745 B. C.) are known to us from the limu list alone, where the brief references to years without campaigns, to pestilence and revolt, tell the melancholy story of imperial decay, until, with the last of the three, the dynasty fell, and a usurper seized the crown.

173. Beyond a few facts, little is known of the political organization and economic development of Assyria during this century. In the time of Shalmaneser II. and his two successors, the spoil of subject peoples continued to flow in abundantly, precious metals and manufactured articles from the west, corn, wine, and domestic animals from the north and east. Among the latter, two-humped dromedaries, received from the far northeast, obtained special mention as novelties, and point to the control of a trade route from the upper Iranian plateau. Shalmaneser seems to have taken a step forward, in the imposition of a regular and definite yearly tribute upon certain communities. Thus the kingdom of Patin paid one talent of silver, two talents of purple cloth, and two hundred (?) cedar beams; another king, at the foot of Mount Amanus, ten mina of silver, two hundred cedar beams, and other products of cedar; Karkhemish paid sixty mina of gold, one talent of silver, and two talents of purple cloth; Qummukh, twenty mina of silver, and three hundred cedar beams. A prescribed number of horses broken to the yoke was required from the northern tribes. These requisitions are more moderate than were the spoils gained in the descents of the armies upon the various subject regions, and indicate that already the Assyrian kings perceived the wisdom of adjusting their demands to the resources of the lands under their sway. Much less harshness in the wars is recorded. Measures like those of Ashurnaçirpal were reserved for the few peoples whose rebellious spirit or persistent hostility seemed to justify extreme penalties. Indeed, revolts became less frequent, because during this period the empire was becoming more compact by the direct incorporation of regions long subject to Assyrian authority. A striking illustration of this fact is found in the limu list, in which a regular order in the succession of officials seems to be established. In it appear governors of cities and districts along the borders, such as Raçappa (Reseph) on the right bank of the Euphrates, Arpakha on the Elamite border, Naçibina (Nisibis) in northern Mesopotamia, Amid and Tushkha in the northern mountains, Guzana (Gozan) in western Mesopotamia, Kirruri, and Mazamua, in the northeastern mountains. To have occupied places in this honorable list, the occupants of such posts must have been in intimate association with the court, and their administrative activity in immediate dependence on the central power.

174. The usual internal troubles that beset oriental monarchies appeared in this century in Assyria, Family difficulties in the reigning house broke out in the rebellion of Shalmaneser's son Ashurdaninpal in the thirty-third year of his father's reign. The cause is not difficult to comprehend. Six years before, Shalmaneser had handed over the leadership of his military expeditions to his Turtan, Damn Ashur. To this evidence of his own growing weakness, and the natural fear, on the part of his sons, of the usurpation of the throne by this general, is, perhaps, to be added a palace intrigue, which threatened the future accession of Ashurdaninpal by the putting forward of another son of Shalm aneser, Shamshi Adad, as a candidate for the throne. The rebellion was a very serious one, involving twenty-seven cities of the empire, among which were Nineveh, Assur, Arbela, Imgur Bel, Amid, and Til-abni. Kalkhi and, apparently, the army were, however, faithful to the king. In the midst of this civil war Shalmaneser died, and, only after it had endured six years, was Shamshi Adad able to bring it to a close and make sure his title to the crown. The blow inflicted upon the centres of Assyrian life must have been very severe.

Sixty years after this, another revolt is chronicled, the causes of which are to be found in the foreign politics of Assyria. The rising kingdom of Urartu was steadily encroaching upon

Assyria all along the northern border as far as the Mediterranean, and the kings were being forced into a defensive attitude in spite of all their efforts. Thus Assyrian military pride was wounded, and mercantile prestige was crippled. A total eclipse of the sun occurring on June 15, 763 B. C., was thought the favorable moment for raising the standard of rebellion in the city of Assur. A line drawn across the limn list at this year suggests the setting up of a rival king in that city. The revolt spread to Arbakha in the east, and Gozan in the west, but was finally subdued. In 746 B. C., however, another insurrection broke out in the imperial military city of Kalkhi. Ashurnirari II. had been satisfied to spend more than half his regnal years without making any military expeditions, and, though in itself the fact does not account for the revolt, since the latter half of the great Ashurnaçirpal's reign is likewise unmarked by wars, it reveals the manifest inability of this ruler to cope with the threatening foreign difficulties. The attitude of the army was decisive, and Ashurnirari disappeared before a military leader who became king in 745 B. C. under the title of Tiglathpileser III.

175. While in these last troubled years the prosperity of the state must have been severely shaken, the earlier and more successful kings show, in their inscriptions and public works, that they were not behind Ashurnagirpal in the development of the higher life of the nation. Shalmaneser II. seems to have resided at Assur and Nineveh in his early years, and in each of these cities traces of his building operations remain. Kalkhi, however, was his real capital, and here, in the centre of the great mound (sect. 170), he built his palace, of which, unfortunately, but few remains have been found. In it stood the "Black Obelisk" (sect. 172), and two gigantic winged bulls carved in high relief on slabs fourteen feet square, inscribed with accounts of the royal campaigns (Layard, N. and R., I. pp. 59, 280 ff.). Toward the close of his reign the king rebuilt the wall of Assur in stone, and left there a statue of himself seated on his throne. At Imgur Bel, nine miles east of Kalkhi, were found the most splendid remains of the artistic skill of his reign, the bronze sheathings of what seems to be a wooden gate with double doors, twenty-seven feet in height. These bronze plates were ornamented with scenes done in repoussé work, representing events in the various expeditions of the king. A sacrifice on the shores of Lake Van, the storming of a fortress in Nairi, the receipt of tribute from Syria, the burning of a captured city — are some of the subjects, the treatment of which is bold and spirited, and differs from the work of the earlier period chiefly in the variety of detail, suggestive of the different localities in which the scenes are placed. Skill in the handling of the metal, sharpness of observation, and an artistic eye in the choice of scenes testify to the remarkable attainments of the royal artists. The inscriptions of the several kings do not differ largely from the conventional form adopted from earlier models. That of Shamshi Adad, indeed, evinces a certain freedom of characterization, indicating some independence in the details of literary expression, but otherwise the same annalistic form and traditional figures of speech prevail. Few other literary remains have survived. To Shalmaneser II. is ascribed the foundation at Kalkhi of the royal library. It had a librarian who cared for its collections. The works were chiefly Babylonian classical religious texts, either in originals brought from the south as the spoil of war, or copies made by scribes. The stock of books was still further increased under Adadnirari III. and Ashurnirari II. Under the former king was produced the diplomatic document known as the "Synchronistic History of Assyria and Babylonia," a summary of the political relations between the kings of these countries from the earliest period (sect. 30). The influence of Assyrian culture of the time on its environment is illustrated by the royal inscriptions of the kings of Urartu, who at first write in the Assyrian language, and later employ the Assyrian script for their native speech.

176. The religious life of the times receives light from several sides. The inscriptions of the kings, while still emphasizing the warlike side of religion and glorifying the gods of war, reveal a tendency to exalt the ethical element. Particularly the ranging, of the sun-god Shamash alongside of the national deity Ashur as the guide and inspirer of the king, and the

epithets applied to him such as "judge of the world," "ordainer of all things," "director of mankind," and — though this is uncertain — "lord of law," suggest the development of a sense of order and justice in the government (Jastrow, Rel. of Bab. and Assyr., p. 210). A new emphasis on culture is indicated by the high place ascribed in the reign of Adadnirari III. to the Babylonian god of wisdom and learning, Nabu. A temple was built for him on the mound of Kalkhi, and his statues were placed within it. On one of them, prepared in honor of the king and the queen, an inscription, glorifying the god as the clear-eyed, the patron of the arts, the holder of the pen, whose attribute is wisdom, whose power is unequalled, and without whom no decision in heaven is made, closes with the exhortation "O Posterity, trust in Nabu; trust not in any other god!" Whatever may have been the occasion to make so much of this god at this time, it is clear that he represented to the Assyrians an ideal of life never before so attractive to them and suggestive of their higher aspirations.

177. Turning to the first of those fields of aggressive activity in which Assyria made distinct advance, it appears that in the year 852 B. C. Babylonia engaged the attention of Shalmaneser II. Nabupaliddin, its king, a vigorous defender of his state against the Arameans, had succeeded in keeping free from hostilities with Ashurnaçirpal and had even made alliance with Shalmaneser II. After a long reign of at least thirty-one years, his people deposed him, and his son Marduknadinshum succeeded to the throne, which was contested by his brother, Mardukbelusate. The latter, having his strength in the eastern provinces with their more vigorous population, was pressing hard upon his brother, who held Babylon and the other cities of western and middle Babylonia. Marduknadinshum appealed to Shalmaneser II. for aid, which was promptly granted. In the two campaigns of 852-851 B. C. the Assyrian king overthrew and killed the usurper, and restored the kingdom to Marduknadinshum, who naturally became a vassal. As a sign of supremacy and with the customary reverence of an Assyrian king for the shrines of Babylonia, Shalmaneser visited the temples of Babylon, Borsippa, and Kutha, and made rich offerings to the gods. Two hundred and fifty years had passed since an Assyrian king had entered Babylon, and now the Assyrian suzerainty was acknowledged by the legitimate Babylonian king, of his own accord. Shalmaneser found the kingdom beset by its southern neighbors, the Kaldi (sect. 155), who had organized petty kingdoms and were constantly pushing up from the coast. He advanced against them, defeated one of their kings, and laid tribute upon them. The suzerainty of Assyria was thrown off by Babylon, possibly in the time of the rebellion of Ashurdaninpal, and was reestablished by Shamshi Adad in 818 B. C., who, however, according to the limu list, occupied the last five years of his reign in expeditions to Babylonian cities, and bequeathed the problem to his successor. Adadnirari III., after an expedition in his first years, in which he fully restored Assyrian, supremacy, appears to have entered into very close relations with the southern kingdom. The completion of the so-called "Synchronistic History" in his reign marks a final stage in the boundary dispute between the two states, The building of the Nabu temple at Kalkhi is an evidence of his regard for things Babylonian. The mention in the inscription on the statue of Nabu (sect. 176) of the Queen Sammuramat, the "lady of the palace," to whom, together with the king, the statue is dedicated, has given rise to a variety of interesting comment. That she should be named in this connection suggests that she was active in the new Babylonian worship, and that, therefore, she may have been herself a Babylonian princess, either wife or mother of the king. The similarity of the name Semiramis, the famous queen mentioned by Herodotus (I. 184) as ruling over Babylon, has suggested the identity of the two royal ladies, but without much gain to history thereby. The activity of the three last kings of the family, so far as Babylonia was concerned, was consumed in expeditions against the Ituha, Aramean tribes in lower Mesopotamia, who evidently interfered with the communications between the two countries. Adadnirari had already found them troublesome. Whether the later kings of the dynasty exercised supremacy over the southern kingdom is uncertain with the probabilities against it in view of the growing weakness of the royal house. A remarkable and

as yet inexplicable fact is that with Nabunaçir, who became king in Babylonia in 747 B. C., the famous Canon of Ptolemy begins, as well as the Babylonian Chronicle, as though the accession of this ruler marked an epoch in the development of the state. Yet no historical memorials in our possession suggest any special change in Babylonian affairs.

178. The Babylonian problem was neither so serious nor so insistent as those of the west and the north. Ashurnaçirpal had subdued the west Mesopotamian states up and down the Euphrates, and, in his one Syrian expedition, had made the Assyrian name known as far as the Mediterranean. His successors proceeded to make that name supreme between the great river and the sea, from the Amanus to the Lebanons. Before advancing thither, however, Shalmaneser had to make good his title to the Aramean states which had yielded to his father. Upon his accession Akhuni of Bit Adini (sects. 163 f.) rebelled, and four years (859-856 B. C.) were needed to subjugate him. With great ability he had formed a league of states on either side of the Euphrates, as far as Patin, to repel the Assyrian advance, — a method of resistance in which the southern Syrian states were soon to imitate him with greater success. Unfortunately the league fell to pieces on its first defeat. Akhuni fought on alone desperately for three years, but was finally captured and taken to the city of Assur. Northern Syria as represented in the states of Karkhemish, Samal, and Patin, had already done homage. The way was open to the south. Planting Assyrian colonists at important centres and leaving garrisons in the chief cities of Bit Adini to which he gave Assyrian names, the king marched to the southwest in 854 B. C. A new country lay before him, as yet untrodden by an Assyrian army.

179, Three leading states divided the region between them; namely, Hamath, Damascus, and Israel. Eighty miles south of Khalman, the southern border of Assyrian authority in Syria, lay Hamath, at the entrance to Coele Syria; one hundred miles farther south was Damascus; the border of Israel met the confines of Damascus yet fifty miles west of south. Each state controlled the country round about it. Israel dominated Judah, Moab, and Edom; Damascus and Ha-math were in treaty relations with the Phoenician ports on the coast near to them. With one another they were in more or less continuous war, the outcome of which at any particular time might be the temporary suzerainty of the one or the other. Ever since Asa of Judah had made the fatal blunder of inviting the king of Damascus to attack Baasha of Israel in his interest, Damascus had been involved with Israel. Omri, founder of a new dynasty and of a new capital of his country at Samaria, had been worsted in the war. His son, Ahab, seems also to have reigned under Damascene influence. In the face of Shalmaneser's advance and in imitation of the example of Akhuni, a coalition was made under the leadership of the three kings, Irkhuleni of Hamath, Benhadad II. of Damascus, and Ahab of Israel, to which the kings of nine other peoples contributed troops. With an army of nearly four thousand chariots, two thousand cavalry, one thousand camel riders, and sixty-three thousand infantry, they met the Assyrian king at Qarqar on the Orontes, twenty miles north of Hamath (854 B. C.). The Assyrian won the battle, no doubt, as he claims, but the victory was indecisive, and he retired beyond the Euphrates without capturing any of the capitals of his enemies or receiving their tribute. Indeed, his own domains in Syria withheld tribute, and in 850 B. C. he was compelled to chastise the kings of Karkhemish and Bit Agusi, In the next year, 849 B. C., he encountered the southern coalition again, and again withdrew. In 846 B. C. he called out the militia of Assyria and attacked the twelve allied kings with an army of one hundred and twenty thousand soldiers, but without any recorded success in the form of tribute. The situation was critical. Three years later (843 B. C.) he visited his Syrian provinces, marching to the Amanus without venturing southward. Meanwhile, either his intrigues or the inconstancy of Syrian princes had been working for him. Revolutions had taken place in Damascus and Israel. Benhadad II. had been overthrown by Hazael, and the house of Omri by Jehu. Shalmaneser II. developed new tactics. Marching westward, in 842 B. C., as though making for the sea at the mouth of the Orontes, he suddenly turned southward, leaving Khalman, Hamath, and Damascus on his left.

He thus took the allied states unprepared and divided. Hazael was isolated, but met the Assyrians on the eastern slopes of Mount Hermon. They drove him back to Damascus and ravaged the territory down into the Hauran, but could not capture his city. The cities of Tyre and Sidon "sent tribute." Hamath appears to have submitted, though the fact is not mentioned. More significant still was the attitude of Israel, "whose king Jehu sent tribute," "silver, gold, golden bowls, golden chalices, golden cups, golden buckets, lead, a royal sceptre and spear shafts (?)." Yet so long as Hazael remained unsubdued, these gifts were empty. A last expedition against him in 839 B. C. was equally unsuccessful in subjugatiug him, though the Phoenician cities again sent presents. Assyria had been virtually halted. Shalmaneser's armies never again marched south of Hamath. Hazael was free to take vengeance on his recreant southern allies, and soon was lord of the south; as far as the Egyptian border. Israel was humiliated; Jehu and his son Jehoahaz became vassals. Shalmaneser II. was forced to be content with northern Syria; but with the southern trade routes cut off, he must find new outlets for Assyrian commerce. He therefore turned toward the northwest where Tiglathpileser I. had warred with the same purpose (sect, 144). Three campaigns are recorded against Qui (Cilicia), where he reached Tarzi (Tarsus) in the rich Cilician plain (840, 835, 834 B. C.); in 838 B. C. Tabal, in the vicinity of the modern Marash, was his objective point; in 837 B. C. he renewed Assyrian authority over Milid (sect. 144). In 832 B. C. his Turtan put down a rebellion in Patin. Thus the land route to the west and with it the rich trade of Asia Minor were secured for Assyria, and the civilization of the Tigris began directly to affect the less advanced peoples of these regions.

180. The civil war in Assyria was not without influence in the west. Khindanu, on the western bank of the Euphrates, and Hamath are mentioned among the rebellious cities. Shamshi Adad gives no indication that he ever crossed the Euphrates, and the presumption is that Assyrian authority in these districts was at a discount. Adadnirari, however, has another story to tell. In the summary of his achievements he says, "From above the Euphrates, Khatti, Akharri to its whole extent, Tyre, Sidon, the land of Omri, Edom, Palastu as far as the great sea of the setting sun I brought to submission, [and] taxes and tribute I laid upon them" (see ABL, p. 52). Special mention is made of an expedition to Damascus, where a certain Mari (Benhadad III.?), who had succeeded to Hazael, was shut up in his capital, and compelled to submit and pay .tribute. In the limu list the objective points of attack are Arpad (806 B. C.), Azaz (805 B. C.), Sahli (804 B. C.), the seacoast (803 B.C.) that is, the Mediterranean (?), Alauvate (797 B. C.). The two former cities are in northern Syria, the others in the central region. It is impossible, therefore, to date the victory over Damascus, and to determine whether the king ever traversed Israel and Palestine with his armies, or merely received "tribute" from them. The latter is more probably the case. The situation suggested is the breaking down of the dominance of Damascus in the south, and the practical recovery of independence on the part of the southern communities, by the easy method of sending gifts to the Assyrian conqueror. The subjugation of Damascus would signify to the king authority over all the regions owning Damascene supremacy. It is thought that some indication of what this victory meant for Israel still lingers in the late passage of 2 Kings xiii. 5, where the "saviour" may be identified with the Assyrian king. At any rate, as no expedition of Adadnirari after 797 B. C. is recorded, and Mancçuate, situated not far from Damascus, was the objective point of that year, Israel, with its northern enemy weakened, was able to recover strength, and, unmolested by Assyrian authority, make headway against its foes. Nor did the Assyrian kings that belong to the following years of decline disturb the southern states. A new centre of opposition to Assyria developed at Hatarika (Hadrach), south of Hamath, against which Ashurdan is said to have marched in 772 B. C. and 765 B. C. Either he or his successor attacked it again in 755 B. C., and one expedition of Ashurnirari against Arpad took place the next year (754 B. C.). It is evident that, if northern Syria remained faithful, the central and southern regions were practically free from Assyrian control after the reign of Adadnirari III. It is easy to understand, therefore, how in

this period so brilliant a reign as that of Jeroboam II. of Israel was possible (2 Kings xiv. 23-29).

181. The relations to the peoples of the northern and eastern frontier form a not less important phase of Assyrian history during this period. The mountain valleys through which the upper Tigris flows had been subjugated and brought under direct Assyrian control by Ashurnaçirpal (sects. 159 f.) These gave the later kings little trouble. But the movements of peoples to the east and north of this district, already in progress in his time (sect. 159), had produced a remarkable change in the political situation. In the mountains from the southern slopes of which the Euphrates takes its rise, peoples were forming into a nation calling itself Khaldia, after the name of its god Khaldis, but to the Assyrians known as Urartu. They appear in history as they come down from the flanks of Ararat in the far northeast, or from homes on the banks of the Araxes, and move toward the southwest in the direction of Lake Van, attracted by the rich valleys on its eastern shore. Ashurnaçirpal is the first to mention them as in this region, but does not fight with them. The first kings of the new nation were Lutipris and Sarduris I., followed — whether immediately or not is uncertain — by Arame. Under this ruler the state made great strides westward and southward, controlling the valley north of the Taurus almost to Maid, and the eastern shores of Lake Van. Young, vigorous, aggressive, and eager for progress, Urartu was ready to take part in the larger life of the world. Already it had borrowed from Assyria its alphabet (sect. 175), and was preparing to dispute the older nation's pre-eminence in the northern lands.

182. Disturbances in the northeast brought Shalmaneser II., in the year of his accession (860 B. C.), into conflict with this new state. He traversed the land of Khubushkia, lying to the southwest of Lake Urmia, and thence fell upon Urartu. In 857 B. C., after defeating Akhuni on the Euphrates (sect. 178), he suddenly turned northward and marched along the western slope of Mount Masius over the Taurus to the upper waters of the Euphrates. Laying waste this region, he faced eastward and made for Urartu. Far up on the slopes of Ararat he destroyed Arzashku, Arame's capital, devastated the land and returned through Gilzan (Kirzan), on the northwestern shores of Lake Urmia, whence came the two-humped dromedaries, and through Khubushkia, coming out of the mountains above Arbela, a march of nearly a thousand miles. Similar expeditions from the sources of the Tigris to those of the Euphrates are recorded for 845 B. C. and 833 B. C. The latter was under command of the Turtan. In the interval Arame had been succeeded by Sarduris II., whom the Turtan of Shalmaneser II. attacked again in 829 B. C, In the Ushpina of "Nairi," with whom the general of Shamshi. Adad fought in 819 B. C., has been recognized Ishpuinis, successor of Sarduris II. The steady expansion of Urartu toward the south and west in these years caused uneasiness among the peoples already settled along the Assyrian border, and compelled the kings to make many expeditions into districts which hitherto had not come within the range of Assyrian aggression. A large extension of Assyrian territory, therefore, is traceable, although the royal authority was not at all times very insistent. Thus appear the Mannai, to the west and northwest of Lake Urmia; Mazamua and Parsua, to the south of the same lake, and the Madai, or Medians, further to the east. In these latter people is to be recognized the first wave of that Indo-European migration which was to exercise so important an influence upon the later history of Western Asia. It has been plausibly conjectured that the movement of the Medes from the steppes of central Asia had forced the advance of Urartu toward the south, and that, swinging off to the southeast, they were pressing on along the mountain barrier that overlooks the eastern Mesopotamian plain. As in the case of Urartu, so with them, the Assyrian kings, without being conscious of the magnitude of the interests involved, felt that they must be stopped, if Assyria was to keep its position in the oriental world. Adadnirari III. marched against them in not less than eight campaigns. From him, indeed, they received more attention than did Urartu. The latter under the son of Ishpuinis, Menuas, pushed east, west, and north, from the Araxes to the land of the Khatti

(Hittites) and Lake Urmia. His son Argistis I. passed beyond the Araxes in the north; in the west he conquered Milid, and in the southeast overran the Mannai, Khubushkia, and Parsua. Shalmaneser III. for more than half his years fought with him without success, The Assyrians were compelled to see their northern and eastern provinces torn away by this vigorous rival, whose intrigues in the west were also threw en ing their possessions there. It was in this fierce storm of assault upon the outworks of the empire that the house of Ashurnaçirpal III. and Shalmaneser II. fell.

183. In summing up this epoch of Assyrian history, the first impression created is that of intense and superabounding energy. The long roll of military expeditions is kept up almost to the end. Where details are given, as in the reign of Shalmaneser II., these campaigns are seen to involve long marches, often in mountainous countries, and frequent battles with not insignificant antagonists. Both method and design in the expeditions are traceable, revealing the fact that they were planned in advance and with a broad outlook. The outcome of the whole was twofold. On the one hand, was a significant extension of Assyrian territory. New regions were opened up. Thus Shalmaneser II. made Assyria dominant on Lake Urmia. It is inferred, from hints in the inscriptions of Adadnirari III., that he reached the Caspian sea. Indeed, a remarkable summary of the wide range of Assyrian predominance is given in the laudatory inscription of the latter king:

Who conquered from the mountain Siluna, toward the rising sun . . as far as the great sea of the rising of the sun; from above the Euphrates, Khatti, Akharri to its whole extent, Tyre, Sidon, the country of Omri, Edom, Palastu as far as the great sea of the setting of the sun, I brought to submission, (and) taxes and tribute I placed on them....The kings of Kaldu, all of them, became servants. Taxes (and) tribute for the future I placed on them. Babylon, Borsippa (and) Kutha supported the decrees of Bel, Nabu (and) Nergal (Slab Iosc., 5-24; see ABL, pp. 51 f.).

184. On the other hand, obstacles of a character not hitherto encountered and, in part, rising out of the very policy of Assyria, confronted these kings. Nations, contemplated in their plans of conquest, began to unite for self-defence. To overcome this concentration of opposition called forth might and skill never before required. Assyrian pressure combined with movements of peoples as yet without the zone of historical knowledge, moulded border tribes into nations with national impulses and aspirations that rivalled those of the Assyrians themselves. New and vigorous tribes were at the same time brought upon the horizon of Assyrian territory. In grappling with such problems, the royal family, which had contributed so many warriors and statesmen to the throne of Assyria, found its strength failing and was constrained to disappear. Would the state itself go down before the same combination of difficulties, or would it regather its energies, and, under other and abler leaders, rise superior to opposition and hold its place of predominance for years to come? The next century contains the answer to this question.

IV.THE ASSYRIAN REVIVAL. TIGLATHPILESER III AND SHALMANESER IV. 746-722 B. C.

185. THE gloomy outlook for the future of the Assyrian state, consequent upon the encroachments of hostile peoples from without and the inner convulsions that shook the government and overthrew the ruling dynasty, was speedily transformed upon the accession of the new king. With him opens an inspiring chapter of splendid Assyrian success. This sudden

change makes it likely that the causes of disaster were due, not so much to decline in the energies of the body politic, as to the weakness or unwisdom of the later members of the ruling dynasty. It has been plausibly conjectured that these rulers identified their interests with the priestly class, the centre of whose power was the city of Assur and who dominated the commercial activities of the realm. As in Babylonia, the temple was the bank and the trading centre of every community as well as the seat of the divine powers. Over against these heads of the spiritual and mercantile world stood the army, recruited chiefly from the free peasantry, and led by their local lords, as royal officers. The disasters on the frontiers brought commercial stringency, which, as in every ancient state, bore most heavily, not upon the men of wealth, but upon the poorer classes. The king unwisely threw himself into the hands of the priests. Sooner or later this attitude was bound to antagonize the army. King, priestly lords, and merchant princes went down before a rebellion, starting from Kalkhi, the seat of the army. The new king represented, therefore, the reassertion of the strongest forces in the state, the native farmers and soldiers, led by the ablest general among them (Peiser in MVAG, I. 161 f.; KAT 3, 50 f.).

186. It is significant that in his inscriptions no stress is laid by the new king upon his ancestral claims to the throne. In a popular leader this would be natural. Among his building activities no temples figure, and the long lists of gods who presided over the careers of his predecessors do not appear on his monuments. Ashur, the representative of the state as a conquering power, is his hero and lord, whose cult he established in the cities subjugated by him. His throne name was Tiglathpileser, chosen, presumably, for its historical suggestions of the first great king of that name, rather than for its theological significance. In military vigor he was a worthy follower of his brilliant predecessor, and surpassed him in statesmanlike foresight and achievement. Cinder his direction the tendencies and measures hitherto observed, looking to the incorporation of the subject peoples, were intensified and consummated. The Assyrian state was revived; the Assyrian empire was founded.

187. The memorials of the king consist of annals, which were written on the slabs adorning the walls of his palace at Kalkhi, and of laudatory inscriptions, containing summary records of his campaigns arranged geographically. All were found in the royal mound at Kalkhi, with the exception of a few bricks from Nineveh which testify to the erection of a palace there. The palace at Kalkhi and its contents suffered a strange fate. To build it the king seems to have removed a smaller structure of Shalmaneser II., which stood in the centre of the terrace, and to have greatly increased the size of the mound toward the south and west by extending it out into the Tigris. On the river side the mound was faced with alabaster blocks. The palace looked toward the north, where it had a portico in the Syrian style with pylons flanking the entrance. In construction it was distinguished from former structures by a predominance of woodwork of cedar and cypress. Double doors with bands of bronze, like those of Shalmaneser II. at Imgur Bel (sect. 175), hung in carved gateways. "'Palaces of joy, yielding abundance, bestowing blessing upon the king, causing their builder to live long,' I called their names. 'Gates of righteousness, guiding the judgment of the prince of the four quarters of the world, making the tribute of the mountains and the seas to continue, causing the abundance of the lands to enter before the king their lord,' I named their gates" (ABL, p. 58). Whether on account of its rapid decay or to do despite to the usurper, a later king of another line, used the materials of this structure for his own palace on the southwestern corner of the mound (sect. 236). The latter, however, was never finished, and to this fact is due the preservation of the fragments of the annals of Tiglathpileser III. on the slabs which had been removed and redressed, preparatory to their use in the walls of the later building. This fragmentary and confused condition of his inscriptions makes the task of reconstructing the historical order and the details of his activities difficult. No certain conclusions can in some instances be attained. Happily, the limu list for the king's reign is complete, and its brief notes form a basis for

arranging the rest of the material. The contributions of the Old Testament, also, become now of special value.

188. Nearly all of the eighteen years of the king's reign (745-727 B. C.) were marked by campaigns on the various borders of the realm. These expeditions were characterized, even more clearly than those of his predecessors, by imperial purposes. The world of Western Asia, in expanding its horizon, had become at the same time more simple in its political problems, owing to the disappearance of the multitudinous petty communities before the three or four greater racial or political unities that had come face to face with one another. In the south the Kaldi were becoming more eager to lay hold on Babylon. In the north Urartu was spreading out on every side to absorb the tribes that occupied the mountain valleys, and even to reach over into northern Syria. In the west the tendency to unification brought this or that state to the front, as the suzerain of the lesser cities of a wider territory, and the representative of organized opposition to invasion. Egypt was preparing again to appear on the scene and to recover its place as a world-power west of the Euphrates. Thus, everywhere, with the exception of the eastern mountain valleys where the Medes had not yet realized that nationality the advent of which was to mark the new order, the movement toward a larger unity, based on political rather than on racial grounds, was growing stronger. The politics of the day were international in a new and deeper sense, and the ideal of world-empire was appearing more and more distinctly, as the controlling powers assumed more concrete and imposing forms. Thus, while the details of Assyrian activities are more complex, the main issues in them are more easily grasped and followed.

189. Tiglathpileser III. ascended the throne toward the last of April 745 B. C. Six months were occupied in establishing himself in his seat, and late in the year (September–October) he took an army to the south. Aramean tribes, forever moving restlessly across the southern Mesopotamian plain from the Euphrates to the Tigris, had grown bolder during these years, and, in spite of the endeavors of the Assyrian kings (sect. 177), had entered Babylonia, occupied the Tigris basin from the lower Zab to the Uknu, and were in possession of some of the ancient cities of Akkad. Aramean states were forming, similar to those of western Mesopotamia which had been overcome with so much difficulty by Ashurnaçirpal III. and Shalmaneser II. The king fell upon the tribes furiously, blockaded and stormed the cities, drove the intruders from Dur Kurigalzu, Sippar, and Nippur, and deported multitudes to the northeastern mountains; he also built two fortresses, dug out the canals, and organized the country under direct Assyrian rule. From Babylon, Borsippa, and Kutha came the priests of the supreme divinities, offering their rikhat ("gifts of homage"?) to the deliverer, who returned to Assyria, claiming the ancient and proud title of "King of Shumer and Akkad."

190. A natural corollary of this campaign was the expedition of the second year (744 B. C.) to the southeast, which, with the expedition of 737 B. C. to Media, completed the operations in the east. In this direction the Assyrian armies reached Mount Demavend, which overlooks the southern coast of the Caspian sea. Fortresses were built, Assyrian rule established among the Namri, the restless Medes chastised, and made temporarily at least to respect the Assyrian power.

191. The four years (743-740 B. C.) following the first eastern campaign were occupied in the west, where a striking illustration was given of the new international situation. All the region west of the Euphrates had practically been lost to Assyria in the last years of the house of Ashurnaçirpal. The centre of reorganization in northern Syria was the city-state of Arpad, lying a few miles north of Khalman (Aleppo), the capital of King Mati'ilu of Agusi. That state had apparently succeeded in breaking up the formerly strong kingdom of Patin (sect. 165), the western part of which formed a separate principality called Unqi (Amq), and was, with the

other contiguous districts, under the suzerainty of Aipad. The work of his predecessors must apparently be done over again by Tiglathpileser. But that was not all. Hardly had he reached the scene of operations, when he learned that he must confront a more formidable antagonist in the king of Urartu. Not contented with robbing Assyria of her tributaries on the northern frontier from Lake Urmia to Cilicia, the armies of Urartu had descended through the valleys along the upper Euphrates, overran Qummukh, and were supporting the north Syrian states in opposition to Assyria. The Urartian throne was occupied at this time by Sarduris III., successor of the brilliant conqueror, Argistis I. (sect. 182). He had advanced over the mountains into the upper Euphrates valley as the Assyrian king moved westward into Syria.

Whether Tiglathpileser III. had already reached Arpad is not clear, but, if so, he retraced his steps, and crossing again the Euphrates, marched northward into Qummukh, where his unexpected arrival and sudden attack threw the army of Sarduris III. into confusion. The king himself barely escaped and, with the relics of his force, ignominiously fled northward over the mountains, pursued by the Assyrians as far as the "bridge of the Euphrates." This defeat effectually cured Sarduris of meddling in Syrian politics, but by no means crippled the resistance of the Syrian states under Mati'ilu. Three years longer the struggle went on before Arpad. It must have fallen in 740 B. C. The fragments of the annals give only scattered names of kings and states that hastened to pay their homage after its overthrow. Qummukh, Gurgum, Karkhemish, Qui, Damascus, Tyre, are mentioned in the list, to which in all probability should be added Milid, Tabal, Samal, and Hamath. Tutammu of Unqi held out and was severely punished. His kingdom was made an Assyrian province, as was doubtless the former state of Agusi. Thus all of northern Syria again became Assyrian territory, and the chief states of the central region paid tribute.

192. In 738 B. C. the king made another step forward in the west. Middle Syria, about Hamath, became involved in trouble with Assyria. Just how this arose it is very difficult to understand, owing to the confused and fragmentary condition of the inscriptions. They mention a certain Azriyau of Jaudi, as inciting these districts to rebellion against the king. At first thought, this personage would seem identical with Azariah (Uzziah) of Judah; but chronological and historical obstacles outweigh the probability of this view, and serve, with other more positive considerations, to lead to the conclusion that the state of Jaudi was situated in northern Syria, adjoining and at times a part of Samal. A prince of this state, Panammu, the son of Karal, had already headed an uprising against the reigning king, Bar-çur, and cut him off with seventy of his house, though, unfortunately, as it proved for the new ruler, a son of Bar-çur, also called Panammu, succeeded in making his escape. It is not unlikely that Azriyau was a successor of the ambitious usurper and, as lord of Jaudi and Samal, was seeking, like so many other princes, to make his principality the centre of a larger Syrian state. This would inevitably bring him into hostility to Assyria. But, with considerable shrewdness, he sought to avoid conflict as long as possible by intriguing with cities of middle Syria as yet unvisited by Tiglathpileser III., among which the most prominent was the city of Kullani. The Assyrian king overthrew the rebel leader, devastated the districts about Hamath, and placed them under an Assyrian governor. Subject states hastened to pay tribute. Among them, besides the rulers of northern and central Syrian states already mentioned (sect. 191), appeared Menahem, king of Israel, and Zabibi, queen of Arabia. Panammu of Jaudi and Samal, the second of that name, had, it seems, fled to Tiglathpileser, and now reaped his reward in being placed upon his father's throne as a vassal of Assyria. His name appears on the tribute list. This was also in all probability, the occasion referred to in 2 Kings xv. 19, 20, where Tiglathpileser is called; by his Babylonian throne name, Pul (sect. 198). The acceptance of Menahem's gift by the Assyrian, as recorded in that passage, may well have been regarded in Israel as "confirming" him in the kingdom, and as a deliverance of the land from the presence of the Assyrian army.

193. With the western states thus pacified, Tiglathpileser turned his attention to his northern enemy whom he had so vigorously ejected from Qummukh in 743 B. C. The campaigns of 739 B. C. and 736 B. C. in the Nairi country may have been intended as preparatory essays in this direction, re-establishing, as they did, Assyrian authority as far as the southern shores of Lake Van. The expedition of 735 B. C. made straight for the heart of Urartu. There is no definite indication as to the route taken, whether the Assyrian came in from the west or from the southeast. The capital of Urartu, by this time pushed forward to the eastern shore of the lake in the vicinity of the present city of Van, was called Turuspa. It consisted of a double city, the lower town spread out along the rich valley, and the citadel perched upon a lofty rock that jutted out into the lake. The Assyrians destroyed the lower town, but besieged the citadel in vain. At last, having ravaged and ruined the country far and wide, from the lakes to the Euphrates as far as Qummukh, they retired, leaving to Sarduris III. a desolate land and an impoverished people. The years of Assyrian humiliation were thus amply avenged.

194. After three years of peace in the west, Tiglathpileser III. was again called thither in 734 B. C. The occasion was one of which the Assyrians had elsewhere often taken advantage. In Israel a new king, Pekah, had joined with Rezon, king of Damascus (2 Kings xvi. 5; Isa. vii. 1 f.), and the princes of the Philistine cities (2 Chron. xxviii. 18), chief of whom was Hanno of Gaza, in a vigorous attack upon the little kingdom of Judah. Edom, also, took up arms against her (2 Chron. xxviii. 17). It has been conjectured that these states had organized a league to resist Assyrian aggression, and were seeking to force Judah to join it. But of this there is no evidence. The real purpose seems to have been to take advantage of the weakness of Judah, and of the youth and incapacity of Ahaz its king, to plunder and divide the country among the assailants. In his extremity, Ahaz, in opposition to the urgent advice of Isaiah the prophet (Isa. vii. 3 ff.), determined to appeal to Tiglathpileser III., preferring vassalage to Assyria to the almost certain loss of kingdom and life at the hands of the league. The Assyrian king seems promptly to have responded to so attractive an invitation to interfere in the affairs of Palestine, hitherto undisturbed by his armies. For three years (734-732 B. C.) he campaigned from Damascus to the border of Egypt. The order of events cannot be determined with certainty. The limu list gives for 734 B. C. an expedition against Philistia. This suggests that he made in that year a rapid march to the far south in order to relieve Judah from the immediate and pressing danger of overthrow at the hands of her enemies, and then proceeded at his leisure to punish them, beginning with the nearest, the Philistines. Gaza suffered the most severely; Hanno fled southward to Munri; the city was plundered, but a vassal king was set up, perhaps Hanno himself, on making his submission. The other cities yielded without much resistance.

195. Israel next received attention. The Book of Kings (2 Kings xv. 29) tells how all Israel, north of the plain of Esdraelon, and east of the Jordan, was overrun. Pekah had thrown himself into his citadel of Samaria, where the Assyrian king would have soon beleaguered him and taken possession of the rest of the country, had not a conspiracy broken out in which Pekah was killed, and Hoshea, its leader, made king. His immediate submission to Tiglathpileser III. was accepted, and his position as vassal king confirmed. The northern half of his kingdom remained, however, in Assyrian possession.

196. In dealing with Damascus, Tiglathpileser III. first defeated Rezon in the field, and then shut him up in the city. How long the siege lasted is uncertain. The entire district was mercilessly devastated. During the siege Panammu II. of Samal, who brought his troops to the aid of his Assyrian suzerain, died, and his son and successor, Bar Rekub, thus records the event upon the funeral stele:

Moreover my father Panammu died while following his lord, Tiglathpileser, king of Assyria, in the camp... And the heir of the kingdom bewailed him. And all the camp of his lord, the king of Assyria, bewailed him. And his lord, the king of Assyria, (afflicted) his soul, and held a weeping for him on the way; and he brought my father from Damascus to this place. In my days (he was buried), and all his house (bewailed) him. And me, Bar Rekub, son of Panammu, because of the righteousness of my father, and because of my righteousness, my lord (the king of Assyria) seated upon (the throne) Of my father, Panammu, son of Bar-çur; and I have erected this monument for my father, Panammu, son of Bar-çur.

The Assyrian account of the capture of the city has not been preserved, but the summary statement of 2 Kings xvi. 9 tells what must have been the final result: "The king of Assyria... took it and carried (the people of) it captive to Kir and slew Rezin." The kingdom of Damascus was destroyed, and the district became an Assyrian province.

197. In the course of the three years other states of middle Syria and Palestine came under Assyrian authority. Sainsi, Queen of Arabia, who had withheld her tribute, was followed into the deserts, and, after the defeat of her warriors, paid for her rebellion with the loss of many camels, and the assignment of an Assyrian qipu, or resident, to her court. Other Arabian tribes to the southwest, among whom the Sabeans appear, sent gifts, and, as qipu over the region of Muçri, a certain Idibi'il was appointed. In the tribute list of the years 734-732 B. C. appear the kings of Ammon, Moab, Edom, and various cities of Phoenicia, hitherto independent. Even the king of Tyre, Mitinna, was compelled to recognize Assyrian suzerainty with a payment of one hundred and fifty talents of gold. The authority of Tiglathpileser III. was supreme from the Taurus to the Gulf of Aqaba and beyond. To slight it meant instant punishment. The king of Tabal, in the far north, ventured to absent himself from the king's presence, and was promptly deposed by the royal official. The king of Askalon, encouraged by the resistance of Rezon, suffered his zeal for Assyria to cool, and merely the news of the fall of Damascus threw him into a fit of sickness which forced him to resign his throne to his son whom the Assyrian king graciously permitted to ascend it. Ahaz of Judah, according to 2 Kings xvi. 10 ff.,. paid his homage in person to his lord Tiglathpileser III. in Damascus after the fall of that city, and caused to be built in Jerusalem a model of the Assyrian altar, set up in the Syrian capital for the worship of Assyrian gods. It has been thought, not without reason, that the biblical narrative intimates that this Jerusalem altar was prepared for the use of the Assyrian king himself, who honored his Judean vassal with a personal visit to his capital (Klostermann, Komm. Sam. u. Kön., in loc.). Such a visit was certainly due to that king whose personal appeal to Tiglathpileser III. had opened the way for this unprecedented extension of Assyrian power.

198. It was reserved for the last years of this vigorous king to see the crowning achievement of his vast ambitions. Thirteen years had passed since he had entered Babylonia and re-established Assyrian suzerainty over that ancient kingdom. Meanwhile Nabunaçir (sect. 177) had been succeeded (in 734 B. C.) by his son, Nabunadinziri (Nadinu), and he after two years was killed by one of his officials, who became king under the name of Nabushumukin. This usurpation was sufficient pretext for the interference of the Kaldi. Ukinzir, chief of the Kaldean principality of Bit Amukani, swept the pretender out of the way two months after his usurpation, and seated himself on the Babylonian throne (732 B. C.). On Tiglathpileser's return from the west he must needs intervene to restore Assyrian influence. In 731 B. C. he advanced against Ukinzir, moving down the Tigris to the gulf, and attacking Bit Amukani. He shut the Kaldean up in his capital, Sapia, cut down the palm-trees and ravaged his land and that of other neighboring princes. Evidently he found the enterprise a serious one, for he remained in Assyria the next year, preparing, it seems, for a decisive stroke. The campaign of 729 B. C. resulted in the capture of Sapia and the complete overthrow of Ukinzir, who disappeared from the scene. Among the Kaldean princes who offered gifts to the victor was a certain Mardukbaliddin, chief of Bit Jakin, far down on the gulf, who is to be heard of again in the

years to come. With the passing of the usurper, the Babylonian throne was vacant, and in 728 B. C. the Assyrian king "took the hands of Bel" as rightful heritor of the prize. Not as Tiglathpileser, but as Pulu, either his own personal name or a Babylonian throne-name, did he reign as Babylonian king. The cause of this change of name is thought by some to be a rescript of Babylonian law, which forbade a foreign king to rule Babylon except as a Babylonian. It may be that the complicated mass of legal and ritual requirements which in the course of the centuries had gathered about the position of the king of Babylon made it necessary, particularly in the case of the Assyrian ruler, to distinguish thus formally between his authority in the two countries. In his native land he was political and military head; in Babylon his authority consisted chiefly in his relation to the gods and their priesthoods. As such, the new position may be considered as much a burden as an honor, and Maspero thinks that this act of Tiglathpileser III. saddled Assyria with a heavy load. On the other hand, it marks the culmination of the centuries of struggle between the motherland of immemorial culture and the younger and more aggressive military state of the north. It was the attainment of the goal toward which, with deep sentiment and inextinguishable expectation, king after king of Assyria had been striving, and which Tukulti Ninib five centuries before had achieved (sect. 121). To rule and guard the ancient home at the mouth of the rivers, as suzerain of its kings, was not enough; it was far worthier to assume in person the holy crown, to administer the sacred laws, to come face to face with the ancestral gods, and to mediate between them and mankind. Something of this feeling may have come to Tiglathpileser III. at this supreme moment. He enjoyed the honor only a little over a year, however, for in 727 B. C. he died, and in his stead Shalmaneser IV. became king in the two lands.

199. Tiglathpileser III., in his eighteen years of ruling, had succeeded in raising Assyria from a condition of degenerate impotence to be the first power of the ancient world, with an extent of territory and an efficiency of administration never before attained. He combined admirable military skill and energy with a genius for organization, to which former kings had not, indeed, been by any means strangers, but which they had not exercised with such ability, or with results so solid. The custom of establishing fortified posts in conquered countries and of appointing military officials to represent Assyrian authority in them was continued by Tiglathpileser III., but it is his merit to have undertaken to attach these subjugated lands much more closely to Assyria, and to give these officials much more significant administrative duties. Taking as a basis the local unit of the city and the land dependent upon it, he united a not too large number of these districts under a single government official, called, ordinarily, the shuparshaku, whose duty it was to administer the affairs of these districts in immediate dependence on the court. As such, he was called bel pikliati, "lord of the districts." In other words, the king introduced a system of provincial government corresponding to the social and political organization of the Semitic world. Of these provinces, two were established in eastern Babylonia, two in the eastern highlands, one in northern Syria out of the kingdom of Unqi (sect. 191), two in central Syria, that of Damascus, and that of the nineteen districts about Hamath, two in Phoenicia, and one in northern Israel. The collection of a regular tribute and the preservation of order were, as before, the chief duties of these provincial officers. They served also as protectors of the districts from attack, and as guardians of Assyrian interests in surrounding tributary states. Such tributary states with their vassal kings were permitted to continue on the same terms as of old. Tiglathpileser III. also followed his predecessors in the custom of carrying away the peoples of conquered lands, but his genius is seen in the system and method introduced. In the first place, the deportations were made on an immensely larger scale, and, second, the majority of those deported were sent, not to Assyria as before, but to other regions already subjugated. In other words, immense exchanges of conquered populations were made by him. Thus, more than one hundred and thirty-five thousand persons were removed from Babylonia, sixty-five thousand from the eastern highlands, seventy thousand from the northern highlands, and thirty thousand from the districts about Hamath,

and these are not all that the inscriptions mention. The Syrians were taken to the north and east; the Babylonians to Syria. The result of this policy was to remove the dangers of insurrection arising out of local or national spirit, and to strengthen the Assyrian administration in the provinces. It has been admirably stated by Maspero as follows:

The colonists, exposed to the same hatreds as the original Assyrian conquerors, soon forgot to look upon the latter as the oppressors of all, and, allowing their present grudge to efface the memory of past injuries, did not hesitate to make common cause with them. In time of peace the governor did his best to protect them against molestation on the part of the natives, and in return for this they rallied round him whenever the latter threatened to get out of hand, and helped him to stifle the revolt, or hold it in check until the arrival of reinforcements. Thanks to their help, the empire was consolidated and maintained without too many violent outbreaks in regions far removed from the capital, and beyond the immediate reach of the sovereign (Passing of the Empires, pp. 200, 201).

200. Receiving from the hands of so able an administrator an empire thus organized, Shalmaneser IV. might look forward to a long and successful reign. Certain badly mutilated inscriptions, if they have been read correctly by modern scholars, indicate that he was the son of Tiglathpileser III. and had already been entrusted by him with the governorship of a Syrian province. No inscriptions of his own throwing light upon his reign have been discovered. This is not strange, as the limu list indicates that his reign lasted but five years (727-722 B. C.) The Babylonian Chronicle states that he succeeded to the Babylonian throne, and the Babylonian kings' list gives his throne name as Ulula'a. The limu list, containing the brief references to campaigns, is here badly mutilated and affords little help. All the more important, therefore, are the biblical statements concerning his relations to Israel, and a difficult passage of Menander of Tyre (in Josephus, Ant., IX. 14, 2) in regard to his dealings with that city.

201. The west had been quiet since the decisive settlement of its affairs made by Tiglathpileser III. in 732 B. C. (sect. 197). The accession of Shalmaneser IV. was generally acquiesced in, and tribute was promptly paid. The Babylonian Chronicle mentions the destruction of the city of Sabarahin (in Syria?) Ezek. xlvii. 16), which may have taken place in his first year (727 B. C. fait which time the payment of tribute by Hoshea of Israel (2 Kings xvii. 3) may have been made. The year 726 B. C. was spent by the king at home. The policy of Tiglathpileser III. seemed to insure the fidelity and peace of the empire. Trouble, however, soon appeared among the tributary kings of Palestine, owing to the intrigues of a certain "Sewe (So), king of Egypt (Miçraim)," (2 Kings xvii. 4), the Assyrian equivalent for whose name is probably Shabi. According to some scholars, the trouble was made by the north Arabian kingdom of Muçri over which Tiglathpileser III. had appointed a gipu (sect. 197). Whatever may be the solution of that question, the results of the intrigue were successful. Hoshea of Israel refused to pay tribute, and it is probable that the king of Tyre followed suit. Shalmaneser IV. came upon the ground in 725 B. C. Menander states that he "overran the whole of Phoenicia, and then marched away after he had made treaties and peace with all;" and a broken inscription, containing a treaty of the king of Tyre with a later Assyrian king appears to substantiate this account (Winckler, AOF, II., i, 15) so far as the submission of Tyre is concerned.

202. Israel was not as easily mastered. Hoshea and his nobles saw clearly that no mercy could be hoped for, in the face of their repeated contumacy, and prepared for the worst. They threw themselves into Samaria, hoping to be able to hold out until their allies brought them relief. By 724 B. C. the blockade began. No help came, yet still they defied the Assyrian army. The country must have been utterly laid waste. The siege continued through the year 723 B. C. The next year Shalmaneser IV. died. The circumstances are not known. The rebellious and beleaguered capital was left to be dealt with by his successor, Sargon, who ascended the

throne in January of 722 B. C.

V.THE ASSYRIAN EMPIRE AT ITS HEIGHT SARGON II. 722-706 B. C.

203. ALTHOUGH Sargon gives no indication in his inscriptions that he was related by blood to his immediate predecessors, the fact that he ascended the throne without opposition in the month that Shalmaneser IV. died, shows that he was no usurper, but was recognized as the logical successor of that king. In his foreign politics and his administrative activity he followed in the footsteps of Tiglathpileser III., and thereby carried forward the empire to a height of splendor, solidity, and power hitherto unattained. In one respect, indeed, and that a very important one, it is claimed that he reversed the policy of the two preceding kings. He favored the commercial and hierarchical interests as over against the peasantry (sects. 185 f.). I, "who preserved the supremacy of (the city) Assur which had ceased," and "extended" my "protection over Haran and in accordance with the will of Anu and Dagan wrote its charter," — are two statements in his cylinder inscription which, as doing honor to these centres of priestly rule, illustrate his friendly attitude toward the hierarchy and their interests. His name in one of its forms, Sharru-ukin, "the king has set in order," may embody a reference to this policy, which he conceived of as a restoration of the old order, the re-establishment of justice and right, ignored by his predecessors. While the king's opposition to them may not have been so intense or express as to warrant the claim that he deliberately threw himself into the hands of the other party, facts like those already mentioned and others, which will later appear, are explicable from this point of view.

204. The abounding religiosity of his inscriptions is in manifest contrast to the ritual barrenness of those of Tiglathpileser III. Long passages glorify the gods, whose names make up a pantheon surpassing in number and variety those of any preceding ruler. A devotion to ecclesiastical archæology, characteristic of a priestly régime, appears in the resuscitation of old cults like that of Ningal, the recognition of half-forgotten divine names such as Damku, Sharru-ilu, and Shanitka (?). The reappearance of the triad of Anu, Bel, and Ea (sect. 89) suggests a revival of the old orthodoxy. Sin, Shamash, Ninib, and Nergal are honored with temple, festival, or gift. As though in express contrast with Tiglathpileser (sect. 187), though perhaps unconsciously, Sargon, when he built his lordly palace and city, gave its gates names which testified directly to the overmastering power and presence of the gods and illustrate the extent of his pantheon.

In front and behind, on both sides, in the direction of the eight winds I opened eight city-gates: "Shamash, who granted to me victory," "Adad, who controls its prosperity," I named the gates of Shamash and Adad on the east side; "Bel, who laid the foundation of my city," "Belit, who gives riches in abundance," named the gates of Bel and Belit on the north side; "Anu, who gave success to the work of my hands," "Ishtar, who causes its people to flourish," I made the names of the gates of Anu and Ishtar on the west side; "Ea, who controls its springs," "Belit-ilani, who grants to it numerous offspring," I ordered to be the names of the gates of Ea and Belit-ilani on the south side. (I called) its inner wall "Ashur, who granted long reign to the king, its builder, and protected his armies;" and its outer wall "Ninib, who laid the foundation of the new building for all time to come" (Cyl. Inscr., 66-71).

205. The siege of Samaria, a bequest of Shalmaneser IV. (sect. 202), was in its final stage when Sargon became king, and the city fell in the last months of 722 B. C. The flower of the

nation, to the number of twenty-seven thousand two hundred and ninety persons, was deported to Mesopotamia and Media. The rest of the people were left in the wasted land, and a shuparshaku (sect. 199) was appointed to administer it as an Assyrian province. Later in the king's reign, captives from Babylonia and Syria were settled there.

206. Sargon could hardly have been present at the fall of Samaria, though, doubtless, the measures connected with its organization into a province were directed by him. The necessary adjustments of his home government and, particularly, the problem of Babylonia would require his presence in Assyria. Three months after his accession in Assyria, he would have to be in Babylon on New Year's day (Nisan) to "take the hands of Bel" as lawful Babylonian king. But what must have been an unexpected obstacle brought his purpose to naught. Tiglathpileser's annihilation of the Kaldean principality of Bit Amukani (sect. 198) had served to consolidate and strengthen the power of another Kaldean prince, Mardukbaliddin, of Bit Jakin, who at that time had paid rich tribute and now pressed forward to seize the vacant throne. He was supported, if not in his claims to the throne, at least in his opposition to Assyria, by Elam, a power which for centuries had not interfered in the affairs of the Mesopotamian valley. The Babylonian kings' list, indeed, records the rule of an Elamite over Babylon somewhere in the eleventh century, but nothing is known of his relation to the Elamite kingdom. Two new forces brought Elam upon the scene, and made it, from this time forth, an important element in Babylonio-Assyrian politics. First, the pressure of the new peoples from the far east, represented by the Medes in the northeastern mountains, was being felt in the rear of Elam, insensibly cramping and irritating the eastern and northern Elamites and forcing them westward. Second, the aggressive campaign of Tiglathpileser III. against the Aramean tribes on the lower Tigris had cleared that indeterminate region between the two countries and brought the frontier of Assyria up to the border of Elam. Collision was, therefore, as inevitable as between Assyria and the Median tribes farther north. Elam entered promptly into the complications of Babylonian politics and naturally took the anti-Assyrian side. While Mardukbaliddin advanced northward, Khumbanigash, the Elamite king, descended from the highlands and laid siege to Dur Ilu, a fortress on the lower Tigris. Sargon moved rapidly down the east bank of the river and engaged the Elamite army before the Kaldeans came up. The result of the battle was indecisive, a fact which practically meant defeat for the Assyrians. After punishing some Aramean tribes that had taken the side of the Kaldi and transporting them to the far west (Samaria), he turned back, leaving Mardukbaliddin to the possession of Babylon and the kingship, which he assumed in the lawful fashion on the first day of the new year (Bab. Chr., I. 32).

207. This serious set-back in Babylonia involved, at the beginning of Sargon's reign, a loss of prestige that had its effect upon all sides. It encouraged the rivals of Assyria to intrigue more actively in the provinces, and gave new heart to those among the subject peoples inclined to rebellion. In the west, Egypt, after centuries of impotence, was ready to engage in the affairs of the larger world. The innumerable petty princes who had divided up the imperial power among them had been formed into two groups, — one, the southern group, under the dominance of Ethiopia; the other, the northern group, under the authority of the prince of Sais, a certain Tefnakht. His son, Bok-en-renf (Greek, Bocchoris), unified his power yet more distinctly. He has gained a place in the Manethonian list as the sole representative of the twenty-fourth dynasty. About the year. 722 B. C. he assumed the rank of Pharaoh. Shut off from the south by his Ethiopian rivals, he looked to the north for the extension of his power, and naturally began to interfere in the affairs of Syria, whither, both by reason of immemorial Egyptian claims to the suzerainty and in view of commercial interests, his hopes were directed. His representatives began to appear at the courts of the vassal kings, and made large promises of Egyptian aid to those who would throw off the Assyrian yoke. Already representations of this sort had induced Hoshea of Israel to refuse the tribute, though in his

case rebellion had been disastrous (sect. 201). Now a new conspiracy was formed, and the unlucky Babylonian campaign of Sargon gave the occasion for its launching. A certain Ilubidi, also called Jaubidi of Hamath, a man of the common people, usually the greatest sufferers from Assyrian oppression, had succeeded in deposing the king of that city, and took the throne as representing the anti-Assyrian party. He secured adherents in the provinces of Arpad, Çimirra, Damascus, and Samaria. Allied with him was Hanno of Gaza, who was ready to try once more the dangerous game, relying upon his Bedouin friends. Gaza, the end of the caravan routes from south and east, was a centre of trade for the Bedouin, and they were likewise hampered by Assyrian authority. Among these Arabian communities were the Muçri, already referred to (sect. 197), the likeness of whose name to that of Egypt (Muçur) probably led the Assyrian Scribes into a confusion of the two peoples, which was encouraged by the geographical proximity of the localities. This confusion appears also in the Hebrew writings, where Sewe (So) is called "king of Egypt" (Miçraim) rather than of Muçri; here it is due to the fact that the impulse to conspiracy came from the Egyptians, although the Muçri were members of the league against Assyria (sect. 201).

208. Sargon hastened to the west in 720 B. C. and took the rebels in detail. Ilubidi was met at Qarqar, where the king defeated, captured, and flayed him alive. Sargon pushed southward and fought the southern army at Rapikhi (Raphia). Shabi (Sibi, Sewe, So), called, by a mixture of titles in the Assyrian account, "turtan of Piru (Pharaoh), king of Muçri," — a statement which has led some scholars to regard him as a petty Egyptian prince under the Pharaoh, — fled into the desert "like a shepherd whose sheep have been taken." Hanno was captured and brought to Assur. Nine hundred thirty-three people were deported. The Arabian chiefs offered tribute, — Piru of Muçri, Samsi of Aribi, and Itamara of Saba. The rebellion was crushed, punishments were duly inflicted, and provinces were reorganized. Having clearly demonstrated the consequences of revolt from Assyria, Sargon returned home. Seven years passed before trouble appeared again in Palestine, stirred up from the same sources as before. In the intervening period Sargon had, according to his annals, in 715 B. C. made an expedition into Arabia in consequence of which Piru of Muçri, Samsi of Aribi, and Itamara of Saba again paid tribute. The Pharaoh, Bocchoris, had fallen before the aggressive Ethiopian king, Shabako, who about 715 B. C. united all Egypt under his sway, and ruled as the first Pharaoh of the twenty-fifth dynasty. He did not wait long before undertaking the same measures as the Saite king to extend Egyptian influence in Asia. His agents began their work at all the vassal courts in Palestine. In Judah, Edom, Moab, and the Philistine cities, Egyptian sympathizers were found everywhere. Proposals were made for a league between these states. In Judah the chief opponent of this policy was the prophet Isaiah, who was moved to the strange action mentioned in Isaiah xx. 2. He kept it up for three years, at the end of which time the air had cleared. In Ashdod King Azuri openly favored the new movement, but so vigilant were the Assyrians that he was promptly deposed, and his brother Akhimiti substituted. This seems only to have added fuel to the flame, and by 711 B. C. the fire broke out. Akhimiti was overthrown; the leader of the mercenaries, a man from Cyprus, was made king, and allegiance to Assyria thrown off. The Assyrian, however, was now wide awake, and the conspirators were again taken unprepared. Sargon sent some of his finest troops in a forced march to Ashdod. The rebel leader was driven from his city before his allies could gather, and fled into the desert, where, in the fastnesses of the Sinaitic peninsula, he fell into the hands of a chieftain of Milukhkha, who delivered him up to the Assyrians. Ashdod and its dependencies, Gath and Aslidudimma, were put under a provincial government. Judah, Edom, and Moab hastened to assure the Assyrian of their faithfulness, and fresh gifts were required of them by way of punishment for their evil inclinations. Some time later, even Ashdod was permitted to resume its own government under a king Mitinti. Another instructive evidence had been given the Palestinians of the folly of seeking the aid of "Pharaoh of Egypt, a king who could not save them."

209. By far the greater number of Sargon's expeditions were directed toward the north, and occasioned by the renewed efforts of the kingdom of Urartu to unite the northern tribes against the Assyrians. Sarduris III. had left Assyria in peace after his punishment by Tiglathpileser III. in 735 B. C. (sect. 193), and was succeeded about 730 B. C. by Rusas I., called in the Assyrian inscriptions Rusa or Ursa. Under his vigorous and ambitious measures, Urartu entered upon its supreme effort for the control of the north and the overthrow of Assyrian supremacy. A combination was formed of states extending from the upper Mediterranean to the eastern shores of Lake Urmia, and the struggle that ensued lasted, in its various ramifications, for more than ten years (719-708 B. C.). The eastern peoples were led by Urartu itself; in the west the Mushki were the leading spirits under their king, Mita; both nations, however, evidently in mutual understanding and sympathy sought the same ends and used the same means.

210. After the humiliation of Urartu, Tiglathpileser III. had sought to build up, in the district between the two lakes, Van and Urmia, a kingdom which, in close dependence on Assyria, would offset the influence of Urartu. This was the kingdom of the Mannai, which had already attained some degree of unity under its king, Iranzu, and controlled a number of principalities, among which were Zikirtu, Uishdish, and Bit Daiukki. Unable to break down Iranzu's fidelity to Assyria, Rusas succeeded in drawing away the principalities from their allegiance and even detached some cities of the Mannai from Iranzu. Sargon promptly punished these latter in 719 B. C. In 716 Iranzu was succeeded by his son Aza, whose declared fidelity to his Assyrian overlord provoked a storm. The chiefs of the rebellious principalities succeeded in having him murdered, and raised Bagdatti of Uishdish to the throne. Sargon appeared again upon the scene, seized Bagdatti and flayed him alive. The rebels raised to the throne Ullusunu, brother of Bagdatti, who, after a brief struggle, submitted to Sargon and was permitted to remain king. The next year, 715 B. C., under the influence of Rusas, Daiukki, chief of another Mannean principality, rebelled against Ullusunu and was deported by Sargon. Expeditions to the east and southeast carried Sargon's armies among the Medes, who were evidently pressing more closely upon the mountain barrier and absorbing the tribes of that region. The campaign of 714 B. C. brought him face to face with Rusas himself. He entered Zikirtu, overthrew its prince, and devastated the country. The army of Rusas, which came to its relief, he utterly defeated, and drove the king himself in hasty flight to the mountains. The Assyrian narrative reports that, seeing his land ravaged, his cities burned, and portions of his territory given to the king of Man, in despair Rusas slew himself. It seems, however, according to Urartian inscriptions, that he lived to fight again. The reduction of the other districts followed without difficulty. From Illipi, in the far southeast on the borders of Elam, westward beyond Lake Van, and eastward as far as the Caspian, gifts and tribute were the signs of Assyrian authority. usual citadels were built, and provinces established for administrative purposes, where vassal kings were not continued in their authority. Urartu, however, somehow escaped incorporation. A new king, Arglstas II., continued to maintain the independence of his country, and even to interfere in Assyrian affairs, but with no success. The aggressive power of the state was broken, and the Assyrians were satisfied to let well enough alone. That Urartu was practically left to itself and yet was closely watched, is illustrated by a despatch which has been preserved from the Crown Prince Sennacherib, who in the last years of Sargon was the commanding general, stationed on the frontier between Urartu and Assyria.

211. In the northwest the Mushki were situated as advantageously for disturbing the Assyrian borders as was Urartu in the east. Perched high up among the Taurus mountains, they saw beneath them Qui (Cilicia) to the southwest, Tabal and the north Syrian states to the south, Qummukh to the southeast, and Milid to the east, beyond which Urartu extended to the mountains of Ararat. They themselves were moved to activity, doubtless, by the pressure of peoples behind them, caused by the westward movement of the Indo-European tribes, of

whom the Medes in the east formed one branch, and who were to make themselves felt more distinctly within half a century. They entered heartily, therefore, into the schemes of Rusas of Urartu, and did their part toward breaking down Assyrian influence on these frontiers. A beginning was made in Tabal in 718 B. C. by a rebellion in Sinukhtu, one of its principalities. The rising was put down, the guilty tribe deported, and its territory given to a neighboring prince. The next year, tempted by the promise of help from Mita, King of Mushki, Pisiris, king of Karkhemish, threw off the yoke, but, if a general rising was expected, it was prevented by the vigilance and promptness of Sargon, who stormed the ancient city, carried away its inhabitants, and settled Assyrians in their places. The city became the capital of an Assyrian province. Mita had, meanwhile, been making advances to Qui. Its king had been faithful to Assyria at first. He was consequently attacked by the Mushki and lost some of his cities. Finally he fell away to the enemy, however, and was punished with the loss of his kingdom for, later in Sargon's reign, an Assyrian provincial governor administered Qui and conducted campaigns against the Mushki. In 713 B. C. the king of Tabal, son of the prince raised to the throne by Tiglathpileser III. (sect. 197), and himself married to an Assyrian princess, declared his independence, in spite of the fact that his territory had been twice enlarged by Sargon. The Assyrian overran the country, carried away the king and his people, settled other captives in the land, and brought it directly under Assyrian authority. The year following, it was the turn of Milid to revolt. Its king had overrun Kammanu, a land under Assyrian protection, and had annexed it. Sargon punished this aggression by the removal of the royal house, the deportation of the inhabitants, and the settlement of people from the Suti in the land. The country was fortified by a line of posts on either side over against Mushki and Urartu. Certain of its cities were conferred upon the king of the Qummukhi. In Gamgum, a small kingdom on the southern slopes of the Taurus, the reigning king had been murdered by his son, who seized the throne. Sargon, regarding this usurpation as inspired from the same source as the other movements in these regions, sent, in 711 B. C., a body of troops thither, by whom the same measures were carried through as elsewhere, and a new Assyrian province established. Meanwhile the governor of Qui had succeeded in his campaigns against Mita of Mushki, who in 709 B. C. made his formal submission to Sargon. At the same time seven kings of the island of Cyprus, who had somehow been involved in the wars of these states in the northwest, sent gifts to the king, who, in return, set up in that island a stele in token of his supremacy. That an Assyrian administration was introduced there, is not clear. Finally, the hitherto faithful kingdom of Qummukh, seduced by Argistis II., the new king of Urartu, threw off the Assyrian yoke. Sargon was then engaged in the thick of the struggle with his Babylonian rival. With its triumphant conclusion in 708 B. C., the king of Qummukh lost heart and did not await the advance of the Assyrian army. His land was overrun, and another province was added to the empire. Already, during these years, the kingdom of Samal, whose kings had been so loyal to Tiglathpileser III. (sect. 196), had disappeared, so that now all the west and north, with the exception of some of the Palestinian and Phoenician states, was directly incorporated into the Assyrian empire.

212. The overthrow of the northern coalition, by the defeat of Rusas of Urartu and Mita of Mushki, left Sargon free to finish the task which he had abandoned in the first year of his reign after the doubtful victory over the king of Elam (sect. 206). For more than a decade had Mardukbaliddin ruled in Babylon, undisturbed by his Assyrian rival. But now his turn had come to feel the weight of Assyrian vengeance, made all the heavier by delay, and by the added might of the Assyrian power, everywhere else victorious. The Kaldean king had, meanwhile, found it no easy task to administer his new domain. The Babylonian priesthood, while nominally acquiescing in his supremacy, were at heart enemies of Kaldean rule and devoted to Assyria, especially since Sargon was inclined to favor hierarchical assumptions. Nor had Mardukbaliddin seized the throne with any other purpose than to give his Kaldeans the supreme positions in Babylonia, and, in pursuing this policy, he appears to have

dispossessed not a few Babylonian nobles in favor of his own partisans. A document which has been preserved recites his purpose "to give ground-plots to his subjects in Sippar, Nippur, Babylon, and the cities of Akkad," and describes such a gift to Bel-akhi-erba, mayor of Babylon, who was most probably one of his own people (ABL, 64 ff.). While Sargon's claims that his rival despised the Babylonian gods are disproved by the pious tone of that document, it appears that southern Babylonia particularly had been so rebellious that the Kaldean king had carried away the leading citizens of such cities as Ur and Uruk along with their city-gods to his capital, and even held confined there people of Sippar, Nippur, Babylon, and Borsippa. The Aramean tribes, also, had been permitted to resume their former independence as a bulwark against Assyria on the lower Tigris, and the Suti were active along the northern frontiers of Babylonia. Moreover, in 717 B. C., Khumbanigash of Elam, the ally of the Kaldean king, was succeeded by Shuturnakhundi, whose zeal for his support had not yet been put to the test. Under such conditions Mardukbaliddin was forced to meet the advance of Sargon.

213. The campaigns of the years 710-709 B. C. were occupied with this war in Babylonia. The weakness of the Kaldean king was apparent immediately. Sargon's account of his operations has been variously interpreted. Some assume two Assyrian armies, — one directed toward the east of the Tigris and the other, led by Sargon himself, moving west of the Euphrates. No good reason for the western trans-euphratean movement can possibly be imagined; indeed it was the worst sort of tactics to separate the two armies so widely. The campaign becomes clear however, if, in the annals (1. 287), we read "Tigris" for "Euphrates." The Assyrian army advanced down the eastern bank of the Tigris without opposition from Elam, and encountered only the Aramean tribes. The chief resistance was offered by the Gambuli, whose city of Duratkhara, though garrisoned by a corps of Kaldean troops in addition to its native defenders, was taken by storm, rebuilt and, as Dur Nabi, made the capital of an Assyrian province. The whole region down to the Uknu, and eastward into the borders of Elam, was overrun, devastated, and made Assyrian territory. Thus Elamite intervention was cut off. The Elamite king drew back into the mountains. Then the army turned westward toward Babylonia, crossed the Tigris (?), and entered the Kaldean principality of Bit Dakurri. Now Sargon stood between Mardukbaliddin and his Kaldean base; hence the Kaldean king must meet his enemy in Babylon. But his resources were not yet exhausted.

He recognized his danger, abandoned Babylon, and hurried eastward with his forces into the region just traversed by the Assyrians, to the border of Elam, to unite with the Elamite forces, and follow up the Assyrian army. It was a bold, but thoroughly strategic move. Shuturnakhundi, however, had lost heart, and no inducements could avail to secure his co-operation. Now one resource only remained for the Kaldean. He moved rapidly to the south, eluded the Assyrians, and threw himself into a citadel of his own principality, Bit Jakin, and there, fortifying it strongly, awaited the Assyrian attack.

214. Sargon, meanwhile, had fortified the capital of Bit Dakurri, and was preparing to advance northward toward Babylon. The news of Mardukbaliddin's escape was followed by the coming of the priesthoods of Borsippa and Babylon, who brought their rikhat (sect. 189) and, accompanied by a deputation of the chief citizens, invited Sargon to enter the city. He accepted the invitation, and showed his gratification by royal gifts and services befitting a devoted worshipper of the gods of Babylon. Sippar, which had been seized by an Aramean tribe driven westward by his advance down the Tigris, was recovered by a detachment sent out from Babylon. The next year (709 B. C.), Sargon "took the hands of Bel" and became lawful king of Babylon. The punishment of Mardukbaliddin followed. His principality of Bit Jakin was fiercely attacked, his citadel stormed in spite of a desperate resistance, the land laid waste, the inhabitants deported, and new peoples settled there. The Kaldean prince, however, succeeded m making his escape, and was destined still to be a troubler of Assyria. The

landowners, dispossessed under the Kaldean régime, were restored to their estates. The imprisoned Babylonians were released, and the city-gods of Uruk, Eridu, and other ancient shrines were brought back and honored with gifts. From the king of Dilmun, an island "which lay like a fish thirty kasbu out in the Persian gulf," came gifts in token of homage.

215. Little is known of the course of events in Sargon's reign after 708 B. C. It is clear, however, that during this period his city and palace of Dur Sharrukin were completed and occupied. The king had lived principally at Kalkhi, where he had restored the famous Ashurnaçirpal palace (sect. 170). But his overmastering ambition suggested to him an achievement which had not entered into the minds of his predecessors. They had erected palaces. He would build a city in which his palace should stand. For this purpose, with an eye to the natural beauty of the location, he chose a plain to the northeast of Nineveh, well watered and fertile, in full view of the mountains. A rectangle was marked out, its sides more than a mile in length, its corners lying on the four cardinal points. It was surrounded by walls nearly fifty feet in height, on which at regular intervals rose towers to a further height of some fifteen feet. Eight gates elaborately finished and dedicated to the gods (sect. 204) gave entrance through these walls into the city, which was laid out with streets and parks in a thoroughly modern fashion, and was capable of housing eighty thousand people. Upon the northwest side stood the royal palace on an artificial elevation raised to the height of the wall. This mound was in the shape of the letter T, the base projecting from the outer wall, the arms falling within and facing the city. An area of about twenty-five acres thus obtained was completely covered by the palace, which consisted of a complex of rooms, courts, towers, and gardens, numbering in all not less than two hundred. The main entrance was from the city front through a most splendid gateway which admitted to the central square. From its three sides opened the three main quarters of the palace, to the right the storehouses, to the left the harem, and directly across, the king's apartments and the court rooms. This latter portion was finished in the highest artistic fashion of the period. The halls were lined with bas-reliefs of the king's campaigns; the doorways were flanked with winged bulls, and the archways adorned with bands of enamelled tiles. In the less elaborate chambers colored stucco and frescoes are found. The artistic character of the bas-reliefs, however, is not distinctly higher than that of previous periods. The variety of detail already noted as appearing in the bronzes of Shalmaneser II. (sect. 175) is the most striking characteristic of these sculptures. It is in the mechanical skill displayed, in the finish of the tiling, in the coloring of the frescoes, in the modelling of the furniture, in the forms of weapons and the like, that the art here exhibited is chiefly remarkable. In addition, the colossal character of the whole design of city and palace, culminating ill the lofty ziggurat, with its seven stories in different fe t ors, rising to the height of one hundred and forty from the court in the middle of the southwest face Of the palace mound, gives a vivid impression of the wealth, resourcefulness, and magnificent powers of the Assyrian empire as it lay in the hand of Sargon, who brought it to its height and gave it this unique monument.

216. Sargon's administration of the empire reveals a curious mixture of progressiveness and conservatism, of strength and weakness, which makes the task of estimating his ability and achievement not a little difficult. His reign was one series of wars, yet a large number of his campaigns were against petty tribes and insignificant peoples. Over against his good generalship, illustrated in the skilful campaign of 710 B. C. against Mardukbaliddin, must be placed the serious reverse in the same region in 721 B. C. Good fortune did much for him in Babylonia and in the west, where rebellious combinations never materialized. He overthrew his enemies in detail or found them deserted by those who had promised help. It is evident that Urartu itself offered him nothing like the resistance it had shown to Tiglathpileser III. His system of provincial government, involving the exchange of populations, was an inheritance from his predecessors. He carried it out more extensively, establishing provinces on all borders

and deporting peoples from one end of the empire to the other in enormous numbers. His new city of Dur Sharrukin was composed almost entirely of the odds and ends of populations from every part of his domains. So intent on making provinces was he, that he seems at times to take advantage of insignificant difficulties in vassal kingdoms to overturn the government and incorporate them into the empire. Was he wise in this? or was the policy of Tiglathpileser III. more far-sighted? He, while establishing provinces in important centres, not only permitted vassal kings to hold their thrones, but even encouraged the growth of such states, as in the case of the kingdom of the Mannai. The task of organizing and unifying this mass of provinces and of meeting the responsibilities of their administration was certainly severe. National spirit had disappeared with the deportation of the people, and imperial attachment had to be fostered in its place. All the details of government and administration, left otherwise to local and tribal officials, must be taken over by the imperial administration. Officials had to be obtained and trained. Military forces must be maintained for their protection and authority. If Sargon had before him the vision of a mighty organization like this, he had not wisely estimated the difficulties of its successful maintenance. As ruler of Babylon, he particularly felt the inconvenience of presenting himself yearly at the city to receive the royal office at the hands of Bel, and therefore contented himself with the title of "Governor" (Shakkanak Bel), by which he exercised the power, even if he must forego the honors, of kingship.

217. A severer indictment against Sargon is found by those who hold that he reversed the policy of Tiglathpileser III. relative to the priesthood (sect. 203). An immediate result of this would be the substitution of a mercenary soldiery for the usual native troops. Sargon certainly revived the policy instituted by Shalmaneser II. of incorporating the soldiers of conquered states into his armies. His inscriptions testify to this in the case of Samaria, Tabal, Karkhemish, and Qummukh. But the maintenance of mercenary troops involves their employment in constant wars to keep them active and secure them booty. When these fail, they sell themselves to a higher bidder, or turn their arms against the state. The policy of Sargon also involved the subordination of the Assyrian peasantry to the commercial and industrial interests of the state or to the possessors of great landed estates. The burdens of taxes fell upon the farmers even more heavily. They dwindled away, became serfs on the estates, or slaves in the manufactories, and their places were supplied by aliens from without, transplanted into the native soil. Thus the state as organized by Sargon became more and more an artificial structure, of splendid proportions, indeed, but the foundations of which were altogether insufficient. Whether this judgment is unduly severe or not, it is clear that none of these evils appeared in the king's time. Assyria was never so great in extent, never so rich in silver and gold and all precious things, never so brilliant in the achievements of art and architecture, never more devoted to the gods and their temples. Nor was Sargon unmindful of the economic welfare of his country, as his inscriptions testify. He directed his attention to the colonization of ruined sites, to the planting of fields, to making the barren hills productive, and causing the waste dry lands to bring forth grain, to rebuilding reservoirs and dams for irrigation. He sought to fill the granaries with food, to protect the needy against want, to make oil cheap, to make sesame of the same price with corn, and to establish a uniform price for all commodities. When he had settled strangers from the four quarters of the earth in his new city, he sent to them Assyrians, man of knowledge and insight, learned men and scribes, to teach them the fear of God and the king (Cyl. Inscr., ABL, pp. 62 ff.). These were high conceptions of the responsibilities of empire, however imperfectly they may have been realized.

218. Hardly had Sargon been settled in his new city and palace when his end came. A violent death is recorded, but whether in battle or by a murderer's hand in his palace, the broken lines of the inscription do not make clear. His son and heir, Sennacherib, was summoned from the frontier, where he was acting as general, and without opposition ascended the throne toward the close of July, 705 B. C.

VI.THE STRUGGLE FOR IMPERIAL UNITY SENNACHERIB. 705-681 B. C.

219. THE reign of Sennacherib, though longer by six years than that of his father, is marked by fewer military expeditions, but the campaigns recorded are, with one or two exceptions, of a much more serious character than those which brought Sargon booty and fame. It is true that for his last eight years (689681 B. C.) he has left no memorials of his activities. Yet that very fact indicates how Assyrian rule was changing from aggression and conquest to the administration of an organized and compact state as the outcome of a long series of experiments in government, brought to a climax in the reign of Sargon. A demonstration of Assyrian strength by a raid into the southeastern mountains in 702 B. C., when the Kassites and Illipi were again punished, an expedition to the northwest among the tribes of Mount Nipur and into Tabal, which, perhaps, reached as far as Cilicia, in 697 B. C., and a campaign among the Arabian tribes in his later years, — these constitute the sum total of the minor wars waged by Seunacherib. Along the eastern and northern borders and in Syria provincial governors kept strict ward over the motley populations under their sway, and carefully watched all signs of movement in the outlying peoples beyond, among whom, for a season, a strange and perhaps portentous quiet seemed to prevail.

220. Only on the two extremities of the long semicircle of lands making up the empire did serious difficulty appear. Babylonia and Palestine, the former especially, were the two problems given to Sennacherib to solve. The complexities which they involved, the new factors appearing there, the daring attempts at solution, and the tragic elements concerned in them make Sennacherib's reign one of the most interesting and baffling studies in all Assyrian history.

221. The Babylonian difficulties were not new. How they troubled his predecessors has already been described (sects. 189, 198, 206). Babylonia was no longer a unity under the rule of kings of Babylon, but a number of separate principalities, each eager for possession of the capital city and thus the nominal headship of the land. Aramean communities lay on the north and east, Arabians on the west, and Kaldean states on the south, while over the borders were the rivals Assyria and Elam, the latter just beginning to assert itself, both determined to enter and possess the land. Babylon itself, the genial fountain-head of religion, culture, and mercantile activity, alike flattered and preyed upon by these various states, containing a great population made up of heterogeneous elements with inclinations divided between all the parties that invited their favor, had no unity except in the self-interest concerned with the maintenance of its religious authority and its commercial supremacy. Tiglathpileser. III. had entered the city as a deliverer from the anarchy threatened by incursions of Arameans and Kaldeans, and, as king by the grace of Bel, had been welcomed. Between his rule and the assumption of the throne by Sargon had come the decade of Mardukbaliddin's reign, which had doubtless accustomed the Babylonians to Kaldean authority and had strengthened Kaldean influence there. After the first year, Sargon relinquished the title of king for that of regent (sect. 216) and, on his retirement to his new residence, Dur Sharrukin, must have ruled Babylonia by a royal governor. It is suggested by a passage of Berosus that he placed a younger son over it who retained his position on the accession of Sennacherib. If the king thought this flattering to the Babylonians, he was disappointed. They would have none but the great king himself, and he must rule as king of Babylon, not of Assyria. Sennacherib had reigned hardly a year, when his brother was murdered, and a Babylonian, Mardukzakir-shum, made king. The latter was, after a month, put out of the way by the Kaldeans, and Mardukbaliddin again seized the throne (704 B. C.). He renewed his alliance with the

Aramean communities and with Elam, and prepared to meet the Assyrians. Sennacherib came in 703 B. C., defeated the Kaldean at Kish, and drove him out, after his nine months' reign. He entered Babylon, seized the palace and treasures of Mardukbaliddin, cleared the capital and other Babylonian cities of the Kaldeans and their sympathizers, marched into Kaldu and laid it waste, and returned by the way of the Aramean states, from which he carried away two hundred and eight thousand people and a vast spoil in cattle. For Babylon Sennacherib provided a new arrangement which he might expect to be altogether agreeable. He took a young Babylonian noble, Belibni, who had been reared at his court, and made him king of Babylon. Naturally, Belibni would be maintained under Assyrian protection, but, as a native king, he would represent to the jealous Babylonians the preservation and maintenance of their ancestral rights. The arrangement seemed to promise well.

222. Meanwhile, in the opposite quarter of the empire, Mardukbaliddin, during his nine months' possession of Babylon, had succeeded in stirring up disaffection which began to threaten serious trouble for Sennacherib. On the Phoenician coastland the kings Of the rich and energetic city of Tyre had been gradually extending their authority over the neighboring communities, until King Luli, who was reigning at this time in Tyre, could claim supremacy from Akko to Sidon and beyond, and was ready to bring no little strength to an organized movement for throwing off the Assyrian yoke. In Palestine the young Hezekiah had succeeded his father, Ahaz, upon the throne Of Judah, the leading vassal kingdom in that region. Its faithfulness to Assyria had been sorely tried during the reign of Sargon, but had apparently Stood every strain, and its reward was freedom from Assyrian interference and a high degree of material prosperity. Hezekiah, however, was ambitious and restless under the Assyrian yoke. He was already entertaining proposals to rebel, when he suddenly fell ill (2 Kings xx. 1). The desperate situation of his house and people, should he die at this time, stirred him to a struggle for life, which, under the ministrations of Isaiah, prophet of Jehovah, was successful. Interpreting this event as a sign of Jehovah's approval, the king proceeded more boldly with his rebellious plans. A visit of emissaries from Mardukbaliddin (2 Kings xx. 12 f.), who, though driven from Babylon, was still active in organizing opposition to Assyria (702 B. C.), secured Hezekiah's adherence to a league which included the Tyrian and Palestinian states, Ammon, Moab, and Edom, the Bedouin on the east and south, as well as the Egyptians. All disguise was thrown off. Padi, the king of the Philistine city of Ekron, who would not join the rebels, was deposed and delivered to Hezekiah. Open defiance was thus offered to Sennacherib.

223. The Assyrian was, however, apparently well apprised of the designs of the leaguers, and determined to forestall them. Early in 701 B. C. he appeared on the Mediterranean coast and received the submission of the Phoenician cities with the exception of Tyre. Ammon, Moab, and Edom hastened, also, to pay homage at that time. Luli of Tyre, called king of Sidon in the Assyrian account, retired to Cyprus, and his newly acquired Phœnician kingdom fell to pieces. The omission of Tyre from the submissive cities makes it evident that Sennacherib was unable to capture it at this time. But he determined to set up a rival which would effectually prevent it from giving him trouble and from re-establishing its influence among the Phoenician cities. For this purpose he chose Sidon, appointed, as king over it, Itobaal (Assyr. Tubalu), and gave him suzerainty over the cities which had acknowledged the authority of Tyre. It is probable that an attack was made upon Tyre by a naval force collected from these cities, under Sidon's leadership; but the assailants were repulsed, and Tyre remained independent (Menander in Jos. Ant., IX. 14, 2).

224. Sennacherib, without waiting for the issue of the attack on Tyre, hurried forward, down the coast road, to strike at Askalon, the southernmost of the Philistine cities that was in rebellion. Having reduced it and captured its king, Çidqa, he turned toward the northeast, and,

on his advance to Ekron, was confronted at Altaqu with an army led by the chiefs of Muçri and Ethiopian-Egyptian generals. The force, hastily gathered and poorly commanded, was dispersed without difficulty. Altaqu and Timnath were despoiled, and Ekron surrendered. All opposition on the coast was thus crushed. Hezekiah was isolated, and the Assyrian attack could concentrate on Judah. The king therefore marched up the valleys leading to the plateau. His own words describe the punishment he inflicted upon the unhappy land:

But as for Hezekiah of Judah, who had not submitted to my yoke, forty-six of his strong walled cities and the smaller cities round about them, without number, by the battering of rams, and the attack of war-engines (?), by making breaches by cutting through, and the use of axes, I besieged and captured. Two hundred thousand one hundred and fifty people, small and great, male and female, horses, mules, asses, camels, cattle, and sheep, without number, I brought forth from their midst and reckoned as spoil. (Hezekiah) himself I shut up like a caged bird in Jerusalem, his royal city. I threw up fortifications against him, and whoever came out of the gates of his city I punished. His cities, which I plundered, I cut off from his land and gave to Mitinti, King of Ashdod, to Padi, King of Ekron, and to Çil-Bel, King of Gaza, and (thus) made his territory smaller. To the former taxes, paid yearly, tribute, a present for my lordship, I added and imposed on him. Hezekiah himself was overwhelmed by the fear of the brilliancy of my lordship, and the Arabians and faithful soldiers whom he had brought in to strengthen Jerusalem, his royal city, deserted him. Thirty talents of gold, eight hundred talents of silver, precious stones, guhli daggassi, large lapis lazuli, couches of ivory, thrones of elephant skin and ivory, ivory, ashu and urkarinu woods, of every kind, a heavy treasure, and his daughters, his palace women, male and female singers, to Nineveh, my lordship's city, I caused to be brought after me, and he sent his ambassador to give tribute and to pay homage (Taylor Cyl., III. 11-41).

225. The course of the campaign, as here presented, is also described in 2 Kings xviii. and xix. (see Isa. xxxvi. and xxxvii.), and a harmonization of the narratives, though difficult, is not impossible. Sennacherib did not, at first, attack Jerusalem, but only blockaded it, and leaving fear and famine to accomplish its surrender, moved southward, devastating the land on every side, until he came to Lachish and Libnah. The capture of these towns made an end of rebellion in the southeastern plain, and completed his Palestinian campaign, which had swung around in a great circle from Askalon in the southwest to these southeastern cities. Meanwhile Hezekiah had decided to submit; he set free Padi, king of Ekron, and sent to Sennacherib, at Lachish, for terms of surrender, which were promptly forthcoming and as promptly met. His failure to present himself in person, however, angered the Assyrian. Recognizing also the danger of leaving behind him Jerusalem the only city which had not opened its gates in submission, Sennacherib demanded the surrender of the capital. Meanwhile he himself, it appears, advanced farther to the south. But the year was now far spent. News came from the east that Mardukbaliddin had appeared again in Babylonia. Sennacherib had already decided to return, when it seems that pestilence fell upon his army. He was, accordingly, forced to withdraw the detachment from Jerusalem and beat a hasty retreat. Having laid greater tribute upon the subdued states, he returned to Nineveh with the heavy spoil of the west. If the close of his campaign had been inglorious, he had succeeded in his purpose. Never again during his reign did the kings of the west raise the hand of revolt against him. The punishment had been effectual. Sennacherib entered the west only once again, and then only to make a foray against Arabian tribes whose constant restlessness needed frequent restraint and sometimes severe chastisement.

226. Sennacherib's well-meant effort to conciliate the Babylonians had ended in failure. During the king's absence in the west, Belibni, either from weakness or seduced by the opposition, had not maintained his fidelity to Assyria. Babylonia was in commotion, and in

700 B. C. the Assyrian king was again called there by an alliance of the Kaldeans and Elamites. Along with Mardukbaliddin appeared another Kaldean chieftain, Shuzub. The combination was dispersed by Sennacherib, who advanced far into the marsh lands of the south. Shuzub disappeared in the swamps. Mardukbaliddin, with his people, emigrated in a body down the eastern coast of the gulf into a district of Elam. He must have died soon after, for he played no part in the succeeding events. Bit Jakin, his principality, was utterly devastated. A new experiment was tried at Babylon. Sennacherib made his eldest son, Ashur-nadin-shum, king of the city, and carried Belibni and his counsellors, in disgrace, back to Assyria. The failure of the coalition against Assyria caused, also, the downfall of the Elamite king, who was dethroned by his brother Khallushu. The way seemed, thus, to be cleared for the new régime in Babylonia and, in fact, Ashurnadinshum occupied the throne for six years (700694 B. C.). But the end of his career was tragical, and opened another period of trouble for the unhappy land.

227. Sennacherib employed these years of quiet in preparations for a military expedition which was as unique in its method as it was audacious in its conception. The Kaldi, whom Mardukbaliddin had carried off with him in ships to the eastern shore of the Persian gulf and brought under the immediate shelter of Elam, were settled on the lower courses of the river Karun, the waterway from the south into the heart of Elam. If an army could be landed here, it might be able not only to destroy these enemies, but even make its way to the Elamite capital Susa, and strike a deadly blow at the power of Elam. Two conditions were essential for the success of this enterprise, a fleet at the head of the gulf for the transport of troops, and secrecy as to the goal and the preparations for the expedition. Accordingly Phoenician ship-builders and sailors from the vassal state of Sidon, recently favored by the king (sect. 223), were secured, and a shipyard was set up at Til Barsip on the upper Euphrates; ships were also gathered in Assyria. At an appointed time both fleets were sent down the rivers; the Assyrian ships, for the sake of secrecy, had been transferred at Upi to the Arakhtu canal, and were thus brought into the Euphrates above Babylon; all were concentrated at the appointed place, where the troops were encamped, awaiting their arrival. An unexpected flood tide delayed them for some days, but, the embarkation once made, the distance was quickly traversed, the troops landed and the surprised Kaldeans overwhelmed (695-694 B. C.). The captives were loaded into the ships and transported to Assyria, the main body of the troops apparently being left behind to push forward into Elam. But in some way, probably by the treachery of the Babylonians, news of the expedition had come to Elam, and Khallushu determined upon a stroke as bold as that of Sennacherib himself. Hardly had the fleet sailed, when, with his Elamites, he rushed down upon northern Babylonia. Sippar was taken by storm, and Babylon, cut off from Assyrian help both north and south, and probably unprepared for so sudden an onslaught, surrendered (694 B. C.). Ashurnadinshum was captured and carried away to Elam, where he was probably put to death. A Babylonian noble, Shuzub, was placed on the throne under the name of Nergal-ushezib, and supported by Elamite troops. He immediately marched southward to overcome the Assyrian garrisons and cut off the army operating in southern Elam. But news of the disaster had reached the king, and he had hastily returned. He made Uruk his headquarters, and awaited the coming of the enemy, who were occupied about Nippur. The battle between the two armies took place in September (693 B. C.), and Nergalushezib was defeated, captured, and carried off to Assyria.

228. Whatever arrangements Sennacherib had made for the government in Babylon, on the fall of the usurper, were speedily brought to naught by the Babylonians themselves, who made the Kaldean prince Shuzub (sect. 226) their king, under the name of Mushezib Marduk (693 B. C.). Meanwhile another revolution had broken out in Elam by which Khallushu was set aside and Kudur-nakhundi became king. The Assyrian king was, as it seems, already marching down the eastern bank of the Tigris again to settle affairs in Babylonia, when the news from

Elam induced him to turn his arms against that enemy. He swept through the lower valleys with fire and sword, and, though the winter was approaching, determined to advance into the mountains whither the Elamite king had withdrawn. But hardly had he entered the highlands when the inclemency of the weather forced him to retire (692 B. C.). He had, however, broken the prestige of Iiudurnakhundi, who lost his throne to his brother, Umman-menanu, after hardly a year's reign. Mushezib Marduk knew that his turn would soon come for punishment, and made a vigorous effort to defend himself. He called for aid upon the new Elamite king, who for his own security must also show a bold front to Assyria. The Babylonians likewise felt that vengeance would fall upon them for their treachery, and committed an act which revealed their desperate fear and hatred of Sennacherib. They opened the treasuries of the temples, and offered the wealth of Marduk for the purchase of Elamite support. All through the winter of 692 B. C. the preparations went on to meet the Assyrian advance. A great army of Elamites, Arameans, Babylonians, and Kaldeans was gathered. Sennacherib compared its advance to "the coming of locust-swarms in the spring." "The face of the heavens was covered with the dust of their feet like a heavy cloud big with mischief." The battle was joined at Khalule, on the eastern bank of the Tigris, in 691 B. C., and, after a long and fierce struggle, the issue was drawn. Sennacherib claimed a victory, but, though the coalition was broken, his own forces were so shattered that he advanced no farther, and left to Mushezib Marduk the possession of the Babylonian throne for that year.

229. During the next two years Sennacherib grappled with the Babylonian problem and brought it to a definite solution. On his advance in 690 B. C. he met with no serious opposition. Ummanmenanu of Elam could offer no aid to Mushezib Marduk, who was Speedily seized and sent to Nineveh. Babylon now lay at the mercy of the Assyrian, whose long-tried patience was exhausted. He determined on no less a vengeance than the total destruction of the ancient city. The work was systematically and thoroughly done. The temples and palaces were levelled. Fortifications and walls were uprooted. The inhabitants were slaughtered; even those who sought refuge in the temples perished. Images of Babylonian gods were not spared. Two images of Assyrian deities, which Marduknadinakhi had carried away from Ekallati (sect. 145), were carefully removed and restored to their city. The canal of Arakhtu was turned from its bed so as to flow over the ruins. The immense spoil was made over to the soldiers. The district was then placed under a provincial government, as had already been the case with the lands of the Kaldeans and Arameans round about it. Sennacherib thus ruled Babylon till his death. The Babylonian kings' list names him as "king" both for the years 705-703 B. C. and also during this last period, 689-681 B. C., although the source from which Ptolemy drew his information denominated both these periods "kingless." The Assyrian had made a solitude and called it peace.

230. The last years of Sennacherib were evidently embittered by family difficulties, of which some traces appear in the inscriptions. When the unfortunate Ashurnadinshum was carried away to Elam, another son of the king, Ardi-belit, was recognized as crown prince. Two other sons are mentioned, Ashur-munik, for whom a palace was built, and Esarhaddon. This latter prince, for reasons not now discoverable, began gradually to supplant his brothers in the king's favor. It seems probable, though absolute proof is not yet available, that he was appointed governor of the province of Babylon (680 B. C.), and a curious document has been preserved in which his father confers upon him certain gifts, and changes his name from Esarhaddon (Ashur-akh-iddin, that is, "Ashur has given a brother") to Ashur-itil-ukin-apla, that is, "Ashur the hero has established the son." The bestowal of the name suggests the choice of him as heir and successor to the throne in preference to his elder brother. His mother, Naqia, who plays an important rôle in her son's reign, may have had her part in the affair. At any rate, the embittered and disgraced brother sought betimes the not unusual revenge. Associating, it may be, another brother with him, as 2 Kings xix. 36 f. states, he slew his father while worshipping

in a temple of "Nisroch" (Nusku?). Thus, once more, a brilliant reign ended in shameful assassination, and revolution was let loose upon the empire.

231. The name of Sennacherib is intimately associated with the city of Nineveh, which owes its fame, as the chief capital of the Assyrian empire, to his choice of it as a favorite dwelling-place. He planned its fortifications, gave it a system of water-works, restored its temples, and built its most magnificent palaces. The city, as it came from his hands, was an irregular parallelogram that lay from northwest to southeast along the eastern bank of the Tigris, its western side about two and one-half miles long, its northern over a mile, its eastern more than three miles, and its southern half a mile in length, making in all a circuit of about seven miles. Through the middle of the city flowed, from east to west, the river Khusur, an affluent of the Tigris. Sennacherib built massive walls and gates about the city, and on the eastern side toward the mountains added protecting ramparts. A quadruple defence was made on this side. A deep moat, supplied with water from the Khusur, was also led along the eastern face. Diodorus estimates the height of the walls at one hundred feet. Their general width was about fifty feet, and excavations have indicated that in the vicinity of the gates they were more than one hundred feet wide. The arrangements for furnishing the city with water are described by the king in an inscription, carved upon the cliff of Bavian, a few miles to the northeast of Nineveh among the mountains. Eighteen mountain streams were made to pour their waters into the Khusur, thus securing a constant flow of fresh water. A series of works regulated at the same time the storing and the distribution of the water, and made it possible for the city to maintain an abundant supply in time of siege. Two lofty platforms along the Tigris front of the city had served as the foundations of the palaces already erected, but both palaces and platforms had fallen into decay. The northern platform, now known as the mound of Kouyunjik, lay in the upper angle formed by the junction of the Khusur and the Tigris. Sennacherib restored and enlarged this platform, changed the bed of the Khusur so that it half encircled the mound, and built in the southwest portion of it his palace. It has been only partially excavated, yet already seventy-one rooms have been opened; in the judgment of competent investigators, the palace is the greatest built by any Assyrian monarch. On the southern platform, now called Nebiyunus, the king built an arsenal for the storing of military supplies. His ideal for these buildings is stated by himself to be that they should excel those of his predecessors in "adaptation, size, and artistic effect." His success in the latter respect is no less remarkable than in the two former. No series of bas-reliefs hitherto executed in Assyria, or even in the ancient world, reaches the height of artistic excellence attained by those of Sennacherib. In variety of subject-matter, strength and accuracy of portraiture, simplicity and breadth of composition, they are among the most remarkable productions of antiquity. The tendency to the development of the background and setting of the principal subject, already observed in previous work (sects. 175, 215), has reached its climax. The delineation of building operations and the sense for landscape are two new features which illustrate the larger outlook characteristic of the higher civilization and broader culture of the time. Similar characteristics appear in the literary remains of the king. Official as they are, they reveal, as compared with similar documents of earlier kings, a feeling for literary effect, an element of subjectivity, a color and breadth of composition, which are unusual. The description of the battle of Khalule, in the Taylor inscription (ABL, pp. 77-79), in spirit and vigor leaves little to be desired, while the free characterization of personages and measures, indulged in throughout the inscription, introduces a distinctly fresh note into these usually arid and stereotyped annalistic documents. The culture of the time may, perhaps, also be illustrated by the subtle and effective speech of the Assyrian royal officer to the people of Jerusalem, preserved in 2 Kings xviii. 19-35, — an argument in content and form worthy of a modern diplomatist.

232. What, after all, shall be said of the central figure of this brilliant time and of the work which he did for Assyria? The verdict has, in general, been unfavorable, ranging from the

moderate statement that, "though great, he was so by no desert of his own," "to the thoroughgoing condemnation of him as boastful, arrogant, cruel, and revengeful," whose "vindictive cruelty was only equalled by his almost incredible impiety," exhibiting "blind rage" and the "ruthless malignity of the narrow-minded conqueror." The chief basis for the extreme view must lie, in part, in the striking subjectivity of his inscriptions as already referred to, and, for the rest, in the judgment passed on his destruction of Babylon. But the former ground is a very hazardous basis for estimating the character of an Assyrian king, since he cannot be regarded as the author of the inscriptions in which he thus speaks. Nor should the destruction of Babylon be singled out from his whole career as the sole test of his character and work. A broader view may be able to make a fairer estimate of his contribution to Assyrian history, and thereby to see even in the overthrow of Babylon something more than one of "the wildest scenes of folly in all human history." As a soldier he was active and brave even to personal rashness in the day of battle. In his conduct of a campaign he will, in energy and rapidity of movement, bear the comparison and with any of his predecessors, and in the daring and originality of his strategy he surpasses them. His Palestinian campaign and his naval expedition to southern Elam are conclusive illustrations. It is true that disasters attended both these campaigns, but they were such as could hardly have been foreseen and prepared for. The most that can be said against him as a soldier is that he may have been hasty in forming plans, and possibly obstinate in carrying them through, and that unexpected difficulties robbed him of complete success.

233. From the larger point of view his dealings with Babylon may, perhaps, be most justly estimated. As the heir of the political programme of Sargon, he found himself face to face with the problem of Babylonian prerogative. The unity of the empire, with its system of vassal kingdoms and of provincial government, could not harmonize with the claims of Babylonian equality. Sennacherib tried various methods of incorporating that ancient city into the scheme of imperial unity, but in vain. Finally, he chose, with characteristic audacity and impetuousness, to cut the knot, to maintain the unity of the empire upon the ruins of Babylon. The solution was one which only a man of genius would have conceived and a man of intense and fiery spirit have carried through. It may be that he also desired the ruin of Babylon to redound to the higher glory of Nineveh, or that he was inspired to the act by his anti-hierarchical inclinations and his wrath at Babylonian obduracy and treachery. These were, however, surely secondary to his main impulse, his determination that the unity of the empire should be secured, so far as it involved Babylonia, even by the destruction of the proud city that would not lower her head and for whose favor the nations round about were forever at strife. So far as the immediate problem was concerned, he was, indeed, successful, but he overestimated his power, if he thought himself able to wipe out a past so ancient and glorious, and to prevent the gathering of man- kind to a spot so manifestly intended by nature and history as , a centre of commerce and culture. The future of the Assyrian empire, in its relation to the Babylon soon to be rejuvenated, holds the answer to the question whether his successors, who reversed his policy in this respect, were wiser than he.

VII.IMPERIAL EXPANSION AND DIVISION ESARHADDON. 681-668 B.C.

234. No contemporary narrative has been preserved which gives in clear detail the story of the critical months that followed the murder of Sennacherib. The deed was done on the twentieth of Tebet (early in January), according to the Babylonian Chronicle. Second Kings xix. 37 states that his murderers escaped into the land of "Ararat," that is, Urartu. The Chronicle adds that the insurrection in Assyria ceased on the second of Adar (middle of February), and that

Esarhaddon became king sixteen (?) days thereafter (18th (?) of Adar). An inscriptional fragment of Esarhaddon seems to refer to events of these days and describes the climax of the struggle:

I was fierce as a lion, and my heart (liver) was enraged. To exercise the sovereignty of my father's house and to clothe my priestly office, to Ashur, Sin, Shamash, Bel, Nabu and Nergal, Ishtar of Nineveh, Ishtar of Arbela, I raised my hands, and they looked with favour on my petition. In their eternal mercy they sent me an oracle of confidence — viz.: "Go, do not delay; we will march at thy side and will subjugate thine enemies." One day, two days, I did not wait, the front of my army I did not look upon, the rear I did not see, the appointments for my yoked horses, the weapons for my battle I did not inspect, provisions for my campaign I did not issue. The furious cold of the month of Shebat, the fierceness of the cold I did not fear. Like a flying sisinnu bird, for the overthrow of mine enemies, I opened out my forces. The road to Nineveh, with difficulty and haste, I travelled. Before me in Hanigalbat, all of their splendid warriors seized the front of my expedition and forced a battle. The fear of the great gods, my lords, overwhelmed them. They saw the approach of my mighty battle and they became insane. Ishtar, the mistress of onslaught and battle, the lover of my priestly office stood at my side and broke their bows. She broke up their compact line of battle, and in their assembly they proclaimed, "This is our king." By her illustrious command they joined themselves to my side (Cyl. B. 1. 1-25).

235. While it is possible that Esarhaddon was in the far northwest when he received news of the murder, and that he proceeded hastily toward Nineveh only to find the army of his brothers barring his way, his more probable starting-point was Babylonia, where he was governor (sect. 230), whence his march would take him northward through Nineveh, the murderers retiring before his advance, until the decisive battle was fought on the upper Euphrates. The desertion of a part of the hostile forces sealed the fate of the insurrection. The brothers escaped to Urartu, and Esarhaddon became king (March, 681 B. C.).

236. The inscriptions of the king, which are available for his reign, are not chronologically arranged, and hence some uncertainty exists as to the duration and order of his various activities, which is not altogether dispelled by the useful chronology of the Babylonian Chronicle. They describe, however, the important movements, both of war and peace, in sufficient fulness and with a variety of picturesque detail that suggests the influence of the literary school of the time of Sennacherib. No such splendid battle-scenes as that of Khalule (sect. 231) decorate the narratives, which, indeed, reveal a decline in energy and an inclination to fine writing that reaches its climax in the following reign. The numerous building inscriptions illustrate a prominent and important feature of the king's rule. On the southern platform of Nineveh, he erected a palace and arsenal on the site of the building of Sennacherib (sect. 231), which had grown too small. At Kalkhi his palace occupied the southwestern corner of the mound; it was partially excavated by Layard. The indications are that it was unfinished at the time of the king's death. Curiously enough, there were found piled up in it a number of slabs, from the palace of Tiglathpileser III.; these had been trimmed off, preparatory to recarving and fitting them for use in the new edifice (sect. 187). A characteristic of both of his palaces, indicative perhaps of a new architectural impulse, is the great hall of unusual width, its roof supported by pillars and a medial wall. Another striking feature is the use of sphinxes in decoration. No bas-reliefs of any significance have as yet been discovered. A tunnel was built by the king to bring the waters of the upper Zab to Kalkhi, a renewal of the channel dug by Ashurnaçirpal. Esarhaddon was also pre-eminently a temple-builder. He rebuilt the temple of Ashur at Nineveh. In Babylonia he was especially active, the temples at Uruk, Sippar, Dur Ilu, Borsippa, and elsewhere being restored by him. Not less than thirty temples in all bore marks of his work.

237. His crowning achievement in this respect was the reconstruction of the city of Babylon, to the account of which he devotes several inscriptions. The wrath of Marduk at the spoiling of his treasure in order to send it to Elam (sect. 228) had been the cause of the city's destruction. "He had decreed ten years as the length of its state of ruin, and the merciful Marduk was speedily appeased and he drew to his side all Babylonia. In the eleventh year I gave orders to re-inhabit it" (The Black Stone Inscr., ABL, p. 88). For Marduk had chosen him in preference to his elder brothers for this work. With profoundly solemn and impressive religious ceremonies, the enterprise was undertaken, all Babylonia being summoned for service and the king himself assuming the insignia of a laborer. The temple, Esagila, the inner wall, Imgur-bel, the ramparts, Nemitti-Bel, began to rise in surpassing strength and magnificence. The royal bounties for the service of the sanctuary were renewed. The scattered population was recalled. It is not unlikely that the city had not been so utterly destroyed as Sennacherib's strong language suggests. The walls, temples, and palaces were, indeed, demolished, but there is no evidence that the site had been utterly abandoned during these years. As the destruction involved the taking away of the religious, political, and commercial supremacy of the city in punishment for its rebelliousness, but not necessarily its complete desolation, so the rebuilding signified that its former headship and prerogative were restored under the fostering favor of the ruler of the empire. Hence the king called it "the protected city." The same conclusion follows from the fact that the work was practically completed in three years (680-678 B. C.). The estates of the nobility in the vicinity of the city, which had been appropriated by the Kaldeans of Bit Dakurri, were restored to them, and the king of that principality paid for his crime by the loss of his throne.

238. This important enterprise had a political as well as an architectural significance. It involved the reversal of Sennacherib's policy, and reinstated Babylon among the problems of imperial rule. The motives which induced Esarhaddon to take this step have been variously conceived. He himself ascribes it to the mercy and forgivingness of the gods. But religion in antiquity, particularly official religion, usually gave its oracles in accordance with royal or priestly policy, and the question therefore still remains. A clew may be found in the personal interest taken by the king in Babylon and its affairs owing to his residence there as governor, or to family ties, if, as is assumed, his mother or wife belonged to the Babylonian nobility. He may have thus paid off a political debt, as his accession to the throne had been made possible by the immediate acknowledgment of him as king in Babylon and through the aid furnished him by Babylonian troops. By some scholars the fundamental political division in the empire is assumed to account for the undertaking. This division appeared originally between hierarchy and army (sect. 185), but now took the more concrete form of Nineveh against Babylon without losing the inveterate opposition of a military and secular policy to a peaceful and commercial, a cultural and religious ideal. Sennacherib devoted himself to the interests of Nineveh and the army; Esarhaddon took the opposite course, and the rehabilitation of Babylon naturally followed. This theory is too rigorously maintained and applied by its advocates; one cannot conceive that any Assyrian ruler or party would voluntarily undertake to set Babylon above Nineveh, or that the ambitions of the Babylonian hierarchy would not be offset by the equally pretentious claims of the Assyrian priesthood. Yet it is quite probable that at the Assyrian court Babylonian influences emanating from personal, religious, and commercial interests alike, were strong, and at this time may have overruled, in the king's mind, the counsel of those who regarded the rebuilding of the city as inimical to the welfare of the state. The very violence of Sennacherib's measures would tend to produce a reaction of which the representatives of Babylon's wrongs would not fail to take advantage. Whatever may have been Esarhaddon's motive, his inscriptions reveal the lively interest he took in the work, and the importance he attached to its completion.

239. In connection with the rebuilding of the city Esarhaddon, as shakkanak of Babylon (sect. 216), was engaged in the reorganization and administration of Babylonia. During the troubles connected with the succession, the Kaldi, under the leadership of a son of Mardukbaliddin, named Nabu-zer-napishti-lishir, took up arms and besieged Ur. The energetic advance of the provincial governor of southern Babylonia into his domain compelled the Kaldean to retreat and finally to flee to Elam, his father's old resort in time of trouble. There Ummanmenanu had been succeeded by Khumma-khaldash I., and he by another of the same name. Khummakhaldash II., however, contrary to the policy of his predecessors, put the fugitive to death. His brother Na'id Marduk, who had accompanied him, fled to Assyria and threw himself on the mercy of Esarhaddon, who promptly made him vassal-lord of the Kaldi, and thereby not only widened the breach between the Kaldi and Elam but also secured the allegiance of the former. The Gambulians, an Aramean tribe of the southeast, were likewise won to the Assyrian side, and their capital fortified against Elam. Still, though thus isolated, the Elamites ventured a raid into northern Babylonia (674 B. C.), while Esarhaddon was in the west, and his mother, Naqia, was acting as regent. They stormed Sippar and carried away the gods of Agade, but were evidently prevented from doing further damage by the well-organized system of Assyrian defence. It seems that this somewhat unsuccessful expedition cost Khummakhaldash II. his throne. The same year he died "without being sick," and was succeeded by his brother, Urtagu (Urtaki), who signalized his accession by returning the gods of Agade. He continued the policy of peace with Assyria during Esarhaddon's reign. It is probable that not only the Assyrian defensive arrangements, but also troubles arising on his northern and eastern frontiers from the encroachments of the Medes, explain this attitude.

240. Assyria, likewise, had her problem to solve upon the northern frontier. During the quiet which reigned here in the years of Sennacherib (sect. 219), the Medes of the northeast had been passing from the condition of tribal independence into a somewhat consolidated confederacy, which now acknowledged as leader a certain Mamitiarshu, who is called in Assyrian documents "lord of the cities of the Medes." In the north the kingdom of Urartu was held in check by the Mannai, who owed their place and power to Assyrian favor (sect. 210); but in the last years of Sennacherib, a new wave of migratory peoples came rolling down from the Caucasus. It broke on the Assyrian border and produced confusion and turmoil. These peoples were called by the Assyrians Gimirrai (anglicized, through the Greek, as "Kimmerians"). Reaching the high and complex mountain-mass behind which lay Urartu, they seem to have split into two divisions, one moving westward along the Anti-Taurus into Asia Minor, the other likewise following the mountains in their southeasterly trend toward Iran. In both directions they emerged upon territory under Assyrian influence, and came into conflict with Assyrian troops. The western body came out above the upper Euphrates, in the provinces of Milid and Tabal, where Esarhaddon met them under the leadership of a certain Teushpa, whom he claims to have defeated. If the restoration of the reading in a broken place in the Babylonian Chronicle is correct, this battle took place as early as 678 B. C. The result of it seems to have been to drive the Gimirrai farther to the northwest, where they fell upon the kingdom of Phrygia. The complications in the northeast were much more formidable. Urartu became restless, and it is not surprising therefore, that the sons of Sennacherib, who murdered him, fled northward, made their stand on the upper Euphrates, and finally took refuge in Urartu. Their presence there may have had something to do with the disturbances which soon arose on the frontiers. These broke out, however, not in Urartu, but in the pro-Assyrian state of the Mannai, which seems to have united with the Gimirrai, and threatened Assyrian supremacy in the mountains. Then, as the Gimirrai pushed farther to the southeast, they sought alliance with the Medes. Before the Assyrians were awake to the situation, they were startled to find that the Gimirrai, Mannai, and Medes were forming a league under the leadership of Kash-tarit, lord of Karkashshi. A series of curious documents, apparently official inquiries made of the sun god with reference to these disturbances and the king's measures taken to quiet them,

reveals at the same time the gravity of the situation and the procedure prerequisite to Assyrian diplomatic and military activity (Knudtzon, Assyrische Gebete). The Assyrian plan is laid before the god for his approval; an oracle as to the outcome of the king's policy or of the enemy's reported movements is requested in a fashion which, though introduced and accompanied with a stately and elaborate ritual, is in essence similar to that employed by the kings of Israel (1 Sam. xxx. 8; 1 Kings xxii. 5, 15). From Esarhaddon's own report and the hints given in these prayers, the details of the wars can be recovered and the general result stated. How many years the struggle continued is quite uncertain; it was brought to an end before 673 B. C. The league against Assyria failed to do serious harm, as much because of its own weakness as through Esarhaddon's attacks upon it. Promises which were made to some tribes detached them from the alliance; a King Bartatua seems to have secured as his reward a wife from the daughters of Assyria's royal house; some Median chieftains, who were being forced into the league, made their peace with Assyria and sought protection. Campaigns were made against the Mannai and their Kimmerian or Scythian ally, king Ishpaka, of Ashguza (Bibi. Ashkenaz?), and against Median tribes in the eastern mountains. Intrigues were set on foot to array the different peoples one against another. Urartu, even, came to terms with Assyria, and in 672 B. C., when Esarhaddon was recovering from the Gimirrai the fortress of Shu-pria, he set free Urartians who were found there and permitted them to return home. Esarhaddon had succeeded in averting the storm and in protecting his frontiers, as well as in inflicting punishment upon the intruders by campaigns which he had made into the regions of disturbance; but there is no evidence that he extended Assyrian authority there, or even that he established on a firm basis in the border-lands the Assyrian provincial system. On this side of his empire the stream of migration was neither turned aside nor dissipated; it was merely halted at the frontier. In such a situation the future was ominous.

241. If Esarhaddon had been able to do little more in the north than maintain his frontier intact, his activity in the west was productive ef a far more brilliant result. It is a signal testimony to Sennacherib's administration of the empire that for more than twenty years after the expedition of 701 B. C. no troubles appeared in the western provinces, not even when the new king came to the throne in circumstances so favorable to uprisings in dependent states. Several years after the accession of Esarhaddon the first difficulty arose, in connection with Sidon. This city owed its power and prosperity to Assyria, favored as it had been by Sennacherib as a rival to Tyre (sect. 223). Its king, Itobaal, had been succeeded by Abdimilkuti. He proceeded to withhold the usual tribute (about 678 B. C.), relying apparently upon a league formed with Sanduarri, a king of some cities of Cilicia (?), and hoping also for assistance possibly from the kings of Cyprus and Egypt. In this he was disappointed, and when Esarhaddon appeared (676 B. C.?), he made little resistance, fled to the west, and, together with his ally, was after a year or two caught and beheaded. Sidon was treated as Babylon; it was utterly destroyed, the immense booty transported to Assyria, and a new city built near the site, called Kar Esarhaddon, in the erection of which the vassal kings of the west gave assistance. In the list of these kings appears Baal of Tyre, who, either at this time or in Sennacherib's reign, had yielded to Assyria. The same kings, together with the kings of Cyprus who renewed their allegiance on Sidon's downfall, contributed materials for the building of Esarhaddon's palace in Nineveh. The list is instructive, as showing the states which at this date (about 674 B. C.) retained their autonomy in vassalage to Assyria.

Ba'al of Tyre, Manasseh of Judah, Qaushgabri of Edom, Muguri of Moab, Chil-Bel of Gaza, Metinti of Askelon, Ikausu of Ekron, Milkiashapa of Byblos, Matanbaal of Arvad, Abibaal of Samsimuruna, Buduil of Ammon, Ahimilki of Ashdod, twelve kings of the seacoast; Ekishtura of Edial, Pilagura of Kitrusi, Kisu of Sillua, Ituandar of Paphos, Eresu of Sillu, Damasu of Kuri, Atmesu of Tamesu, Damusi of Qartihadashti, Unasagusu of Sidir, Bu-ou-su of Nure, ten kings of Cyprus in the midst of the sea, in all twenty-two kings of Khatti (Cyl. B. Col. v. 13-

242. Esarhaddon's activities in the west, however, contemplated something more than the restraining of uneasy vassals or the conquest of rebellious states. Egypt was his goal. It is conclusive for the view that the enmity of Egypt had for a long time been the chief hindrance to Assyrian aggression in the west, and its overthrow a standing purpose of the Sargonids, that Esarhaddon, at the first moment of freedom from complications elsewhere, proceeded to lay plans for attacking it. The breadth of the plans and the persistency of his activities show that he regarded Egypt as "an old and inveterate foe." Ever since the Ethiopian dynasty had unified Egypt, the interference of Egypt with Syria and Palestine, first under Sabako, then under his successor, Shabitoku (about 703-693 B. C.), and now under the vigorous and enterprising Taharqa (about 693-666 B. C.), had been offensive and persistent. It was now, at last, to be grappled with in earnest by Esarhaddon. In the light of his Egyptian goal his Arabian campaigns are comprehensible. The Assyrian yoke was fixed more firmly on the Aribi, to whose king, Hazael, were returned his gods captured by Sennacherib. A Queen Tabua was appointed to joint sovereignty with Hazael and, upon his death, his son Yailu was seated on the throne. The districts of Bazu and Hazu, somewhere in southwestern Arabia, were subjugated after a march the appalling difficulties of which are imaginatively described in the king's narrative. These campaigns (675-674 B. C.) preceded the first advance against Egypt in 674 B. C., in which the Egyptian border was crossed, and a basis for further progress established. The next year, however, if Kundtzon's reading of the confused statement of the Babylonian Chronicle at this point is correct, the Assyrian army was defeated and driven out. It was this disaster which probably emboldened Baal, King of Tyre, to withhold his tribute. Esarhaddon, nothing daunted, spent two years in more extensive preparations, and was on his way to the west by 670 B. C. Baal was summoned to surrender, and, when he refused and retired to his island citadel, he was besieged, while the army moved on southward. The course of the campaign cannot be described more vividly and tersely than in the royal inscription of Samal:

As for Tanya, King of Egypt and Cush, who was under the curse of their great divinity, from Ishupri as far as Memphis, his royal city — a march of fifteen days — every day without exception I killed his warriors in great number, and as for him, five times with the point of the spear I struck him with a deadly stroke. Memphis, his royal city, in half a day, by cutting through, cutting into and scaling (?) I besieged, I conquered, I tore down, I destroyed, I burned with fire, and the wife of his palace, his palace women, Ushanahuru, his own son, and the rest of his sons, his daughters, his property and possessions, his horses, his oxen, his sheep without number, I carried away as spoil to Assyria. I tore up the root of Cush from Egypt, a single one — even to the suppliant — I did not leave behind. Over all Egypt I appointed kings, prefects, governors, grain-inspectors, mayors, and secretaries. I instituted regular offerings to Ashur and the great gods, my lords, for all time. I placed on them the tribute and taxes of my lordship, regularly and without fail (Mon. 38-51; ABL, p. 92).

243. Twenty Egyptian city-princes, headed by Necho of Sais, were said to have yielded to Esarhaddon, and, after taking the solemn oath of fidelity to Ashur, were confirmed in their authority, subject to the oversight of Assyrian officials (qipani, sect. 167). The usual tribute was required. Last named among these princes was the king of Thebes; yet he could have paid but nominal homage at this time, for only after some years did his city fall into the hands of Assyria. It is evident that Esarhaddon proposed, by these measures, to incorporate at least lower Egypt into his empire. On his return he set up the stele at Samal, in which he appears, endowed with heroic proportions, and holding a cord attached to rings in the lips of two lesser figures, his captives, one of whom on his knees is evidently Taharqa of Egypt, and the other presumably Baal of Tyre. The inscription, however, says nothing of Baal's surrender, and his

submission, if offered, was merely nominal. A. similar image and superscription appears graven on the cliffs of the Nahr-el-Kelb, side by side with the proud bas-reliefs of Egyptian conquerors of former centuries. Another long-sought goal of Assyrian kings had been attained, and Esarhaddon was the first of their line to proclaim himself "King of the kings of Egypt." But a year had hardly passed when he was summoned to Egypt again by a fresh inroad of Taharqa. He set out in 668 B. C., but never returned, dying on the march in the last of October. The expedition was concluded triumphantly by his son and successor.

244. As if anticipating that he would never return from the campaign, Esarhaddon had, in that very year, completed the arrangements for the succession to the throne. At the feast of Gula (last of April, 668 B. C.) the proclamation was made to the people of the empire that Ashurbanipal, his eldest son, was appointed king of Assyria, and a younger son, Shamash-shum-ukin, was to be king of Babylon. Other sons were made priests of important temples. This procedure seems to have been necessitated by court or dynastic difficulties which troubled the last years of the king. The Babylonian Chronicle, at the year 669 B. C., has the significant statement: "The king remained in Assyria; he put to death many nobles with the sword." It is easy to conjecture that this record testifies to a revolt of the Assyrian party against the pro-Babylonian tendencies of the king (sect. 238), and that Ashurbanipal represented this party and succeeded in carrying his point (so KAT3, 91 f.), whereby he secured the Assyrian throne and the primacy in the empire. But this is only conjecture, against which much might be urged. It is sufficient to observe that Esarhaddon, before his death, himself determined upon this method of administering the empire, either to avoid a war of succession, or to secure the future establishment of that form of government which to him appeared likely to be the wisest and the most successful for the state.

245. The verdict upon Esarhaddon has been as uniformly favorable as that upon his father has been condemnatory. He is characterized by a "reasonable and conciliatory disposition," a "largeness of aim peculiarly his own;" he was "a wise and strenuous king who left his vast domains with a fairer show of prosperity and safety than the Assyrian realm had ever presented at the demise of any of his predecessors." He "is the noblest and most sympathetic figure among the Assyrian kings." These are high commendations of both the personal and public worth of the king. The facts, however, require a more balanced judgment. The king's action regarding Sidon was peculiarly cruel. Not only was the city destroyed, and its king beheaded, but, as the royal record declares, on the triumphal march into Nineveh, the heads of the monarchs slaughtered in that campaign were hung upon the necks of their great men. The restoration of captured gods and the establishment of submissive kings upon their thrones must be regarded as political rather than personal acts, a part of the policy followed in other periods of Assyrian history. The king's generalship, personal courage, and force are all that any king before him exhibited, and his success was brilliant. Yet he, too, suffered military disasters as in Egypt and on the northern frontier. In the latter region, moreover, his energy was exhibited rather in beating off his enemies than in aggressive warfare. A Tiglathpileser, it may be said, would have followed up and broken the power of his assailants. In Esarhaddon, also, appears more distinctly than before something of that orientalism in manners and taste which is accustomed to be associated with eastern monarchs. He is the first of the Sargonids to boast of his lineage and to trace it back to a fabulous royal ancestry. Kings from all parts of his realm throng his court and are summoned regularly to do him homage at his capital. As captives, they are represented as in his stele of Samal, as beasts crouching at his feet, with rings in their lips. His religiosity, amounting almost to dependence upon the priesthood and their oracles, is another marked and not altogether favorable trait of character. It is not a mere chance that the largest number of oracle texts of the temples of Ishtar and Shamash come from his reign and relate to his affairs. "A pious man and a friend of priests from the beginning" is Tiele's estimate of him from this point of view, and it is illustrated yet more completely by his

temple-building and his restoration of the city of Babylon. But piety in Assyria was not far removed from superstition, and the facts suggest that this was not absent from the king's disposition.

246. As a statesman, Esarhaddon in many respects shows himself a worthy follower of his predecessors. The provincial system and the policy of deportation are employed by him in the reorganization of Sidon and the province of Samaria (Ezra iv. 2). His relations with vassal kings, indeed, are perhaps more uniformly successful than was the case with former rulers, and in the Kaldean and Arabian states, where he combines various districts under native rulers, he reveals distinct and admirable diplomacy. His larger foreign policy was, however, in every case inadequate, if not disastrous. In the north he stood on the defensive; but under such conditions mere defence was worse than useless. His conquest of Egypt Was brilliant, yet in the end it weakened more than it strengthened the empire. Our larger knowledge of his organization of Egypt makes it clear that he intended to incorporate it into the state by setting up an administrative system, in part directly, in part indirectly, related to the central government. The system failed completely, and the drain on the imperial resources was severe.

247. His internal policy is revealed in his splendid building operations that culminated in the new Babylon. In this direction no king had approached the lavish outlay of treasure which these enterprises must have required. That this treasure was available was due to the resources laid up by Sennacherib in his years of peace, and it is a question whether their dissipation in such operations was wise. No doubt can rest upon the political inexpediency of the rebuilding of Babylon. It revived at once the Kaldean and Elamite problems, as well as the most perplexing problem of all, that of Babylon itself. It led directly to that act which even the most ardent admirers of Esarhaddon concede to have been "an act of folly" and "a colossal failure," — the division of the empire between two rulers, the king of Assyria and the king of Babylon. Sennacherib may have been violent, ruthless, and short-sighted. He was not so witless as his son, who, while he added Egypt to the empire, gave the state, by his deliberately adopted policy of decentralization, a start upon the downward road at the end of which lay sudden and complete destruction.

VIII. THE LAST DAYS OF SPLENDOR ASHURBANIPAL. 668-626 B. C.

248. UPON the death of Esarhaddon the arrangements made by him for the succession were smoothly and promptly carried out; the empire passed to Ashurbanipal, while his brother Shamashshumukin became king in Babylon. The queen mother, Naqia, who had already acted as regent in the absence of her son, issued a proclamation calling for obedience to these, the legally constituted rulers. For Shamashshumukin, however, a further ceremonial was requisite. He must, according to precedent, "take the hands of Bel" in the city of Babylon. But the images of the gods of Babylon, removed to Assur at the time of the destruction of Babylon, had never been returned to the reconstructed capital. At the command of the sun-god, Ashurbanipal ordered their return to their temples, and with stately ceremonial the coronation of the new king of Babylon proceeded in the ancient fashion intermitted for more than half a century. All seemed to promise well for the peace and prosperity of the state. The brothers were well disposed toward each other, and proceeded to the tasks which lay before them, the king of Babylon to continue the rebuilding of his city and to revive its industrial activities, the Assyrian ruler to guard and extend the boundaries of the empire.

249. The affairs of Egypt were the first to require the attention of Ashurbanipal. Esarhaddon's

death, while on the march to Egypt to drive back a new invasion of Taharqa, apparently had not caused a more than temporary delay of the expedition. The presence of an army in the western provinces, indeed, at the time of a change of rulers in Assyria was desirable for holding disaffected peoples to their allegiance. The general of the forces seems to have improved the moment to obtain renewal of homage and gifts, as well as a substantial contingent of troops, from the twenty-two vassal kings of the states already mentioned by Esarhaddon as subject to him (sect. 241). The only new royal names in the list of Ashurbanipal are Iakinlu of Arvad and Amminadbi of Ammon. Manasseh king of Judah again appears there, as also Baal of Tyre, who had evidently submitted so far as nominally to recognize Assyrian supremacy. The Ethiopian king was already in Memphis, and his troops met the Assyrians somewhere between that city and the border. The battle went against Taharqa, who retired to the vicinity of Thebes. Whether the Assyrians pursued him thither, as one of the several somewhat contradictory inscriptions states, is doubtful. With good reason it has been held that the Assyrians were content to renew their sway over lower Egypt only, restoring the vassal princes to their cities under oath of fidelity to Assyria, and did not attempt to advance farther up the river. In the years that followed stirring events occurred.

The princes, led by Necho, Sharruludari, and Paqruru, were discovered to be intriguing with Taharqa; their cities were severely punished, and the two chief culprits sent to Nineveh for punishment. Ashurbanipal determined to try a new policy similar to that employed for Babylon; he pardoned Necho and returned him as a kind of vassal ruler of Assyrian Egypt, sustained by Assyrian troops. The plan worked well. Taharqa was quiet till his death (666 B. C.), and his successor, Tanutamon (Assyr., Tandamani), made no move for at least three years. Then he, in consequence of divine monitions, and also invited, no doubt, by the petty princes who were jealous of Necho, marched northward. Necho and his Assyrians fought bravely, but were too few to make a successful resistance. Necho was slain, and Pisamilku (Psamtik), his son, with his troops, was driven out. In 661 B. C. — the date is attested astronomically — Ashurbanipal sent an army against the Ethiopian invader, to which the latter made but feeble opposition, retiring at last into Ethiopia, never again to return to Egypt. The Assyrian army now for the first time captured Thebes and carried away abundant spoil, returning "with full hands" to Nineveh. The administration of Egypt under Assyrian supremacy continued as before. People from Kirbit in Elam were deported thither, after Ashurbanipal's conquest of that rebellious district. Pisamilku occupied the position held by his father, Necho, sustained, as he had been, by Assyrian troops.

250. During these years, or at the close of this second campaign of 661 B. C., the affairs of the west were placed in order. Baal of Tyre, whose allegiance to Assyria varied according to Assyrian success in Egypt, had finally roused Ashurbanipal's wrath, and was shut up in his island-city so strictly that famine forced him to make terms. He sent his son, as a hostage, and his own daughter with the daughters of his brother for the king's harem, with rich gifts. The women and the gifts Ashurbanipal graciously accepted, but returned the son to his father. Iakinlu of Arvad, who had shown himself only nominally submissive hitherto, now, likewise, sent his daughter to the king, as did also Mukallu of Tabal and Sandasarme, a prince of Cilicia. Some special reason induced the Assyrian king to remove the king of Arvad and place his son Azibaal upon the throne. Tribute was laid upon all these states. It is not improbable that the difficulties which these northwestern communities were having with the Kimmerians induced their kings to seek Assyria's aid in opposing these new enemies. This is the reason assigned by Ashurbanipal for the appeal of king Gyges of Lydia, for Assyrian help. This ruler, under whom the Lydian state comes forth into the world's history, was establishing and extending his power chiefly through the employment of mercenary soldiers from Caria. The Kimmerians assailing him in fresh swarms, he was led, by the revival of Assyrian influence in Tabal and Cilicia, to send ambassadors to Ashurbanipal. Before, however, any aid was rendered, it

appears that the Kimmerian crisis had passed away, and Gyges had no intention of paying tribute to the far-off monarch on the banks of the Tigris. The latter, however, did not hesitate in his inscriptions to make the most of the appeal. The affair is notable, chiefly as showing how the world of international politics was widening toward the west, and new factors were entering to make more complex the political relations of the times.

251. The friendly relations with Elam which characterized the later years of Esarhaddon (sect. 239) gave place, soon after his death, to a renewal of hostilities. By 665 B. C. Urtaki of Elam, in conjunction with Kaldean and Aramean tribes, raided northern Babylonia and besieged Babylon. Ashurbanipal was satisfied to drive the invaders back into their own land, where in a short time Urtaki was succeeded by his brother Teumman, who attempted to kill off all members of the royal house. Sixty of them succeeded in escaping to Assyria. Teumman demanded that they be given up to him. Ashurbanipal's refusal led to another Elamite invasion which was checked by the advance of an Assyrian army to Dur Ilu and thence toward Susa, the Elamite capital. The decisive battle was fought at Tulliz on the Ula River before Susa, and resulted in an overwhelming defeat for Elam. The king and his son were killed; the army cut to pieces. The event marked, according to Billerbeck (Susa, p. 105), the end of the old kingdom of Susa. The Assyrians made Khumbanigash, son of Urtaki, king of Elam; his son, Tammaritu, became prince of Khidal, one of the royal fiefs. The division of power was evidently made with the purpose Of intensifying the dynastic conflicts in the kingdom, which hitherto had contributed more to the overthrow of the Elamite power than defeats of its armies. The punishment of the Gambulians, the Aramean tribe whose secession from Assyria had played so large a part in inducing hostilities, formed another and concluding stage of the war. Their chiefs were captured and suffered shameful deaths in Assyria (about 660 B. C.).

252. For some years affairs in Babylonia and Elam remained on a peaceful footing. The latter country had been too frightfully devastated and left too thoroughly in confusion to permit hostile movements there. In Babylonia, too, Shamashshumukin had ruled in harmony with his brother, content to administer the affairs of his city, to direct the religious ceremonial, and to enjoy the prerogatives which were the prized possession of the king of that wealthy capital and the holy seat of the great gods. In the very nature of the situation, however, contradictions existed which were bound to produce trouble. Babylon's claims to supremacy were secular as well as religious, and her nobles never relinquished their rights to supremacy over the world of nations as well as over the world of the gods. Their king, too, was an Assyrian, with the ambitions of a warrior and a statesman as well as the aspirations of a priest. Yet, in the very nature of things, Ashurbanipal was lord of the empire and the army, the protector of the peace, and conqueror of the enemies of the state, the defender of Babylon from assailants, its head in the political sphere. A clash was therefore inevitable, and it speaks well for the brotherly confidence of both rulers that for fifteen years they worked together peacefully. Nor is it possible to indicate any special reasons which brought on the conflict that in its various ramifications shook the state to its foundations. The ambition of the younger brother was doubtless intensified by the intrigues of his priestly advisers, and his pride wounded by the achievements of Ashurbanipal and the glorification of them. It appears, also, that an economic crisis, caused by a series of bad harvests, was imminent in Babylonia about this time, which may have brought things to a head. Shamashshumukin determined to declare his independence. The course of events shows how carefully he laid his plans and how wide a sweep was taken by his ambitious design, which in its fulness comprehended nothing less than the substitution of Babylon for Assyria as ruler of the world. Two main lines of activity were followed: (1) agents were employed to foment rebellion in the vassal states; (2) the treasures of the temples were freely used to engage the help of the peoples about Babylon in driving the Assyrians from Babylonia, and to raise an army of mercenaries to defend and maintain the new centre of the empire. How far these emissaries succeeded in the former work is not

certain, but Ashurbanipal found traces of their activity in the provinces of southern Babylonia, along the eastern mountains, in Syria, and Palestine and in western Arabia, while Egypt and far-off Lydia are supposed to have been tampered with by them. Northern Babylonia was already secure for Shamashshumukin, and his gold had found acceptance in Elam, Arabia, and among Kaldean and Aramean tribes. Even some Assyrian officers and garrisons had been corrupted.

253. The conspiracy was well advanced before any knowledge of it came to the surface. The prefect of Ur, who had been approached in the interests of the plot, sent word to his superior officer, the prefect of Uruk, that Shamashshumukin's envoys were abroad in that, city. The news was immediately sent to Ashurbanipal, who seems to have been taken utterly by surprise. If he had had suspicions, they had been allayed by a recent embassy of noble Babylonians who had brought to him renewed assurances of loyalty on the part of his brother. His feelings are expressed in the following words of his inscription:

At that time Shamashshumukin, the faithless brother, to whom I bad done good, and whom I had established as king of Babylon, and for whom I had made every possible kind of royal decoration, and had given him, and had gathered together soldiers, horses, and chariots, and had intrusted them to him, and had given him cities, fields, and woods, and the men dwelling in them, even more than my father had commanded — even he forgot that favor I had shown him, and he planned evil. Outwardly with his lips he spoke friendly things, while inwardly his heart plotted murder (Rm Cyl., III. 70-81; ABL, p. 107).

254. Shamashshumukin now threw off the mask and launched the rebellion (652 B. C.). He closed the gates of his fortresses and cut off the sacrifices offered on his brother's behalf before the Babylonian gods. The various kings and peoples were either summoned to his aid, or invited to throw off the Assyrian yoke. The southern Babylonians responded by besieging and overcoming Ur and Uruk. The king of Elam entered Babylonia with an army. Ashurbanipal, though taken unawares, was not disconcerted. Obtaining a favorable oracle from the moon-god, he mustered his troops and sent them against the rebels. Meanwhile his partisans in Elam also set to work. Suspicion and intrigue, however, brought to naught all assistance expected by the Babylonians from that quarter. Khumbanigash lost his throne to Tammaritu, and he, in turn, to Indabigash, who withdrew his forces from Babylonia (about 650 B. C.). Meanwhile Ashurbanipal's army had shut up the rebels in the great cities, Sippar, Kutha, and Babylon, and cleared the south of invaders, driving the Kaldeans under their leader, Nabu-bel-shume, a grandson of Mardukbaliddin, back into Elam. The three sieges lasted a year or more, and the cities yielded only when famine and pestilence had done their work. The despairing king killed himself, apparently by setting fire to his palace and throwing himself into the flames. With his death the struggle was over (648 B. C.). Wholesale vengeance was taken upon all who were implicated in the plot; the streets of the cities ran with blood. Ashurbanipal had conquered, but the problem of Babylon remained. He reorganized the government, and himself "took the hands of Bel," becoming king of Babylon under the name of Kandalanu (647 B. C.).

255. It remained to punish the associates of Shamashshumukin in the great conspiracy. Elam was the first to suffer. Ashurbanipal demanded of Indabigash the surrender of the Kaldean, Nabu-bel-shume, who had not only violated his oath, but had captured and carried away Assyrian soldiers. On the refusal of the Elamite, an Assyrian army entered Elam. Indabigash fell a victim to a palace conspiracy, and was succeeded by Khummakhaldash III., who retired before the Assyrians. They set up in his place Tammaritu (sect. 251), who had escaped and made his peace with Assyria. He, too, soon proved false to his patron and plotted to destroy all Assyrian garrisons in Elam. The plot was discovered and the king thrown into prison.

Khummakhaldash III. remained, and met the advance of the enraged Assyrians in their next campaign. They would not be restrained, but drove the Elamites back on all sides, devastated the land and encompassed Susa, which was finally taken and plundered (about 645 B. C.). The royal narrative dwells with flowing detail upon the destruction wrought upon palaces and temples, the indignities inflicted upon royal tombs and images of the gods, and the rescue and return to its shrine of the famous statue of Nana of Uruk, carried away by the Elamites sixteen hundred and thirty-five years before (sect. 63). Again Ashurbanipal demanded the surrender of the Kaldean fugitive, but the latter saved the wretched Elamite king the shame of yielding him up by falling upon the sword of his shield-bearer. Khummakhaldash himself, together with another claimant to the Elamite throne, Pa'e, finally fell into the hands of the Assyrians. Elam was thus at last subdued under the Assyrian yoke, and disappeared from the scene (about 640 B. C.).

256. The Arabians, also, felt the weight of Assyrian displeasure. Yailu, king of Aribi, who had been placed upon his throne by Esarhaddon (sect. 242), had been persuaded to throw off allegiance to Assyria. He sent a detachment to the aid of Shamashshumukin, and also began to make raids into the Syrian and Palestinian provinces. The Assyrian troops succeeded in holding him back and finally in defeating him so completely that he fled from his kingdom and, finding no refuge, was compelled to surrender. His throne went to Uaite, who, in his turn, made common Cause with the enemies of Assyria, uniting with the Kedarenes and the Nabateans, Bedouin tribes to the south and southeast of Palestine, in withholding tribute and harassing the borders of the western states. Ashurbanipal sent an expedition from Nineveh, straight across the desert, to take the Arabians in the rear. After many hardships by the way, defeating and scattering the tribes, it reached Damascus with much spoil. Then the army marched southward, clearing the border of the Bedouin and moving out into the desert to the oases of the Kedarenes and Nabateans. The chiefs were killed or captured, camels and Other spoil were gathered in such numbers that the market in Nineveh was glutted, camels bringing at auction "from a half-shekel to a shekel of silver apiece (?)." In connection with this campaign the Phoenician cities of Ushu (Tyre on the mainland) and Akko (Acre) were punished for rebellion. It is strange that other states of Palestine had not yielded to the solicitations of the king of Babylon. The Second Book of Chronicles (xxxiii. 11), indeed, tells how Manasseh, king of Judah, was taken by the captains of the host of the king of Assyria and carried in chains to Babylon. Does a reminiscence of punishment for rebellion along with Shamashshumukin linger here? Possibly, though neither the Books of Kings nor the Assyrian inscriptions refer to it. Not improbably the excess of zeal on the part of the rebellious Arabians, which led them to attack the frontiers of these Palestinian states, soon discouraged any inclination in these communities to rise against Assyria, whose armies protected them against just such fierce raids from their desert neighbors, who had withheld tribute must have soon made their peace, among them, it may be, Manasseh of Judah. It was precisely the coast cities, because they were in no danger from the Arabs, that persisted in the rebelliousness for which they now suffered.

257. The policy of his predecessors made the difficulties of Ashurbanipal, upon his northern borders, of comparatively slight moment. That policy which was followed and developed by him, consisted essentially in arraying the northern tribes against one another, and in avoiding, where possible, direct hostilities with them. Thus, friendly relations were cultivated with the kings of Urartu, Ursa (Rusa) III. and Sarduris IV., whose deputations to the Assyrian court were cordially received. The Mannai, however, continued aggressively hostile, and their king, Akhsheri, valiantly resisted an expedition sent against him. When he had been defeated he fled; a rising of his people against him followed in which he was slain; his son, Ualli, was placed by Ashurbanipal upon the throne as a vassal king. Other chieftains of the Medes and Sakhi, and Andaria, a rebellious prince of the Lubdi, were likewise subdued. In the far

northwest Gyges of Lydia (sect. 250) had fallen before a renewed attack of the Kimmerians under Tugdammi, a fate in which Ashurbanipal saw the reward of defection from Assyria. His son, Ardys, renewed the request for Assyrian aid, and the forces of Tugdammi were met by the Assyrians in Cilicia, and beaten back with the loss of their king (about 645 B. C.). Thus, all along these mountain barriers, Ashurbanipal might boast that he had maintained the integrity and the glory of the Assyrian empire. He was not aware what momentous changes were in progress behind these distant mountains, what states were rounding into form, what new masses of migratory peoples were gathering to hurl themselves upon the plains and shatter the huge fabric of the Assyrian state.

258. By the year 640 B. C. the campaigns of Ashurbanipal were over. The empire was at peace. Its fame and splendor had never seemed so great, nor, in reality, had they ever been so impressive. The king, like his predecessors, sought the welfare of his country, and thus bears witness to its prosperity under his rule:

From the time that Ashur, Sin, Shamash, Adad, Bel, Nabu, Ishtar of Nineveh, Queen Of Kidmuri, Ishtar of Arbela, Ninib, Nergal, and Nusku graciously established me upon the throne of my father, Adad has let loose his showers, and Ea has opened up his springs; the grain has grown to a height of five yards, the ears have been five-sixths of a yard long, the produce of the land — the increase of Nisaba — has been abundant, the land has constantly yielded heavily, the fruit trees have borne fruit richly, and the cattle have done well in bearing. During my reign plenty abounded; during my years abundance prevailed (Rassam Cyl. I. 42 ff.).

259. Ashurbanipal, too, was a builder. Temples in Nineveh, Arbela, and Tarbish, in Babylon, Borsippa, Sippar, Nippur, and Uruk were embellished or rebuilt by him. Nineveh owed almost as much to him as to his grandfather Sennacherib. He repaired and enlarged its defences, and reared on the northern part of the terrace, upon the site of the harem built by Sennacherib, a palace of remarkable beauty. In form this palace did not differ from other similar structures, but it was adorned with an extraordinary variety and richness of ornamentation, and with sculptures surpassing the achievements of all previous artists. Sennacherib had led the way, but the sculptors of Ashurbanipal improved upon the art of the former day in the elaboration of the scenes depicted, the delicacy and refinement of details, and the freedom and vigor of the treatment. For some of these excellences, particularly the breadth and fulness of the battle scenes, it has been said that the new knowledge gained of Egyptian mural art was responsible. But in the hunting sculptures and the representations of animals, the Assyrian artist of Ashurbanipal's time has attained the highest range of original and effective delineation that is offered by antiquity. The reliefs of the wounded lioness, of the two demonic creatures about to clinch, and of a dozen other figures represented in the hunting scenes, are instinct with life and power; they belong to the permanent æsthetic treasures of mankind.

260. Within the palace was, also, the remarkable library which has made this king's name famous among modern scholars. Whether it was founded upon the nucleus of the royal library which Sennacherib had gathered in Nineveh, or was an original collection of Ashurbanipal, is uncertain, but in size and importance it surpasses all other Assyrian collections at present known. Tens of thousands of clay tablets, systematically arranged on shelves for easy consultation, contained, besides official despatches and other archives, the choicest religious, historical, and scientific literature of the Babylonio-Assyrian world. Under the inspiration of the king's literary zeal, scribes copied and translated the ancient sacred classics of primitive Babylonia for this library, so that, from its remains, can be reconstructed, not merely the details of the government and administration of the Assyria of his time, but the life and thought of the far distant Babylonian world. It is not surprising, then, that the inscriptions of

this king, produced in such an atmosphere, are superior to all others in literary character. The narratives are full and free; the descriptions graphic and spirited, with a Sense for stylistic excellence which reveals a well-trained and original literary quality in the writers of the court. The impulse had been felt in the time of Sennacherib (sect. 231), and was gained, no doubt, from the new literary reinforcements which Nineveh received from Babylon at the time of the destruction of that ancient city. After two generations this school of writers had attained the high excellence which these inscriptions disclose.

261. It is evident that the king himself was personally interested in this higher side of the life which appears in the art and literature of his day. He has left a charming picture of his early years, how, in the harem, which he afterwards transformed into a splendid palace, he acquired the wisdom of Nabu, learned all the knowledge of writing of all the scribes, as many as there were, and learned how to shoot with the bow, to ride on horses and in chariots and to hold the reins" (R. Cyl. I. 31 ff.; ABL, p. 95). The latter part of this statement reveals, also, his training in the more active life characteristic of the Assyrian king. The truth of the description is vouched for by the many representations of the king's hunting adventures, the pursuit of the gazelle and the wild boar, the slaying of wild oxen and lions. His was no effeminate or indolent life. This union of culture and manly vigor is the characteristic of a strong personality.

262. As an imperial administrator, he both resembled and differed from his predecessors. He added nothing to the methods of provincial government, but was content to use the best ideas of his time. Deportation was employed by him in Egypt, where peoples from Kirbit in Elam were settled, and in Samaria, where, on the testimony of Ezra iv. 10, he (there called Osnappar) placed inhabitants of Susa, Babylonia, and other eastern peoples, with the resulting confusion of worships referred to in 2 Kings xvii. 24-41. His father's policy of uniting various districts under one vassal king (sect. 246) was continued; the most striking example of this is found in his dealing with Egypt. His armies were recruited, as before, from subject and conquered peoples. In one remarkable respect, indeed, he departed from past precedents. His armies were, rarely if ever, led by himself in person; his generals usually carried on the campaigns. This has been thought to reflect upon his personal courage and manliness. Yet it may be that the variety of demands made upon the ruler of so vast an empire decided him in favor of this reversal of immemorial policy. It is certain that in his case the change proved wise. No whisper of rebellion among his generals has been recorded. His armies, directed in their general activities from one centre, and given free scope in the matter of detail in the field, reflect credit upon the new system by their almost uniformly brilliant success. His predecessors had worn themselves out by long and severe campaigns, which only iron constitutions like that of Ashurnaçirpal or Shalmaneser II. could endure for many years. During their continuance in the field, moreover, internal administration must be neglected. Ashurbanipal was able to hold his throne for nearly half a century; the victories of peace which he won in the fields of culture and administration rivalled, if they did not surpass, the achievement of his armies.

263. Under Ashurbanipal the tendencies toward "orientalism" which appeared in his father's day reached their height. The splendor of his court was on a scale quite unequalled. It formed the model for future kings, and served as the theme for later tradition. Thus, the Greek historians have much to tell of the famous Sardanapalus, the voluptuary who lived in the harem clad in woman's garb, and whose end came in the flames of his own gorgeous palace. While Ashurbanipal was anything but such a weakling, he loved pomp and show, the pleasures of the court, and the splendor of the throne. If the daughters of kings sent to his harem were, in fact, pledges of political fidelity, it is clear that the senders knew what kind of pledges were pleasing to his royal majesty. A famous bas-relief represents him in the garden, feasting with his queen, while, hanging from one of the trees, is the head of the conquered

Teununan of Elam. In an oriental court of such a type, pomp and cruelty were not far separated.. It is not strange, therefore, that in his finely wrought sculptures and brilliantly written inscriptions are depicted scones of hideous brutality. Plunder, torture, anguish, and slaughter are dwelt upon with something of delight by the king, who sees in them the vengeance of the gods upon those that have broken their faith. The very religiousness of the royal butcher makes the shadows blacker. No Assyrian king was ever more devoted to the gods and dependent upon them. Among all the divine beings, his chief was the goddess Ishtar, the well-beloved who loved him, and who appeared to him in dreams and spoke oracles of comfort and success. As her love was the more glowing, so her hate was the more bitter and violent. Captive kings were caged like dogs and exposed " at the entrance of Temple street" in Nineveh. No more thrilling and instructive picture of the union of religion and personal glorification can be found than that given by the king in the supreme moment of his proud reign when, all his wars victoriously accomplished, he took the four kings, Tammaritu, Pa'e, Khummakhaldash, and Uaite, and harnessed them to his chariot. Then, to use his own words, " they drew it beneath me to the gate of the temple " of Ishtar of Nineveh. " Because Ashur, Sin, Shamash, Adad, Bel, Nabu, Ishtar of Nineveh, Queen of Kidmuri, Ishtar of Arbela, Ninib, Nergal, and Nusku had subjected to my yoke those who were unsubmissive, and with might and power had placed me over my enemies, I threw myself upon my face and exalted their deity, and praised their power in the midst of my hosts " (R. Cyl. X. 31 ff.).

IX.THE FALL OF ASSYRIA. 626-606 B.C.

264. ABOUT the year 640 B. C. all records of the reign of Ashurbanipal cease. That he remained on the throne for yet fourteen years is evident from the Ptolemaic canon, which gives twenty-two years to the reign of Kineladanos (Kandalanu, sect. 254) over Babylon, that is, 648-626 B. C. This silence is properly interpreted as due in part to the tranquillity of these years and in part to the storm and stress which fell upon the state as they were coming to their close. While the victories of the past century had placed Assyria at the height of its glory and had extended its bounds to regions hitherto unsubdued, these achievements and acquisitions proved, in the end, to weaken its power and gave to new enemies the vantage-points for its ultimate overthrow. Egypt, the scene of hard fighting and splendid conquest, was already practically independent. Psamtik, its vassal king, had taken advantage of the Elamite and Babylonian troubles to withhold tribute, and, by an alliance with Gyges of Lydia, another recreant, had obtained Carian mercenaries to overthrow his Egyptian opponents and maintain his independence against his Assyrian Overlord. He is the founder of the twenty-sixth dynasty. Elsewhere, also, though in a different fashion, the same results were preparing.

As has already been remarked, the incessant assaults upon the Median tribes of the east were steadily moulding them into a unity of national life, which, once reached, could not be restrained, and which, in- spired equally with hatred of its Assyrian enemy and the sentiment of nationality, under proper leadership was to prove a dangerous antagonist. The breaking down of the vigorous nations of Urartu on the north and of Elam on the southeast not only cost Assyria heavily in men and treasure, but also made it easier for the peoples who were advancing from the north and east to grapple freshly and hand to hand with her before time had been given for recuperation. Indeed, these conquered territories could not be held by the Assyrians. As Egypt, so Elam, once devastated and made harmless, was practically abandoned; within a few years Persian tribes entered and took up the old feud with Assyria. Thus, instead of peace and prosperity within the broad reaches of the immense empire, as the outcome of the tremendous energy of the century, the Assyrian kings found themselves confronted with yet more serious and threatening difficulties, and at a moment when the state was least able to grapple with them.

265. The two sons of Ashurbanipal followed him in the kingdom. The one, by name Ashur-etil-ili, has left memorials of building activity at Kalkhi, where he reconstructed the temple of Nabu (sect. 176). The remains of his palace bare and petty in comparison with the structures of his predecessors, are found upon the same terrace and speak significantly of his limitations. His brother, Sinsharishkun, succeeded, and has the unenviable reputation of being the last Assyrian king. In a broken cylinder inscription he speaks in the swelling language of his great ancestors, of the gifts of the gods and their choice of him as the ruler of the world. It is only an empty echo of the past. Before his reign was over (608-607 B. C.) Necho II. of Egypt, son of Psamtik, had entered Palestine with an army and, after defeating Josiah of Judah at Megiddo (?), had marched into Syria and occupied it as far as the Euphrates, while Assyria, already in the throes of death, made no resistance. But, in Babylonia, Sinsharishkun had shown a vigor worthy of better days in the attempt to maintain his supremacy. Business documents from Babylonia, one from Nippur dated in the fourth year of Ashuretilili, and another from Uruk of the seventh year of his successor, indicate that each was recognized as ruler over that region. Their authority over Babylon itself was hardly more than nominal, however, for already, probably on the death of their father (626 B. C.), according to the Ptolemaic canon a certain Nabu-paluçur had become king of that city. Another tablet from Nippur is dated in the first year of an Assyrian king, Sin-shum-lisir, but of him and his place in the history of this troubled age nothing is known.

266. In tracing the details of these confused years, the student is dependent on three sources of knowledge, all imperfect and unsatisfactory. There is, first, what may be called contemporary testimony, limited to the indefinite utterances of the Hebrew prophet, Nahum, and to statements of the Babylonian king, Nabuna'id, who lived three quarters of a century. later; second, the Babylonian tradition, preserved in the fragments of Berosus found in other ancient writers (sect. 37); third, Herodotus and the other Greek historians who represent, in the full and picturesque, often fantastic, details of their narratives, the Medo-Persian tradition. From all of them together only approximate certainty on the most general features can be reached, and the opportunity for conjectural hypothesis is large.

267. The Medo-Persian tradition as represented by Herodotus lays emphasis on the part taken by the Medes. According to him Deioces, the founder of the Median kingdom, about the beginning of the seventh century, was followed by his son, Phraortes, who attacked and subdued the Persians. Not satisfied with this success, Phraortes engaged in war with Assyria, now shorn of its allies. The Assyrians, however, defeated him; he lost his life in the decisive battle. His son, Cyaxares, reorganized the Median army and proceeded against Nineveh to avenge his father. The Assyrian army had been defeated and Nineveh was besieged, when the Scythians, led by Madyes, fell upon Media, compelled the raising of the siege, and defeated and overcame Cyaxares. They then overran all western Asia as far as the borders of Egypt, whence, by gifts and prayers, they were induced by Psamtik to retire. Their dominion lasted twenty-eight years. Cyaxares, however, succeeded in recovering his kingdom, by slaying the Scythian leaders assembled at a banquet. He then took Nineveh and brought the Assyrian state to an end.

268. In the Babylonian tradition, Sardanapalus (Ashurbanipal) is succeeded by Saracus (Sinsharishkun ?). Hearing that an army like a swarm of locusts was advancing from the sea, he sent Busalossorus (Nabupaluçur?), his general, to Babylon. The latter, however, allied himself with the Medes by marrying his son, Nebuchadrezzar, to the daughter of the Median prince, Ashdakos, and advanced against Nineveh. Saracus, on hearing of the rebellion of his vassal and the contemplated attack, set fire to his own capital and perished in the flames. In

another form of the story, which seems to combine elements of both traditions, it is said that the Babylonian chief united with the Median in a rebellion against Sardanapalus and shut him up in Nineveh three years. In the third year the Tigris swept away part of the walls of the city, and the king, in despair, heaped up the treasures of his palace upon a funeral pyre, four hundred feet high, and offered himself to death in the fire, together with his wives.

269. The inscriptions of Nabupaluçur contain no reference to his relations to Assyria, beyond his claim to be king of Babylon and to have conquered the Shubari, a people of North Mesopotamia (sect. 143). The stele of Nabuna'id (ABL, p. 158), however, set up about 550 B. C., while it offers difficulties of its own, throws a welcome light upon the exaggerations and confusions in the traditions. It declares that Nabupaluçur found a helper in the "king Umman-manda," who "ruined the temples of the gods of Assyria" "and the cities on the border of Akkad which were hostile to the king of Akkad and had not come to his help," and "laid waste their sanctuaries." Both traditions, therefore, contain elements of truth. The Babylonians were at war with Assyria and in alliance with another people in this war; yet not the Babylonians, but this other people, actually overthrew Assyria. Whether this people, whom the royal chronicler calls the Ummanmanda, is to be identified with the Medes, or was one of the Scythian hordes of which Herodotus writes, is uncertain. So long as this is undetermined, an important part of the historical situation cannot be cleared up. What is tolerably plain, however, is that, when Nabupaluçur set himself up as king in Babylon, the Assyrian rulers sought to maintain their power there and succeeded in bringing the Babylonian usurper into straits. A happy alliance with the people of the eastern mountains, whether Medes under Cyaxares, as is, indeed, most probable, or Scythians, delivered him from his difficulties and opened the war which closed with the destruction of Nineveh and the disappearance of the Assyrian monarchy. The vicissitudes of the struggle, the length and details of the siege, and the fate of the last Assyrian king may well have lived on in the Median and Babylonian traditions, and in their essential features be preserved in the narratives of Herodotus and Berosus. In the series of references of the prophet Nahum to the defences and dangers of the city of Nineveh, have properly been thought to lie the observations of an eyewitness of the splendors of that mighty capital. His predictions of its overthrow and particularly of the one soon to come, "that dasheth in pieces" (Nah. ii. 1), may have had their occasion in his own experiences upon Assyrian soil during these troubled years. A gruesome memorial of the assault is a fractured skull, preserved in the British Museum, "supposed to have belonged to the soldier who Was on guard in the palace of the king" (BMG, p. 102). The date of the capture of the capital, the final blow which crushed Assyria, while not exactly determined, is probably 606 B. C. Scarcely twenty years after the close of the brilliant reign of Ashurbanipal the empire had disappeared.

270. Assyria's sudden collapse is so startling and unexpected as properly to cause surprise and demand investigation. The series of events which culminated in the catastrophe and gave occasion for this fall were, it is true, such as could not have been prepared for in advance and they would have sorely strained the resisting power of any state. Yet evidently the causes for Assyria's disappearance before this combined onslaught of her enemies must lie deeper. The problem involves a consideration of the elements and forces which made this monarchy so great and enabled it to attain so wide and magnificent an empire. Attention has already been called to the conditions Of soil and climate in which a population hardy, vigorous, and warlike would be nourished. This people was from the first environed by adverse forces that called forth its aggressive energies. The wild beasts of the upper Tigris and the rude tribes of the mountains must be held in check, while a hard living was wrung from the ungracious soil. The effect was to give to the nation a peculiarly warlike character, and to weld the comparatively small population into unity Of spirit and action. Leaders were demanded and produced to whom large initiative was given, and in whom the spirit of conquest was supreme, — a spirit

to which religion and culture might contribute energy, but which they could not dominate.

271. To this people, however, from the beginning was given a higher ideal than mere brutal warfare. The relation of Assyria to Babylon, unique in the history of mankind, while it gave an outlet to Assyria's military activity, infused into her heart a patriotic purpose to deliver the mother country from enemies, and stirred a lofty sentiment of reverence for the culture and civilization there achieved. So deep, indeed, was this sentiment, that the Assyrian adopted in its entirety the culture of Babylonia, its language, its art, the essentials of its religion, and manifested little or no desire to improve upon them. This procedure, on the other hand, contributed immeasurably to the successful achievement of the military ideal which lay deep in the Assyrian heart. Most great nations must work out their own civilization with constant toil and distinct sacrifice of energy. But Assyria, inheriting and appropriating the culture of Babylon, had the residue of strength to give to the work of conquest and political administration. She had an immense start in the race for supremacy; no wonder that the race was so splendidly won.

272. Yet Assyria's weakness lay in the very elements of her strength. The early unity of national life led to pride of race and blood which permitted no admixture and, as revealed in Assyrian monumental portraits, resulted in far purer Semitism than was the case with the Babylonians. But purity of blood, in course of time, enfeebles a people. The Assyrian was no exception. The defects essential to a military state were equally manifest. The exhausting campaigns, the draft upon the population, the neglect of agricultural development which is the economic basis of a nation's existence and for which industry or commerce cannot compensate, least of all the spoils of aggressive warfare, the supremacy of great landowners, and the corresponding disappearance of free peasants, the employment of mercenaries and all that follows in its train, — these things, inseparable from a military régime, undermined Assyria's vitality and grew more and more dangerous as the state enlarged. These weaknesses might have been less pronounced had Assyria been able to work out original and fruitful methods of social and civil progress. But, as has been just noted, her civilization, because it was imitative, set free more energy to devote to conquest; hence her achievements only emphasized her inner emptiness. No great distinctively Assyrian poetry, or architecture, or ideals of life and religion ever came into being. The nation stood for none of these things. Living on a past not its own, it could feel no quickening of the inner life. No contribution to the higher ranges of human thought was possible. Moreover, in its administrative activity, one central thing was lacking, — the ability to organize conquered peoples in a way to unite them vitally to the central government. They yielded and lay passive in the grasp of the mailed fist, but no national spirit thrilled through the mass and made it alive. Assyrian pride of race among other things stood in the way of union. Thus in some measure may be understood how the Assyrian monarchy so suddenly fell at the height of its glory, and so utterly disappeared that, as has often been observed, when Xenophon and his Greeks passed by the site of Nineveh some two hundred years later, they did not so much as know that any such capital had ever existed there. The monarchy had stood in proud isolation, ruling its empire from its palaces on the Tigris; with its passing, the great fabric which it reared was neither shattered nor shaken, since between the Assyrian monarchy and the Assyrian empire no vital connection existed. Hence, when the one disappeared, the other passed under the sway of Babylon. In view of the absolutism and tyranny of the monarchy the outburst of hate and exultation at Assyria's overthrow is not surprising. It is voiced most clearly by the prophets of that petty vassal state upon the Judean hills, the history of which is at the same time the wisest commentary upon the career of its haughty and tyrannical master and his severest condemnation.

273. Yet Assyria's contribution to world-history was real and indispensable. Its rulers supplied, for the first time, the realization of an ideal which has ever attracted the world's

leaders, — the unification of peoples in a world-empire, the dominance of one lord, one authority, over all men. In this achievement it worked out the beginnings, necessarily crude and imperfect, of political organization on a large scale. The institutions, forms of government, methods of administration that were devised by its statesmen, formed the basis on which later world-rulers built solider structures. In this empire thus unified, it distributed the elements of civilization, the most fruitful civilization of that day, although not its own. Along the roads under its control trade and commerce peacefully advanced from east to west, and, with these, went art and culture to Asia Minor and to Greece. Even its wars, cruel as they were, served the interests of civilization, in that they broke down and annihilated the various petty and endlessly contending nationalities of western Asia, welding all into a rude sort of unity, which prepared the way for the next onward movement in the world's history. A true symbol of Assyria is offered by that most striking form taken by its art, — the colossal figure standing at the entrance of the royal palaces, a human head upon a bull's trunk; from its shoulders spring the wings of an eagle, but its hinder parts seen still struggling in vain to escape from the massive block of alabaster in which the sculptor has confined them forever.

PART IV. THE NEW BABYLONIAN (OR KALDEAN) EMPIRE

I. THE HEIRS OF ASSYRIA

274. THE two peoples, whose union had accomplished the overthrow of Assyria, had no difficulty about the division of the spoils. The Manda (Medes) were a mountain folk, with problems of organization and aspirations to conquest as yet limited to the regions east and north of the Tigris. Their king, whom the Medo-Persian tradition (sect. 267) names Cyaxares, extended his sway southward over Elam and to the north and northwest to the borders of Asia Minor, where he came into conflict with the kingdom of Lydia. A decisive battle for supremacy was averted only by an eclipse (585 B. C.), and subsequent negotiations temporarily fixed the boundary between the two kingdoms at the river Halys. Cyaxares seems to have been at once a successful warrior and a wise administrator, the true founder of a firm nationality among the widespread and restless peoples of this region. During his lifetime peace between him and the rulers of the kingdom on the Euphrates was unbroken, sealed as it had been by the marriage of his daughter to the son of Nabupaluçur.

275. It was natural that the provinces of Assyria to the west and south of the Tigris and the mountain wall as far as the Mediterranean should fall to the king of Babylon. Various districts of Babylonia seem to have been held by the Assyrians for a time before the fall of Nineveh (sect. 265), but thereafter they were united under Babylonian rule with out a struggle. This fact, coupled with the tradition of the army from the sea which he was sent to oppose (sect. 268), but with which, it appears, he made common cause, suggests that Nabupaluçur was a Kaldean, and that with him these tribes, so long struggling with Assyria for the supremacy over Babylon, had at last attained their goal. Such, also, was the Opinion of the Jewish writers, who call the king and his armies "Chaldean." Hence the new empire may be called the Kaldean Empire. Yet during the past centuries of contact, so intermingled in blood and united in common interests had Kaldeans and Babylonians become, that the empire may with equal propriety be called the New Babylonian Empire. For its history the chief sources available are the Greek writers of a later age. Its royal inscriptions, so far as discovered, are occupied more with the buildings restored by the kings than with the wars waged by them; with slight exceptions, they are silent as to relations with the world without. That the Greek historians were not always accurate is convincingly proved in some crucial instances (sect. 312), and hence the modern Student of the period, who is dependent so largely upon them, treads often on uncertain ground Happily, the contemporaneous accounts of the Hebrew writers, prophets and historians, throw much welcome light on some important details of foreign affairs.

276. Although Nabupaluçur was king twenty-one years (626-605 B. C.), it was not until the later period of his reign that he became active outside the limits of his capital. The alliance with the Manda (Medes) and the beginning of active operations against Nineveh could hardly have been previous to 610 B. C. The few inscriptions that are known to be his, describe his works of peace, the rebuilding of Etemenanki, the temple tower of Babylon, the reopening of the canal at Sippar, and the rearing there of a temple to the Belit, or "mistress of Sippar." One inscription speaks vaguely of the destruction of his enemies, and refers particularly to the overthrow of the Shubari and the turning of "their land into mounds and plough-land." This would indicate a campaign in northern Mesopotamia, and, were it not for the statement of Nabuna'id (Nabonidus) that the Babylonian king had nothing to do with the destruction of the temples of Assyria, might reasonably be regarded as a reference to the final expedition in which Nineveh fell. In fact, however, it suggests that while the siege of Nineveh was going on, the army of Nabupaluçur, under his son Nabukudurriuçur (Nebuchadrezzar), was operating in upper Mesopotamia on the Euphrates. The whole region was in confusion; wandering bands of

mountaineers were pillaging the towns; Haran's famous temple of the moon-god was ruined by such a raid. The army of Necho II. of Egypt (sect. 265) was also threatening the fords of the river, and, having already taken possession of Syria, was prepared to demand a still greater share of the spoils of Nineveh. Nebuchadrezzar, after clearing the country east of the river, crossed it and met the Egyptians on Syrian soil at the famous city of Karkhemish in 605 B. C. (Jer. xlvi. 2). Necho was thoroughly beaten and fled hastily southward, followed by the Kaldean army. The vassal kings paid their homage to the new conqueror. Among them was Jehoiakim of Judah (2 Kings xxiv. 1). Nebuchadrezzar, at the border of Egypt, received news of the death of his father. Fearing difficulties regarding his accession, he made a treaty with Necho by which the latter relinquished his claims to Palestine and Syria, and at once marched rapidly across the desert to Babylon. At Babylon he seems to have found all things in quiet, and ascended the throne at the close of 605 B. C. The heritage of Assyria, so far as it fell to the Babylonian heir, had been secured, with the exception of Egypt, and the new king, while ruling over a region far less extensive than that of the great Assyrian monarchs, possessed a territory that in size, position, and resources still deserved to be called an empire.

II.NEBUCHADREZZAR AND HIS SUCCESSORS

277. THE exact reason for Nebuchadrezzar's haste in returning to Babylon to secure the throne may not be easy to name, but the fear of trouble which such an action suggests was prophetic. A curious passage from the description of the ceremonial at the rebuilding of the Marduk temple in Babylon, found in an inscription of Nabupaluçur, may throw some light upon the situation:

Unto Marduk, my lord, I bowed my neck; I arrayed myself in my gown, the robe of my royalty. Bricks and mortar I carried on my head, a dupshikku of gold and silver I wore; and Nebuchadrezzar, the first-born, the chief son, beloved of my heart, I caused to carry mortar mixed with wine, oil, and (other) products along with my workmen. Nabu-shum-lisher, his talimu, the offspring of my own flesh, the junior, my darling, I ordered to take a basket and spade (?); a dupshikku of gold and silver I placed (on him). Unto Marduk, my lord, as a gift, I dedicated him (II. 59–III. 18; see ABL, p. 132).

278. The struggle of two brothers for their father's throne has already appeared in Assyrian history. In this case the younger seems, from this passage, to have been intended by his father for a special post in the kingdom; the consecration to Marduk indicated, probably, his elevation to the priesthood and, in connection with the epithet talimu, suggests to Winckler (AOF, II. ii. pp. 193 ff.) an appointment as king of Babylon, while the elder brother was to be ruler of the empire and the suzerain. Thus the old problem of Babylonian prerogative reappeared under the Kaldeans. While the fully developed theory, as held by Winckler (l. c.), of a division between the hierarchy and the Kaldean rulers that runs all through the history of this empire and finally causes its ruin, is improbable, the existence of intrigue and the danger of dynastic troubles are obvious. How to be king of Babylon in all the ancient religious meaning of that term and at the same time to harmonize the demands of this position with the administration of the greater state, remained, to the end, the standing problem of the Mesopotamian dynasties. Nebuchadrezzar, however, by the promptness of his appearance on the scene and through the fidelity of his father's counsellors, overcame whatever opposition may have existed, and in his long reign (605-562 B. C.) maintained his supreme position with power undisturbed by revolt and splendor undimmed by rivalry.

279. If the Kaldean empire was of modest proportions in comparison with that of Assyria, it

had the advantage of relief from the wearisome and costly wars with mountain peoples. The absorption of all the northern and eastern Assyrian provinces by the Manda (Medes), and the firm alliance between them and the Kaldean king, left him free to take possession of the more compact and tractable districts which fell to him and to organize their administration. How this was done is not very clear, except as it may be inferred from the details of his relations to the single kingdom of Judah, as preserved in the Old Testament writings. Nebuchadrezzar himself has left no documents of value that bear upon this side of his activity. But the long and instructive biblical story of Judah's fortunes, involved, as they were, with the fate of neighboring peoples, reveals with sufficient fulness the king's modes of procedure and ideals of administration, as well as the problems and difficulties that he was compelled to meet. The study of it is essential to the understanding of Babylonian history. Unfortunately the narratives are not free from confusion and contradictions, the special investigation of which belongs to the student of Jewish rather than of Babylonian history. In general, Egypt was the troublesome factor in this region. The twenty-sixth dynasty had succeeded in reorganizing the Nile principalities into something like unity, and in so adjusting the demands of the various classes as to occupy a firm seat at the head of affairs. Accordingly, it proceeded to reassert its old pre-eminence in western Asia. After Necho's conclusive defeat at Karkhemish, he did not, however, make a new attempt in force upon Palestine (2 Kings xxiv. 7), but preferred to use intrigue to induce the communities there to rebel. Jehoiakim may, in the beginning, have stood by his Egyptian suzerain and suffered punishment from Nebuchadrezzar's army on its first advance (2 Chron. xxxvi. 6 f.); but after his submission he remained faithful to Babylon for three years (2 Kings xxiv. 1), till 601 B. C. At last the situation became intolerable. Palestine was seething with elements of revolution. The Kaldean army had been withdrawn. Bedouin were raiding the border communities, and these, in turn, were harrying the frontiers of Judah (2 Kings xxiv. 2). The Kedarenes were pouring into Syria from the desert at the same time (Jer. xlix. 28), — the whole movement being the result of the removal of Assyrian pressure, which, for the last century, had presented an unyielding barrier to the advance of this last wave of Arabian migration. So Jehoiakim renounced his allegiance. For a year or more he was left undisturbed, until Nebuchadrezzar apparently was forced to send an army to restore his own authority throughout the western border. Jerusalem closed its gates and was besieged. Meanwhile Jehoiakim died, and his son Jehoiachin succeeded to the throne. Nebuchadrezzar had followed his army in order to settle the affairs of the west, and, when he appeared before Jerusalem, Jehoiachin gave himself up to his overlord (597 B. C.). The kingdom was punished by the deportation of the king, his court and from nine to ten thousand of the citizens. Jehoiachin's uncle was appointed king under the name of Zedekiah, and sworn to faithfulness to Babylon. During the same campaign it is probable that the Bedouin were driven back and the other disturbances upon the border quieted. The captured king was imprisoned in Babylon, and his people were settled in central Babylonia near Nippur on the Khebar canal.

280. But quiet had been only temporarily restored. Zedekiah found his people hard to restrain. The states on the east, Ammon, Moab, and Edom, were in ferment, and Judah, if faithful to its suzerain, was in danger of constant inroads from that quarter. Their ambassadors appeared at his court, and at the same time emissaries from Tyre and Sidon were present (Jer. xxvii. 3) to urge common cause against Nebuchadrezzar. Twice, apparently, it was necessary for Zedekiah to explain matters at Babylon, once by sending ambassadors (Jer. xxix. 3), and once by appearing in person before the king (Jer. li. 59). The deported Jews in Babylonia were also intriguing in the interests of rebellion, and even the burning alive of two of the most outspoken of their leaders, by the order of Nebuchadrezzar, could not restrain them. Finally, Pharaoh Hophra, who had succeeded Psamtik II., son of Necho, in 589 B.C. threw himself vigorously into the cause of the conspirators and Zedekiah joined them (588 B. C.). Nebuchadrezzar bestirred himself and advanced in strong force as far as Riblah on the middle Orontes. Thence he sent out a division against Judah, that overran the country and besieged the three

strongholds which held out, Azekah, Lachish, and Jerusalem (Jer. xxxiv. 7). The defence of Jerusalem was particularly desperate; only after a siege of one and a half years was it taken (586 B. C.). The usual punishments were inflicted. The king was blinded by Nebuchadrezzar's own hand; his sons and counsellors were slain, the citizens deported, the city was demolished, and the booty carried away. The people remaining in the land were left under the oversight of a Jewish noble, Gedaliah, and, when later he was slain by one of his fellow chieftains, the region was still further desolated and abandoned. Thus the old tragedy was re-enacted, and for the last time. It is true that Hophra had made a demonstration against the Kaldeans during the siege of Jerusalem that had compelled a temporary raising of the siege, but the lack of concerted action on the part of the rebels was followed by the usual disaster. Edom and Moab had already made their peace with their overlord. Ammon and Tyre do not seem to have played any active part in the struggle. Judah stood alone and perished.

281. Nebuchadrezzar seems to have proceeded against Tyre and besieged it. The siege is said to have lasted thirteen years (585-573 B. C.), after which the city came to terms, although it was not entered by the Kaldean king. The death of its king, Itobaal II., coincided with its submission. Egypt was attacked by Nebuchadrezzar in 568 B. C., at a time when Hophra had been followed by Amasis as a result of internal strife. Of the success or extent of the campaign there is no definite knowledge. It was little more than a punitive expedition, from which Egypt speedily recovered.

282. If the knowledge of Nebuchadrezzar's wars and the administration of his empire must be derived largely from others than himself, the case is different with respect to his activity in Babylonia. To this long inscriptions are devoted, and small tablets, stamps, and bricks from many famous sites add their testimony. He describes, particularly, his building operations in the city of Babylon, the fortifications, the palaces, and the temples reared by him. Utility and adornment were his guiding principles, but not without the deeper motives of piety and patriotism. In Babylonia at large, he labored at the restoration of the canal system, so important for agriculture, commerce, and defence. One canal which was restored by him, led from the Euphrates south of Hit directly to the gulf through the centre of Babylonia; another on the west of the Euphrates opened up to irrigation and agriculture the edge of the Arabian desert. The river, as it passed along before Babylon, was lined with bricks laid in bitumen, which at low water are visible to-day. The city-canals were similarly treated. Those connecting the two rivers and extending through the land between them were reopened. A system of basins, dykes, and dams guarded and guided the waters of the rivers, — works so various and colossal as to excite the admiration of the Greeks, who saw or heard of them. A system of defences was planned by the erection of a great wall in north Babylonia, stretching from the Euphrates to the Tigris; it was flanked east and west, by a series of ramparts of earth and moats filled with water, and extended southward as far as Nippur. It was called the Median wall. Restorations of temples were made in Borsippa, Sippar, Ur, Uruk, Larsam, Dilbat, and Baz. More than forty temples and shrines are mentioned in the inscriptions as receiving attention. Bricks bearing the king's name are said to have come from every site in Babylonia, from Bagdad to the mouth of the rivers. He may well stand as the greatest builder of all the kings of the Mesopotamian valley.

283. An estimate of the policy and achievements of Nebuchadrezzar, while limited by the unequal amount of information on the various phases of his activity, and subject to revision in the light of, new material, can be undertaken with a reasonable expectation of general accuracy. Tiele has called him one of the greatest rulers of antiquity (BAG, p. 454), and, when his operations in Babylonia are considered, that statement has weight and significance. A century and a half of war, in which Babylonia had been the field of battle, had reduced its cities to ruins and its fields to waste lands. Its temples had been spoiled or neglected, and its

gods, in humiliation or wrath, had abandoned their dwelling-places. Warring factions had divided up the country between them, or vied with one another in handing it over to foreign foes. The first duty of the king, who loved his people and considered the well-being and prosperity of his government, was to restore and unite. Recovery and consolidation, — these were the watchwords of public policy for the time, and these Nebuchadrezzar set himself to realize. It is no chance, then, that his inscriptions deal so uniformly with Babylonian affairs, with matters of building and canalization and religion. It has been pointed out, also, that his far-seeing policy contemplated the danger from the Medes, his present allies, and that his elaborate scheme of defences was intended to make Babylon impregnable in the conflict which he saw impending. All this was sagacious and statesmanlike.

284. In the fulfilment of this policy, the king conceived it indispensable to lay the emphasis on the pre-eminence of his capital, the city of Babylon. Here were his most extensive and costly buildings erected. For its protection the vast system of fortifications was designed. To beautify and adorn its streets and temples was his supremest desire, as the exaltation of its gods was the deepest thought of his heart. He, or his successors, even went so far as to destroy the famous temple of the elder Bel in the immemorially sacred city of Nippur, the sanctuary of the whole land, an act which has its explanation only in this purpose to glorify Marduk of Babylon (Peters, Nippur, II. p. 262). But one title is borne by him in all his inscriptions, and that is "King of Babylon;" and in them he declares, "With the exception of Babylon and Borsippa I did not adorn a single city," and "Because my heart did not love the abode of my royalty in another city, in no (other) human habitation did I build a residence for my lordship. Property, the insignia of royalty, I did not establish anywhere else" (ABL, pp. 140, 141). Reasonable question may be raised as to the wisdom of this procedure. The Assyrian kings, while they glorified Nineveh, or Kalkhi, always proclaimed themselves rulers of the state or the empire, and the title assumed was recognized to entail responsibility. But Nebuchadrezzar chose to follow the less laudable feature of the example of his predecessors, and, when the city concerned was Babylon, with the jealousies and rivalries which had gathered around it, the preference was doubtfully wise. To have developed the religious, economic, and even defensive significance of the other cities, while indicating his preference for Babylon, would have removed difficulties which his successors found insoluble.

285. The most serious modification of one's high estimate of Nebuchadrezzar must be made when his administration of his empire is examined. The fundamental principles of his policy in this field are involved in his preference of Babylonia and its capital. It is true that the following passage in his inscriptions must be given due weight:

Far-off lands, distant mountains, from the Upper Sea to the Lower Sea, steep trails, unopened paths, where motion was impeded, where there was no foothold, difficult roads, journeys without water, I traversed, and the unruly I overthrew; I bound as captives my enemies; the land I set in order and the people I made to prosper; both bad and good among the people I took under my care (?); silver, gold, costly precious stones, bronze, palm-wood, cedar-wood, all kinds of precious things, a rich abundance, the product of the mountains, the wealth of the seas, a heavy gift, a splendid present, to my city Babylon I brought (EIH, II. 13 ff.).

This, however, is the only statement of the kind to be found, and its limitations are obvious. The facts, which his dealing with Judah and the other western states reveals, lower its significance yet more. For a century Assyria had maintained its supremacy there with little or no trouble, with what success can be measured in a single instance. On good grounds it has been held that King Josiah's opposition to Necho of Egypt was inspired by his loyalty to Assyria, though that state was now at its last gasp. Its government had been severe, but it had organized and protected its vassals. But the Jewish rebellion against Nebuchadrezzar is explicable, chiefly from the neglect of the Babylonian king to look .after the subject states in the west. There is no evidence that anything but the most general supervision was exercised. Assyrian methods were servilely imitated. The punishment of Judah is a most instructive example. The Jews were deported, but no peoples were put in their place. The system of dealing with a conquered city, developed by Assyria, was employed (McCurdy, HPM, III. pp. 287 ff.), except that the rehabilitation of the wasted and spoiled district was quite overlooked, and it was practically abandoned. Thus, while Babylonia was enriched by spoils of war and captives, a vassal kingdom, paying tribute and important to the well-being of the west, was annihilated. Nor did the deportation accomplish the results which the Assyrian system contemplated. The Jews, segregated in Babylonia and left practically to themselves, preserved their national spirit and were a constant trouble to their master. On the whole, therefore, it is probable that Nebuchadrezzar was interested in the empire only as it contributed to the enrichment of the capital, and where commercial interests were not at stake, he paid little attention to his possessions outside of Babylonia. The Euphrates and the trade-routes to the sea were kept open, because Babylonian merchants demanded this, and the prosperity of the great emporium at the mouth of the rivers was involved in it. Where subject-states not industrially or commercially of the first importance made trouble, they were demolished.

286. Nebuchadrezzar was, in truth, a son of Babylonia, not of Assyria, a man of peace, not of war, a devotee of religion and culture, not of organization and administration. His strength as a world-ruler lay in his inheritance, — the alliance with the Medes made by his father and the methods of imperial organization which. Assyria had bequeathed to him. His Babylonian policy had its strong and its weak points. For the rest, he manifested the cruelty, the luxury, and the ruthless energy characteristic of the great Semitic monarchs. From this point of view, the picture of him in the Book of Daniel is, in not a few respects, strikingly accurate. His inscriptions reveal a loftiness of religious sentiment, unequalled in the royal literature of the oriental world. As a pious worshipper of Marduk and his son Nabu, he utters prayers which, though they may not be of his own composition, were sanctioned by him and bear witness to the height of religious thought and feeling reached in his day. The following is not the least remarkable of these petitions:

O eternal prince ! Lord of all being!
As for the king whom thou lovest, and
Whose name thou hast proclaimed
As was pleasing to thee,
Do thou lead aright his life,
Guide him in a straight path.
I am the prince, obedient to thee,
The creature of thy hand;
Thou hast created me, and
With dominion over all people
Thou hast intrusted me.
According to thy grace, O Lord,
Which thou dost bestow on All people,
Cause me to love thy supreme dominion,
And create in my heart
The worship of thy god-head,
And grant whatever is pleasing to thee,
Because thou hast fashioned my life.
(EIH, I. 55.)

Similar utterances justify Tiele's statement that an Israelite worshipper, by substituting Jehovah and Jerusalem for Marduk and Babylon, could take them upon his own lips. As coming from the king, they indicate a remarkable conception of sovereignty, its ideals and obligations, as well as its source in the righteous character and beneficent will of God Almighty (Jastrow, RBA, pp. 298 f.).

287. The instability of the dynasty of Nebuchadrezzar, in spite of his own vigorous and successful reign, is painfully manifest in the careers of his successors. He was followed by his son Amel Marduk (Evil-merodach), who was slain by his brother-in-law Nergal-shar-uçur (Neriglissar) after a reign of two years (562-560 B. C.). The latter ascended the throne to rule but four years (560-556 B. C.), when he was cut off, apparently, by an untimely yet not violent death. His son, Labashi Marduk (Labosoarchod), followed him as king, but, after ruling nine months (556 B. C.), was made away with by a body of conspirators who chose one of their number, Nabuna'id (Nabonidus), to be king, the last to occupy that seat as ruler of the New Babylonian Empire.

288. Nabuna'id has left an instructive commentary upon the political situation of these years in his stele, recently discovered, describing the events connected with his own accession, the character of his predecessors, and his rule of Babylonia. According to him, Amel Marduk and Labashi Marduk had failed to keep the precepts and fellow the policies of their respective fathers, Nebuchadrezzar and Nergalsharuçur, and hence fate carried them away before their time. The fathers, however, had agreed in their political policy, and this policy Nabuna'id set before himself as ruler. In essential harmony with the testimony of Nabuua'id is that of Berosus (Jos. Cont. Ap., I. 20), who describes Amel Marduk as "lawless and impious" and Labashi Marduk as "not knowing how to rule." Such characterizations of these kings, however, evidently made by their enemies, are so vague as to leave large room for hypothesis as to the particular policy they pursued. Some modern students have regarded them as adherents of the priestly party and, as such, overpowered and removed by the military or official party. For this view support has been sought in the one known specific act of Amel Marduk, the release of Jehoiachin of Judah (sect. 279) from prison and his admission to the royal table (2 Kings xxv. 27 ff.). But the motive for this act is uncertain, and the exactly opposite hypothesis is held by others. All that can be said with certainty is that, beneath the firm rule Of Nebuchadrezzar, intrigues and strifes of parties had been secretly growing the manifestation of which in the following years threw the government into confusion and threatened the collapse of the state. Had Nergalsharuçur lived longer, he might have kept affairs in order and prolonged the life of the empire, for his inscriptions indicate that he was a man Of capacity, active in the restoration of Babylonian cities and temples, quite in the spirit of Nebuchadrezzar. The reign of Nabuna'id introduces new elements into the final scene of Babylon's downfall and deserves, therefore, a separate discussion.

III.BABYLONIA UNDER THE KALDEANS

289. THE accession of the Kaldi to supremacy in Babylonia might be expected to result in the communication of new and original impulses to the somewhat stationary civilization of that ancient land. They had proved their right to exist as a people and their power both to endure hardness and to rise superior to disaster, by centuries of conflict with the mightiest organized force that had as yet appeared in the world. They had even outlived Assyria and divided her spoils, and, unhindered by opposition, were now in a position to realize their national ideals in the fairest region of the ancient world.

290. Materials exist in reasonable abundance from which to gain knowledge of the contribution made by this régime to human progress and to estimate its character. It is true that the ruins of Babylon itself have not, as yet, been so carefully investigated as to yield much information concerning the art and architecture of the city in its Kaldean prime, although this lack will, it is hoped, be supplied by the work of the German commission now excavating there (1902). But a thoroughly representative series of royal inscriptions exists, as an evidence of the literature, and vast collections of business documents, extending from the beginning to the end of the period, open up the social life of the people in all its varied aspects. The writings of the Hebrew exiles in the land and the reports of later Greek travellers and historians make additions of no little value.

291. The examination of these sources of information reveals a general result which is at first thought somewhat surprising. It discloses a life and culture which differ in no essential respects from the Babylonian civilization of the past two thousand years. The sketch of the society of 2500 B. C. (Part I. chaps. iii., iv.) stands in the main without need of alteration for the society of 500 B. C. As in the case of the Kassites (sect. 123), so in that of the Kaldi the age-long Babylonian civilization has absorbed the new elements and has moulded them into its immemorial forms. The same occupations are followed; the same institutions are preserved; the same social classes exist; the same principles of legal, political, and moral action prevail; the same forms of intercourse are maintained. There seems to be almost a conscious effort on the part of the Kaldean leaders to return to the ancient customs. So marked is this movement that the period can properly be characterized as the Renaissance of Old Babylonia. Its most picturesque exemplar is king Nabuna'id, whose archæological activities and his deep interest in them have already been referred to and will be described in the following chapter (sect. 308). Not less manifest is the same tendency in the royal literature, in which, as has been noted, not only the literary style but even the forms of the characters are modelled after the inscriptions of the time of Khammurabi. Winckler has said that an inscription of Nebuchadrezzar must have made an impression upon the Babylonians of this period corresponding to what a German of today would feel in seeing a modern work printed in gothic characters and written in middle-high-German (GBA, p. 320). An interesting historical parallel, not without significance also, is found in the Egypt of the same age which, under the Pharaohs of the twenty-sixth dynasty, reveals a return to the past of exactly similar character.

292. It remains for the student of the period to indicate in this sphere of imitation of the past the distinctive features of the new age, since no epoch can precisely reproduce the features of one long gone by. Of the various occupations followed, industry and commerce seem to have developed beyond agriculture. In the centuries of conflict in Babylonia the farmer suffered most severely, and vast areas of country were devastated. The Kaldean kings sought to remedy the difficulty by importing populations like the Jews, who were settled in the country and appear to have been put to agricultural labor. Later, in the Persian period, the fertility of the land was astonishing to the Greek Herodotus, and his testimony illustrates the outcome of the measures instituted by Nebuchadrezzar (sect. 7). But industrial pursuits and their concomitants, commercial activities, the seat of which was in the cities had grown enormously and were zealously fostered by the rulers. Of all the manufactures, the carpets, cottons, and linens of Babylon were still the most famous in the ancient world. A development of trade with the south and southwest is suggested by the building of the city of Teredon at the mouth of the Euphrates, and by the spice and incense traffic carried on through the Arabian city of Gerrha. The undisturbed possession of the Euphrates valley and of the trade-routes to the west gave impulses to larger commercial energy in that direction. It is Nebuchadrezzar who is doubtless referred to by Herodotus under the name of Nitocris, to whom is ascribed the making of the Euphrates to wind about in its course, that thus its force might be diminished and its use by the frail boats and rafts still employed for traffic facilitated. The other

improvements in canals and in the Euphrates itself, and the building of the quays, not only at Babylon but also at Bagdad and elsewhere by these kings, point to their recognition of the importance of trade and commerce, which never was so enormous as in this period. Ezekiel declares that his people had been carried away into "a land of traffic" and "set in a city of merchants" (xvii. 4), though he also adds that they were "planted in a fruitful soil" and placed "beside many waters" and "set as a willow tree" (ibid. v. 5).

293. The pre-eminence of industrial life illustrates other changes which had come over Babylonian society in this period. Social life, if it had preserved its ancient distinctions of noble and common man, was permeated by the spirit of business. Even kings and princes appear in documents describing ordinary business transactions. Nergalsharuçur borrows money to buy a house. Belshazzar, son of Nabuna'id, sells wool and takes security for the payment, as any other merchant. Indeed, it has been thought that the old aristocracy had practically disappeared, and that the merchant princes and ecclesiastical lords had taken its place. Certain families, like that of the Egibi at Babylon and the Murashu at Nippur, were prominent financiers and handed down their talents, both material and intellectual, through several generations. Gold and silver were the standards of value, and it has been calculated that the ratio between the two was from eleven, or twelve, to one. Coinage had improved, smaller portions of the precious metals being stamped as five shekel and one shekel pieces. Interest varied from twenty per cent to ten per cent.

294. Accompanying this industrial development was the transference of the bulk of the population to the cities, and chiefly to Babylon. In the capital, doubtless, the refinement and luxury of civilized society in the ancient world reached its highest point. Herodotus has an interesting picture of the Babylonian gentleman of the time:

The dress of the Babylonians is a linen tunic reaching to the feet, and above it another tunic made in wool, besides which they have a short white cloak thrown round them, and shoes of a peculiar fashion, not unlike those worn by the Bœotians. They have long hair, wear turbans on their heads, and anoint their whole body with perfumes. Every one carries a seal, and a walking stick, carved at the top into the form of an apple, a rose, a lily, an eagle, or something similar; for it is not their habit to use a stick without an ornament (Her., I. 195).

To this description may be added that of Ezekiel, who pictured "the Chaldeans portrayed with vermilion, girded with girdles upon their loins, with dyed turbans upon their heads, all of them princes to look upon" (Ezek. xxiii. 14 f.).

295. The family life continued to be the basis of social organization. Few changes are traceable, and these were in the direction of a higher standard of morals. The practice of polygamy or concubinage appears to be much restricted, and the custom of marriage by purchase was practically done away with. The wife still brought her dowry. The position of woman was still as free and as high as before. The strange statement of Herodotus as to the religious prostitution of the Babylonian women is, in itself, incredible, as well as his stories of the marriage-market (I. 196, 199). The contemporaneous documents bear quite the opposite testimony.

296. The history of the Kaldean regime is a sufficient illustration of the character of the state during this period. It differed from the earlier Babylonian organization, chiefly because the Assyrian Empire had done its work. It was more centralized; the king was less of a sacred personage and more of a warrior and administrator. Yet there appears here the return to the old-time conception of the ecclesiastical character of the ruler, inseparable from a king of Babylon, and in harmony with this renaissance spirit. That an imperial administration was

possible at all was due to the Assyrian system already in vogue in the provinces, and to an army which was chiefly composed of mercenaries gathered from the ends of the earth. Tradition has preserved the name of a certain Antimenidas, a Greek of Mitylene, who was a prominent figure among the soldiers of Nebuchadrezzar (Strabo, XIII. 2, 3). The character of the soldiery was not high. The impression made upon subject peoples is illustrated by the testimony of the Hebrew prophets. Habakkuk declares, "Their horses also are swifter than leopards, and are more fierce than the evening wolves; and their horsemen spread themselves: yea, their horsemen come from far; they fly as an eagle that hasteth to devour. They come all of them for violence; their faces are set eagerly as the east wind; and they gather captives as the sand" (Hab. i. 8, 9).

297. The glory of Babylonia, however, was in the arts of peace, and this age was not behind in the cultivation of science, æsthetics, and literature. But there is no evidence that, in this direction more than in others, was there any endeavor to outdo the past. The literary art showed, perhaps, greater elaboration of details, but there was no new thought. Its quality and influence are best estimated by the example of the one people of genius that breathed its atmosphere. Hebrew literature, of the exile and after, is in form separated by a great gulf from that of the earlier period. The peculiarities of the style of Ezekiel and of Zechariah — the artificiality of form and the grotesqueness of conception — are Babylonian. But the mechanical correctness of these writers becomes harmony and unity of presentation in such a literary artist as the author of the second part of Isaiah. "His discourse, serene, affluent, and glowing, is an image of a Babylonian landscape. As it unrolls itself, we think of fields and gardens and stately palms and bending willows and gently flowing streams, stretching away over an ample plain, and all standing cut clear in the light of a cloudless sky" (McCurdy, HPM, III. p. 420). For a fuller knowledge of the contribution of the Kaldean period to the artistic development it will be necessary to await further excavation on the site of Babylon; but already it is known that the special type of artistic adornment in the Kaldean palaces was the wall decorated in colors. Bricks enamelled in colors are among the commonest articles picked up on the mounds of Babylon. It is the walls of Nebuchadrezzar's palace to which Diodorus refers in speaking of "every kind of animal imitated according to all the rules of art both as to form and color; the whole represented the chase of various animals, the latter being more than four cubits high — in the middle Semiramis on horseback letting fly an arrow against a panther, and on one side her husband Ninus at close quarters with a lion" (Diod., II. 8, 6). This description is confirmed by the recent discovery of the throne-room of the palace with beautifully colored decorations of this character, which took the place of the bas-reliefs of Ninevite kings.

298. In the sphere of religion the Kaldean period was most active, and yet most characteristically conservative. It was the brief Indian summer of the faith, cherished through so many centuries in the temples by successive generations of zealous priests and devout worshippers. Ancient cults were revived; ruined shrines restored; old endowments renewed. Yet the ideas of the gods and of their place and prerogatives in the pantheon had changed but slightly. Mention has already been made of the preference of the kings for Marduk and Nabu (sect. 284), and of the approach to monotheism and spirituality which appears in the prayers of Nebuchadrezzar. Nabuna'id, it is thought, sought to raise Shamash, the sun-god, to the level of Marduk and Nabu, but the attempt only cost him the enmity of the priests of the capital. Everywhere priestly control made the cult the dominant element in the religion; its materialistic features, its demonology, its incantation ceremonials, and its astrology continued to be the popular elements. The condition of morals was fluctuating, affected, it is true, by noble expressions of faith and devotion such as are found in the hymns and prayers, but elevated and maintained at a worthy standard far more by the secular activities of business. True, it was a commercial and mercantile morality, but a striking testimony is borne to it by a

later writer who mentions, among the other virtues of the Babylonians, their imperturbability and their straightforwardness (Nic. of Damascus, Fr. 131), characteristics of which the Stoics were proud. The influence of the religion upon outside peoples was, however, never as potent as in this period. The international life of east and west, now so close and reciprocal, afforded the most favorable opportunity for the extension of the profound cosmological and theological ideas which, in strange and often grotesque forms, had been wrought out on Babylonian soil. The fertile and inquiring Greek mind was now brought within close range, and the reports of eastern travellers stimulated the curiosity and the thoughts of the philosophers. The Jews, too, drank in the teachings. "The finishing touches to the structure of Judaism — given on Babylonian soil — reveal the Babylonian trade-mark. Ezekiel, in many respects the most characteristic Jewish figure of the exile, is steeped in Babylonian theology and mysticism; and the profound influence of Ezekiel is recognized by modern scholarship in the religious spirit that characterizes the Jews upon the reorganization of their commonwealth" (Jastrow, RBA, pp. 696 f.).

299. This splendid renaissance of the past, which is the achievement of the Kaldi for Babylonia, has its shining example and supreme symbol in the city of Babylon. The devotion of the great Nebuchadrezzar to his capital has already been indicated (sect. 284). To present, however imperfectly, a general picture of the city as it came from the hands of its Kaldean rulers is a service due to their memory. At the same time this supreme interest is the best illustration of the limitations as well as the height of their ideals. It is possible at present, with some certainty, to connect at least two of the three great mounds on the site of the ancient city, now called Babel, Kasr, and Amran, with the special structures, palaces, temple, and gardens which are ascribed to Nebuchadrezzar, even if the many other ruin-heaps in the vicinity cannot be identified. The many royal inscriptions of the Kaldi and the descriptions of the Greek writers permit a sketch of the Babylon of that day. The city proper, the nucleus and heart of it, was that which lay along the east bank of the Euphrates and within the inner wall called Imgur Bel, which stretched in a kind of half. circle out from the river. The chief buildings within this wall were the temple and the palace. Around this inner wall there ran a second wall called Nemitti Bel, roughly parallel to it and at a considerable distance from it, constituting the defence of the larger city. Its circumference, including the river front, was about eight miles. Each of these walls had its moat. Though of about the same size as Nineveh (sect. 231), Babylon was much more thickly populated, the houses being three and four stories in height. The streets of the city ran at right angles, and all the spaces about the temple and between the walls were probably occupied with private houses or buildings for business.

300. The temple, the centre of the inner city, consisted of a complex of structures, situated upon its elevated platform and surrounded by its own wall. Most conspicuous was the ziggurat, or temple-tower of seven stages, which the king rebuilt. Of this Herodotus says: "The ascent to the top is on the outside by a path which winds round all the towers (stages). When one is about half-way up, one finds a resting-place and seats where persons are wont to sit some time on their way to the summit. On the topmost tower (stage) there is a spacious temple, and inside the temple stands a couch of unusual size richly adorned with a golden table by its side. There is no statue of any kind set up in the place." Beside the tower was the shrine of the god Marduk, E-kua, a magnificent structure whose walls glistened with gold, precious stones, and alabaster, and whose roof was of fragrant cedar of Lebanon. At the entrance was the shrine of the goddess, his spouse, and elsewhere were the sanctuaries of Nabu and other deities. Of another sacred chamber Nebuchadrezzar records that:

The shrine of the Fates, where, on Zagmuku, the beginning of the year, on the eighth and the eleventh day, the king, the god of heaven and earth, the lord of heaven, takes up his residence, where the gods of heaven and earth reverently pay obedience and stand bowed down before him; a fate of a far-distant day, as the fate of my life, they determine therein: that shrine, the shrine of royalty, the shrine of lordly power, belonging to the leader of the gods, the Prince Marduk, which a former king had constructed with silver, I decorated with shining gold and brilliant ornaments (EIH, II. 54 if).

From the door of the temple a passage led to the sacred street, A-ibur-shabu, along which the sacred ships of the gods were wont to be borne on festal days, while by the temple's side the sacred canal ran from the Euphrates eastward, bringing water for sacred uses.

301. To the north lay the palace between the canal and the inner wall. Built or renewed by Nabupaluçur, it had fallen into decay and had to be repaired by his son. For so great a king, however, it had become too small. Yet it could not be enlarged without encroaching on the sacred domains of the god. Nebuchadrezzar restored it, therefore, exactly after the old dimensions, but across the inner wall, either to the north or east, within the outer wall, he cleared a space, and within fifteen days the turrets of a splendid palace appeared, uniting the two walls and making, with its own intersecting battlements, a citadel which protected alike the outer and the inner city. Upon the furnishing of this palace were lavished all the resources of his empire. Cedar, cypress, palm, and other costly woods, gold, silver, bronze, copper, and precious stones, brick and marble from the distant mountains, were employed in its construction and adornment.

302. This palace, which was also a citadel, was but one of the many defences which were devised for the city's security. The inner and outer walls were raised and strengthened. Most imposing of all was the system of fortifications placed by Nebuchadrezzar quite outside of the walls already described. It consisted of a combination of earthworks and water-ways. A wall was built of colossal dimensions, four thousand cubits (one and one half miles?) east of Nemitti-Bel. The extremities were connected with canals or earthworks which reached to the Euphrates; it was itself protected by a fortified moat. This was the mighty work which astonished Herodotus. He gave its height as somewhat more than three hundred and seventy feet, and its width more than ninety feet. The summit was lined with battlements and guard chambers, between which on either side a space was left sufficient for a four-horse chariot to turn. The wall was pierced by an hundred brazen gates (Her., I. 178 ff.).

303. Adornment and practical utility as well as defence were in the mind of Nebuchadrezzar when he put his hand to the rebuilding of Babylon. He dug again the sacred canal and lined it with brick; he raised the sacred street, carrying it by a bridge over the canal and lifting higher the gates of the two city walls at the point where it passed through them. He built up the bank of the Euphrates with bricks, making splendid quays, which still exist, walled them in and opened gates at the points where the city streets came down to the water's edge. Later historians dwell on his magnificent hanging gardens, which rose somewhere near his palaces; they were built in lofty terraces to solace his Median queen for the absence of her beloved mountains. Across the river, in the twin city of Borsippa, he rebuilt the city wall and restored the temple tower of the god Nabu, son of Marduk. In time the two cities became more and more united. It is this double city which seems to be in the mind of Herodotus when he describes Babylon as a great square about fourteen miles on each side, the walls making a circuit of fifty-six miles and enclosing an area of two hundred square miles. While the Babylon of the Kaldi was much smaller than this, their devotion to it manifested itself in these initial works that in course of time produced the larger and more famous city. Already it contained at least two of the seven wonders of the world, and its beauty and wealth made it for a long time thereafter the chief centre of the east. "From Nebuchadrezzar to the Mongol invasion" it was well-nigh "the greatest commercial city of the world."

304. For Babylon remained, after the wreck of the Semitic domination of the East, as glorious as before and as imperious in the realm of commerce and of culture. She had succeeded to the varying and petty local powers that, in the beginnings of history, struggled with one another for a transient pre-eminence. She had laid, there and then, the foundations of the state which had endured for millenniums. She had outlasted the empire on the Tigris. She had been the despair of the statesmen of Assyria, and a decisive element in the downfall of that monarchy. She had been the pride of the Kaldean monarchs, and was at last the grave of their glory. She had given to the ancient world its laws, its literature, its religion. In the words of Professor Rawlinson: "Hers was apparently the genius which excogitated an alphabet; worked out the simpler problems of arithmetic; invented implements for measuring the lapse of time; conceived the idea of raising enormous structures with the poorest of all materials, clay; discovered the art of polishing, boring, and engraving gems; reproduced with truthfulness the outlines of human and animal forms; attained to high perfection in textile fabrics; studied with success the motions of the heavenly bodies; conceived of grammar as a science; elaborated a system of law; saw the value of an exact chronology; — in almost every branch of science made a beginning, thus rendering it comparatively easy for other nations to proceed with the superstructure. . . . It was from the east, not from Egypt, that Greece derived her architecture, her sculpture, her science, her philosophy, her mathematical knowledge, in a word, her intellectual life. And Babylon was the source to which the entire stream of eastern civilization may be traced. It is scarcely too much to say that, but for Babylon, real civilization might not even yet have dawned upon the earth" (Gt. Mon., III. pp. 75 f.).

305. Upon the people of Israel, too, Babylon left her mark. Though mistress of their state and its destroyer, she could not rule their spirits. Their prophets looked forward to her fall and rejoiced. To them, the image of all material prosperity, she was set over against that higher ideal of victorious suffering, of spiritual achievement, the triumph of which in their vision was sure. Thus pictured by them, Babylon has lived on in the imagination of Christendom as the supreme symbol of the rich, the cruel, the lustful, the enemy of saints, the Antichrist, destined to destruction. Who shall say that, thus seeing, these prophets did not behold clearly the vital weakness of that ancient civilization in her, its embodiment? With all her glory Babylon was of the earth and is fallen; Jerusalem, which is from above, abideth forever.

IV .THE FALL OF BABYLON

306. THE conspiracy which placed Nabuna'id upon the throne (555-539 B. C.) seems to have involved a transfer of emphasis in the politics of the state. Nabuna'id was not a Kaldean but a Babylonian noble, son of a prince, Nabu-balatsu-iqbi. In his long stele inscription, to which reference has already been made (sect. 288), he declares his purpose to conduct affairs after the example of Nebuchadrezzar and Nabupaluçur. In fact, his rather numerous inscriptions present him not only as a devout worshipper of the gods and a restorer of temples, but also as a vigorous and zealous defender of the imperial authority. The empire stood intact within its old limits when he came into possession of it, and in the first years of his reign he paid no little attention to the maintenance of his authority in the west. In the badly broken first column of his so-called Annals, references made to Hamath and the mountains of Amanus; in connection with military movements, indicate that he was active in Syria, and fragments of Menander suggest that in his reign dynastic troubles in Tyre led to his setting, first, Merbaal (555-552 B. C.), and then Hirom III. (551-532 B. C.), both hostages at his court, upon the Tyrian throne. The impulse to these western expeditions may have been given by the new relations to the Manda (Medes) which the last years had induced, and which may now be described in some detail.

307. During the lifetime of Nebuchadrezzar the alliance with the Manda (Medes) had remained firm, although to Cyaxares had succeeded (about 584 B. C.) his son Ishtuvegu (Astyages). The rapid changes which followed upon the death of the great Kaldean monarch, and particularly the transference of the succession from the Kaldean to the Babylonian line, in the person of Nabuna'id, seem to have been the occasion of estrangement between the two peoples. Nabuna'id asserts that in the beginning of his reign the Manda had been in possession of northern Mesopotamia and were encamped about Haran. But one Of those sudden reversals of supremacy not uncommon in the beginnings of great empires had taken place in Media. Among the communities that acknowledged the sway of Astyages was the province of Anshan in northern Elam, occupied by the Persians under their hereditary chieftains of the house of Teispes. The king of Anshan during these years, a certain Cyrus, raised a rebellion against his suzerain (about 553 B. C.) which resulted in the downfall of Astyages and the supremacy of Cyrus and the Persians (550 B. C.). During these troubles the movement of Astyages against Babylonia was given up, and Nabuna'id reports that by 553 B. C. there were no Manda about Haran. He also dwells with satisfaction upon the overthrow of Astyages by Cyrus, king of Anshan, as a divine intervention in his own favor. The way was open for him to send an expedition not only to Haran to rebuild the temple there, but to advance farther into the west. He was doubtless gratified that inner troubles were breaking up the Median Empire, as had so often been the case among the loose agglomerations of peoples in the northern mountains, and he felt that henceforth neither their friendship nor their enmity was particularly significant, little dreaming that within two decades the young conqueror would be knocking at his own gates. The career of Cyrus is one of the marvels of antiquity. His victory over his Median suzerain was not merely the substitution of one dynasty for another, nor was it followed by internecine wars in which the fresh and vigorous peoples of the north were crippled. With consummate statesmanship the young king united all elements, inspired them with a common spirit, and out of a kingdom in which tribes and peoples had been joined in loose confederation about a common overlord, he built the solid foundations of the Medo-Persian Empire.

308. The immunity from hostile complications with the Medes, enjoyed by Nabuna'id during the years that followed, he improved by pursuing those works of peace in which his prototype Nebuchadrezzar had gained such renown. With the details of such building operations his inscriptions are filled. The peculiar delight which they represent him as feeling in these works and the unique method which he adopted in the prosecution of them have led scholars to regard him as a political weakling, a cultured dilettante, an archæological virtuoso, to whom the discovery Of an ancient foundation stone was more significant than the conduct of the state or the defence of the empire. Further knowledge has proved the accusation unjust, although the facts on which it was based are evident enough. In his zeal for the reconstruction of temples he was not satisfied with clearing off the superficial rubbish of the mound, but must dig down through the successive layers of ruins, until the original foundation had been reached and the inscription of the first builder had been uncovered. Reference has already been made to the value of the data which he thus published (sect. 40) for the construction of a Babylonian chronology. A passage may be here given from an inscription, illustrative at once of his devout piety and his archæological perseverance and of its scientific value for modern scholars:

For Shamash, the judge of heaven and earth, E-babbara, his temple which is in Sippar, which Nebuchadrezzar, a former king, had rebuilt, after searching for its platform-foundation without finding it — that house he rebuilt, but in forty-five years its walls had fallen in. I became anxious and humble; I was alarmed and much troubled. When I had brought out Shamash from within it and made him take residence in another house, I pulled that house down and made search for its old platform-foundation; and I dug to a depth of eighteen cubits, and Shamash, the great lord of E-babbara, the temple, the dwelling well pleasing to him, permitted me to behold the platform-foundation of Naram Sin, the son of Sargon, which during a period of thirty-two hundred years no king among my predecessors had seen. In the month Tishrit, in a favorable month, on an auspicious day, revealed to me by Shamash and Adad in a vision, with silver, gold, costly and precious stones, products of the forest, sweet-smelling cedars, amid joy and rejoicing, I raised its brick-work — not an inch inward or outward — upon the platform-foundation of Naram Sin, the son of Sargon. I laid in rows five thousand large cedars for its roof; I set up in its doorways high doors of cedar.... . I took the hands of Shamash, my lord, and with joy and rejoicing I made him take up a residence therein well pleasing to him. I found the inscription written in the name of Naram Sin, the son of Sargon, and I did not alter it. I anointed it with oil, offered sacrifices, placed it with my inscription, and restored it to its place (Nab. Cyl. II. 47 ff.).

He claims thus to have reconstructed, besides this temple of Shamash in Sippar, that of Anunit, also in Sippar, that of Sin in Haran, the temple E-ul-bar in Agade, the tower and other shrines in Ur and the Shamash temple at Larsam.

309. It was not to be expected that in a hot-bed of intrigue such as Babylon was at this time, the various activities of Nabuna'id were pursued with a successful harmonization of all factions. With Nebuchadrezzar as example, he sought to maintain the empire, while at the same time he honored the gods; but in both respects he appears to have failed. He called himself "patron of Esagila and Ezida," temples of Marduk and Nabu in Babylon and Borsippa; he gave rich gifts to these deities; yet his rearing of temples to other gods, and especially the attention paid to Shamash, the sun-god, are thought to have arrayed against him the priests of Babylon, as though he were planning to put that deity in the place of pre-eminence given by Nebuchadrezzar to Marduk and Nabu. Nor may his hardly concealed satisfaction at the victory of Cyrus over Astyages have pleased those who remembered Nebuchadrezzar's alliance with Media. He certainly left the conqueror unmolested, if indeed, as some think, he did not give him aid in his rebellion, — a policy which, however shrewd, was not acceptable to the Kaldeans. Thus difficulties were inevitable. A hint of the situation is given in the Annals, where, beginning with the seventh year of the king (549 B. C.), it is said that he "was in Tema; the son of the king, the nobles and his soldiers in Akkad. (The king for Nisan) did not come to Babylon. Nabu did not come to Babylon; Bel was not brought forth." In other words, the usual yearly ceremonial, by which a king renewed his royal authority in "taking the hands of Bel" in Babylon, did not take place. The same omission is chronicled in effect for the eighth, ninth, tenth, and eleventh years (548-545 B. C.), and may have continued, though the breaking of the Annals at this point permits no positive statement. It is difficult to understand how he could have maintained himself as king, if this retirement to Tema and the omission Of an indispensable ceremonial had been due to his own carelessness regarding affairs of state and his absorption in his temples and books. The facts are more satisfactorily interpreted by supposing that, with his seventh year, on account of universal dissatisfaction he was forced into retirement, and the conduct of affairs assumed by his son, Bel-shar-uçur (Belshazzar), with whom began more active measures towards protecting the state from its Medo-Persian neighbors.

310. The consequences of this change of attitude towards Cyrus soon became apparent. In the year 547 B. C. he appeared with his army at the Tigris below Arbela, and seems to have taken possession of a border state, so that now the troops garrisoning the frontier cities of the Medo-Persian and Babylonian empires stood face to face. The conflict seemed imminent; but affairs in another quarter of the kingdom demanded the presence and activity of Cyrus, and a few years intervened before the final struggle took place.

311. The extraordinary success of Cyrus alarmed all the older states of the oriental world, and

they bestirred themselves to resist his progress. The initiative was taken apparently by Lydia, which, under its king, Croesus, was now the great power of Asia Minor. Both commerce and culture had brought that state into close association with the Greek cities as well as with Egypt and Babylonia. The advent of the new and aggressive Persian power was disturbing to all parties alike. Accordingly, a quadruple alliance was formed by Croesus of Lydia, Amasis of Egypt, Sparta, as leader of the Greek states, and the war party now in power at Babylon, with the evident purpose of putting a stop to the advance of Cyrus (about 547 B. C.). He accepted the challenge and marched westward against the most formidable and aggressive of his opponents, the king of Lydia, before the troops of the other leaguers could join with him. Croesus, nothing loath, crossed the Halys in 546 B. C., but was beaten and lost his kingdom the next year (545 B. C.).

312. Babylon's time of trial was now at hand. Unfortunately the beginning of the advance of Cyrus into the Mesopotamian valley and the details of the earlier years of the struggle, as well as the ebb and flow of party strife at Babylon are quite unknown, a gap occurring in the Annals at this point. The inscription becomes again intelligible with the seventeenth and last year of Nabuna'id (739 B. C.). The Babylonian king is now in the capital, and the usual religious ceremonials are performed. Cyrus is on the northeastern frontier. Has Nabuna'id been released from his confinement at Tema in consequence of the breaking down of the plans of his enemies? However that may be, he has gathered into Babylon the images of the gods from the length and breadth of Akkad, excepting those of Borsippa, Kutha, and Sippar, with a view either to their protection or to the aid they may supply to the capital. The action was ill-timed from the point of view of the priests of Marduk, Babylon's city god, whose prerogative and power were thus underestimated or even dishonored. Cyrus's attack upon the great system of defences was made at Upi (Opis), at the junction of the Tigris and the Turnat, where he broke through and stood on Babylonian soil in October, 539 B. C. Belshazzar and his army were beaten back. Nabuna'id sought in vain to organize the people for defence. Sippar was taken early in October, and the king fled to Babylon, closely pursued by a detachment of the Persians under Gubaru (Gobryas). It might well be thought that the broad and lofty walls of the capital would long withstand the assaults of an enemy; the narrative of Herodotus (I. 190, 191) tells how, after a tedious siege, Cyrus, in despair, set about diverting the main channel of the Euphrates and by marching his troops into the city through the river gates, thus laid open, took the defenders by surprise and captured the city. Nothing, however, could be farther from the actual event. Gubaru found friends within the walls who opened the gates soon after his arrival; Babylon fell into the hands of the Persians without a struggle. So deeply had the feuds of parties, ecclesiastical and political, eaten into the body politic that the capital was betrayed by its own citizens. The so-called Cyrus cylinder has perpetuated the memory of this infamy. There, in words written under the hand of Babylonian priests, it is said that Marduk, in wrath at the loss of his prerogative and the complaints of his servants, not only abandoned the city, but —

He searched through all lands; he saw him, and he sought the righteous prince, after his own heart, whom he took by the hand. Cyrus, king of Anshan, he called by name; to sovereignty over the whole world he appointed him. . . . Marduk, the great lord, guardian of his people, looked with joy on his pious works and his upright heart; he commanded him to go to his city Babylon, and he caused him to take the road to Babylon, going by his side as a friend and companion . . . without skirmish or battle he permitted him to enter Babylon. He spared his city Babylon in (its) calamity. Nabonidus, the king, who did not reverence him, he delivered into his hand. All the people of Babylon, all Shumer and Akkad, nobles and governors, prostrated themselves before him, kissed his feet, rejoiced at his sovereignty, showed happiness in their faces (Cyrus Cyl., 11 ff).

313. A few days later, Cyrus himself entered the city. Nabuna'id had already been captured. He was treated kindly and exiled to the east. Belshazzar was shortly afterward slain, while, as it seems, making a last stand with the remnant of his forces. The new lord worshipped at the ancient shrines, glorified the gods that had given him headship over their land and people, and received in his royal city Babylon the kings, from all quarters of the world, who came bringing their heavy taxes and kissed his feet. He called himself by the old familiar titles — "Cyrus, king of the world, the great king, the powerful king, the king of Babylon, the king of Shumer and Akkad, the king of the four quarters of the world, . . . whose reign Bel and Nabu love, whose sovereignty they longed for in the desire of their hearts." But the words are empty echoes of a vanishing past. It was, in fact, a new master of the nations, who Stood upon the ruins of the mighty Semitic communities that for millenniums had ruled the world. A man of another race, to whom the valley of the Tigris and the Euphrates was no longer the centre of human power and human civilization, whose ideals of the divine and the human world were formed under other skies, and whose empire stretched far away beyond the boundaries of Assyria in its fairest splendor, was henceforth to direct the destinies of the peoples, whose leadership of human history has been followed from its dawn to its setting. A new force had come to its own, and another chapter of human progress began.

CHRONOLOGICAL SUMMARY

By 5000 B.C.		City-states flourish in South Babylonia.
About 4500-2250		Expansion and Conflicts of City-states.
"	4500	Enshagsagana, of Kengi, victor over Kish.
"	4400	Mesilim, king of Kish, victor over Shirpurla.
"	4200	Dynasty of Ur Nina, king of Shirpurla, victor over Gishban; Stele of

Vultures.

"	4000	Lugalzaggisi, king of Gishban, ruler as far as the Mediterranean.
"	3850	Alusharshid, of Kish, conqueror of Elam.
"	3800-3750	Sargon, king of Agade, and his son Naram Sin, lords of the

Mediterranean coast-land,

of northern Mesopotamia, and of Elam.

"	3500	Ur Bau and other patesis of Shirpurla.
"	3100	Gudea, patesi of Shirpurla,
"	3000	Ur Gur and Dungi I., kings of Ur, kings of Shumer and Akkad.
"	2900	Kings of Uruk and Isin,
"	2800-2500	Second Dynasty of Ur; Dungi IL, lord of the West.
"	2450-2300	Migrations and Invasions: Arabians and Elamites enter Babylon,
"	2400-2100	First Dynasty of kings of Babylon.
"	2290	Rim Sin, Elamite king of Larsam, king of Shumer and Akkad.
"	2297-2254	Khammurabi, king of Babylon, victor over the Elamites,

unifier of Babylonia.

"	2188-2151	Ammiditana, of Babylonia, king of the West.
"	2085-1717	Second Dynasty of Babylonian kings.

In the centuries before 2000 B. C. Babylonian influence, political and commercial, was predominant in the Mediterranean coast-lands.

A SELECTED BIBLIOGRAPHY

I. GENERAL HISTORIES OF ANTIQUITY

Abbreviations

DuHA...........Duncker — The History of Antiquity (translated by Evelyn Abbott). 6 vols. London, 1877-1882.

MeyGA.........Meyer — Geschichte des Altertums. I. Geschichte des Orients bis zur Begründung des Perserreichs. Stuttgart, 1881.

MaDC..........}Maspero — Histoire ancienne des peuples de l'orient classique.

MaSN..........}Translated as three separate volumes: I. The Dawn of Civilization;

MaPE..........}II. The Struggle of the Nations; III. The Passing of the Empires.

SPCK..........}London, 1894-1900 (New York: Appleton).

MeHPM........McCurdy — History, Prophecy, and the Monuments; or, Israel and the Nations. 3 vols. New York, 1894-1901. (3d Ed. revised of Vol. I. 1898, 2d Ed. of Vol. II. 1897).

RawlGM.......Rawlinson — The Five Great Monarchies of the Ancient Eastern World. 3 vols. New York, 2d Ed., 1871.

LenHA..........Lenormant — Histoire ancienne de l'orient jusqu'aux guerres médiques (continued by Babelon). 6 vols. Paris, 1881-1888.

HeWG..........Helmolt — Weltgeschichte. Band III. Westasien (by Winckler). Leipzig, 1901.

Rommel — The Civilization of the East. Temple Primer. (Trans. from the author's Geschichte des alten Morgenlandes. Stuttgart, 1895). London, n. d.

Belck — Beiträge zur alten Geographic und Geschichte Vorderasiens, I., II. Leipzig, 1901.

KrGAG.........Krall — Grundriss der Altorientalischen Geschichte. Erster Theil: Bis auf Kyros. Wien, 1899.

WaESG.......Wachsmuth — Einleitung in das Studium der Alten Geschichte. Leipzig, 1895.

Winckler — Die Volker Vorderasiens. Leipzig, 1899.

II. BABYLONIO–ASSYRIAN HISTORY

TiBAG..........Tiele — Babylonisch–Assyrische Geschichte, Zwei Teile. Gotha, 1886-1888.

HoGBA.........Hommel — Geschichte Babyloniens und Assyriens. Berlin, 1885-1888.

WiGBA.........Winckler, Geschichte Babyloniens und Assyriens. Leipzig, 1892.

MDelGBA......Mürdter–Delitzsch — Geschichte Babyloniens und Assyriens 2teAufl. Calw und Stuttgart. 1891.

RoHBA.........Rogers — A History of Babylonia and Assyria. 2 vols. New York, 1900.

HoHBD.........Hastings' Bible Dictionary — Articles "Assyria" and "Babylonia" by Hommel.

KiEBi...........Encyclopædia Biblica — Articles "Assyria" and "Babylonia" by L. W. King.

MuBA..........Murison — Babylonia and Assyria: A Sketch of their History. (Bible Class Primers.) New York, 1901.

Winckler — Die politische Entwickelung Babyloniens und Assyriens. Leipzig, 1900.

Radau — Early Babylonian History down to the end of the fourth dynasty of Ur. New York, 1900.

BiS..............Billerbeck — Susa. Leipzig, 1893.

III. TEXTS AND TRANSLATIONS
Rawl...........Rawlinson — The Cuneiform Inscriptions of Western Asia. 5 vols. London, 1861-1884.

SchKB.........Schrader (editor) — Keilinschriftliche Bibliothek. Sammlung von assyrischen und babylonischen Texten in Umschrift und Uebersetzung. Bd. I. Historische Texte des altassyrischen Reichs. Bd. II. Historische Texte des neuassyrischen Reichs. Bd. III. 1-Hälfte, Historische Texte altbabylonischer Herrscher; 2-Hälfte, Historische Texte des neubabylonischen Reichs. Bd. IV. Texte juristischen und geschäftlichen Inhalts. Bd. V. Thontafeln von Tel-el-Amarna. (English Translation, New York, 1898). Bd. VI. Assyrisch-Babylonische Mythen und Epen. Leipzig, 1889-1901.

Layard — Inscriptions in the Cuneiform Character. London, 1851. Botta et Flandin, Monuments de Ninevé, I., III., et IV. Paris, 1849.

RP[1],[2]..........Records of the Past — Being English Translations of the Assyrian and Egyptian Monuments. I Series, 12 vols. London; II Series, 6 vols. London, 1888-1892.

ABL.............Assyrian and Babylonian Literature — Selected Translations, with a Critical Introduction by R. F. Harper (The World's Great Books). New York, 1901.

HiOBI..........Hilprecht — Old Babylonian Inscriptions, chiefly from Nippur. Philadelphia, 1893.

Editions of inscriptions of particular rulers are given in the "References."

IV. GEOGRAPHY, TRAVEL, EXPLORATION, ETC.

Rich — Narrative of a Journey to the Site of Babylon in 1811. London, 1839. Narrative of a Residence in Koordistan and on the Site of Ancient Nineveh. London, 1836.

Loftus — Travels and Researches in Chaldea and Susiana. London, 1857.

LayNR..........Layard — Nineveh and its Remains. 2 vols, New York, 1849.

LayD............Discoveries in the Ruins of Nineveh and Babylon. London, 1853.

Chesney — The Expedition for the Survey of the Rivers Euphrates and Tigris. 2 vols. London, 1850.

Rassam — Asshur and the Land of Nimrod. New York, 1897.

Oppert —Expédition scientifique en Mesopotamie. 2 vols. Paris, 1863-1867.

PeN.............Peters — Nippur; or, Explorations and Ad‑ventures on the Euphrates. 2 vols. New York, 1897.

Sachau — Reise in Syrien und Mesopotamien. Leipzig, 1883. Am Euphrat und Tigris, 1897-1898. Leipzig, 1900.

SmAD..........G Smith — Assyrian Discoveries: an Account of Explorations and Discoveries on the site of Nineveh, during 1873 and 1874. New York, 1875.

KaAuB..........Kaulen — Assyrien und Babylonien nachden neuesten Entdeckungen. 5te. Ausg. Freiburg, 1899.

SchKG..........Schrader — Keilinschriften und Geschichts‑forechung. Giessen, 1878.

DelP............Delitzsch — Wo Lag das Paradies? Leipzig, 1881.

HiRR...........Hilprecht (editor) — Recent Research in Bible Lands. Philadelphia, 1896.

EvNL...........Evetts — New Light on the Bible and the Holy Land. London, 1892.

V. RELIGION
The most important editions of texts are: King—Babylonian Magic and Sorcery, being "The Prayers of the Lifting up of the Hand." London, 1896.

Zimmern — Babylonische Busspsalmen. Leipzig, 1885.

Beiträge zur Kenntniss der Babylonischen Religion. I. Die Beschwörungstafeln Shurpu. II. Ritualtafeln für den Wahrsager, Beschwörer und Sänger. Leipzig, 1896-1899.

Tallquist — Die Assyrische Beschwörungsserie Maqlû, 1894.

Knudtzon — Assyrische Gebete an den Sonnengott für Staat und Königliches Hans. 2 Bde. Leipzig, 1893.

Thompson — The Reports of the Magicians and Astrologers of Nineveh and

Babylon. 2 vols. London, 1900.

The Treatises are:

JaRBA.........Jastrow — Religion of Babylonia and Assyria. Boston, 1898.

KiBRM.........King — Babylonian Religion and Mythology. London, 1899.

Lenormant — Chaldean Magic, its Origin and Development. London, 1877. Sayce—Lectures on the Origin and Growth of Religion as illustrated by the Religion of the Ancient Babylonians (Hibbert Lectures, 1887). London, 1887.

Jeremias — (in Saussaye, Lehrbuch d. Religionsgeschichte, 2te Ausg. Bd. I, 163221) — "Die Babylonier und Assyrer." Freiburg, 1897.

Tiele — (in Geschichte der Religion im Alter-turn, Bd. I, 127-216) — "Die Religion in Babylonien und Assyrien." Gotha, 1896.

Eerdmans — (in "Progress," 3d ser. 6, 403415) —"Babylonian-Assyrian Religion," Chicago, 1897.

Jeremias — Houle und Paradies bei den Babyloniern. Leipzig, 1900; English Translation, London, 1902.

VI. MANNERS AND CUSTOMS; ART AND LITERATURE

SaBaA.........Sayce — Babylonians and Assyrians, Life and Customs (The Semitic Series). New York, 1899. Babylonian Literature. London, n. d.

PeiSBG.......Peiser — "Skizze der babylonischen Gesellschaft," in Mitteilungen der Vorderasiatischen Gesellschaft, I. 3, Berlin, 1896.

PCHACA.....Perrot and Chipiez — History of Ancient Art in Chaldæa and Assyria. 2 vols, London.

BMG...........A Guide to the Babylonian and Assyrian Antiquities of the British Museum. London, 1900.

Bezold — Kurzgefasster Ueberblick über die Babylonisch-Assyrische Litteratur. Leipzig, 1886.

Ihering — The Evolution of the Aryan (trans, from the German). New York, 1897.

Babelon — Manual of Oriental Antiquities. New York, 1889.

Maspero — Life in ancient Egypt and Assyria. London, 1892.

Speck — Handelsgeschichte des Alterthums I. Leipzig, 1901.

VII. BABYLONIO-ASSYRIAN MONUMENTS AND THE BIBLE

Price — The Monuments and the Old Testament. Chicago, 1900.

Driver — (in "Authority and Archæology," edited by Hogarth) — "Hebrew Authority." pp. 1-152. New York, 1899.

Sayce — The Higher Criticism and the Verdict of the Monuments. London, 1894.

Hommel — The Ancient Hebrew Tradition as illustrated by the Monuments. London, 1897.

Schrader — The Cuneiform Inscriptions and the Old Testament- 2 vols.

KAT³..........Die Keilschriften und das Alte Testament. 3te Aufl. 1-Hälfte, bearb. von H. Winckler. Berlin, 1902.

Cheyne — (in "The Hexateuch" by Carpenter and Harford-Battersby, vol. I. pp. 164-171).

Wi...............Winckler — (see above under Schrader). Ball—Light from the East, or the Witness of the Monuments. London, 1899.

Vigouroux — La Bible et les découvertes modernes. 6th ed. 4 vols- Paris, 1896.

VIII. COLLECTIONS OF ESSAYS, SERIES, JOURNALS, ETC.
WiUAG........Winckler—Untersuchungen zur Altoriental‑ischen Geschichte. Leipzig, 1889. Alttestamentliche Untersuchungen. Leipzig, 1892.

WiAOF........Winckler — Altorientalische Forschungen. Erste Reihe, Heft 1-6; Zweite Reihe, Bd. I., Bd. II. Heft 1. Leipzig, 1893– .

BA Delitzsch und Haupt — Beiträge zur Assyriologie, Bd. I.–IV. Leipzig, 1890.

MVAG.........Mittheilungen der Vorderasiatischen Gesellschaft (yearly volumes in parts). Berlin, 1896.

ZK..............Bezold (editor) — Zeitschrift für Keitschrift- forschung. Leipzig, 1884-1885.

ZA.............Zeitschrift für Assyriologie. Leipzig, 1886..

EncyBrit......Encyclopædia Britannica.

EBi.............Encyclopædia Biblica, edited by Cheyne.

DB..........A Dictionary of the Bible, edited by Hastings.

AJSL.........The American Journal of Semitic Languages and Literatures (continuing Hebraica).

IX. CHRONOLOGY
Lehmann — Zwei Hauptprobleme der altorientalischen Chronologie. Berlin, 1898.

Niebuhr — Die Chronologie der Geschichte Israels, Aegyptens, Babyloniens u. Assyriens. Leipzig, 1896.

Rost — Untersuchungen zur altorientalischen Geschichte, MVAG, II. 2, 1897.

Winckler — Zur babylonisch-assyrischen Chronologie. UAG. Leipzig, 1889.

REFERENCES

INTRODUCTION

I

THE LANDS OF THE EUPHRATES AND TIGRIS
The classical descriptions of Mesopotamia are those of Herodotus, I. 193, Strabo, XVI. 1, and Pliny, N. H. XVIII. 17, The most complete modern discussion still remains that of Rawlinson in GM, I, 1-42 ("Chaldæa"), and 180-235 ("Assyria"), including land, climate, and productions. Compare EncyBrit, arts. "Babylonia," "Mesopotamia;" MaDC, 547.-560; MaSN, 597602; RoHBA, I. 266-289; TiBAG, I. 50-58; HoGBA, 180-195; KaAuB, ch. ii.; KiEBi, I-cols. 350, 420; HoHBD, I. 176, 214. The books of travel referred to in the Bibliography IV. may also be profitably consulted. Excellent maps in HBD, I. 176; EBi (art. "Assyria").

II

THE EXCAVATIONS IN BABYLONIA AND ASSYRIA
The most exhaustive account of the exploration of the lands of the Tigris and Euphrates, the excavation of the ruin-sites and the decipherment of the monuments, is that in RoHBA, I, 1-253. Less complete but accurate and more or less readable accounts are found in ABL, iii-xxxii (R, F. Harper); a series of articles by the same scholar in the Old and New Testament Student, XIV. 1 and 2, and the Biblical World, I. 4 and 5; VIII. 1; HoGBA, 58-146; KaAuB, chs. Iii., v., vi.; Delitzsch, "Assyrian Grammar," 1-8. Compare also Lyon, "A Half Century of Assyriology," in Bib. World, VIII. 2.

The narratives of the explorers and excavators contain material of the first importance and the deepest interest. The student would do well to dip into LayNR and read vol. I. ch. iii. or vol. II. ch. xiii.; and PeN, vol. I. ch. xi. or vol. II. ch. iii., to catch a glimpse of the actual experiences of the workers.

III

THE LANGUAGE AND LITERATURE
See references for ch. ii. (decipherment of inscriptions) and EvNL, ch. iv.; Mahaffy, "Prolegomena to Ancient History," 167-212; On the "Sumerian" problem the leading discussions on opposite sides are Weissbach, "Die Sumerische Frage" (for "Sumerian"), and Halévy, "Le Sumérisme et l'histoire babylonienne" (against "Sumerian"). Compare also McHPM, T. sects. 79-85; and his article in Pres. and Ref. Review, II. 6; HBD, art. "Accad" and lit. there cited. HoGBA, 237-258, sketches the Old "Sumerian" civilization with

unwarranted certainty.

Besides the works On the literature cited in the Bibliography, the religious literature is treated most fully in JaRBA (see table of cont.); Jastrow has also written on "The Text Book Literature of the Babylonians" in the Bib. World, IX. 4. Compare ABL, xxxiv-lxii, for an excellent summary of the whole subject, as also KaAuB, ch. vii. Translations of these texts are referred to in the Bibliography. See also "References" to Part I. chs. iii. and iv.

IV

CHRONOLOGY AND HISTORY
See Bibliography under IX. "Chronology" for special treatises. Good general discussions are found in RoHBA, I. 312-348; Paton, "Oriental Chronology" in Bib. World, July, 1901. A thoroughgoing article with valuable texts but not altogether up to date is that by Winckler, "Zur babylonisch-assyrischen Chronologie," in UAG, 1-46; see also Wi, "Zur babylonisch-assyrischen Geschichte" in AOF, I. 5. On Herodotus as a trustworthy oriental historian some controversy has arisen; see Sayce in the preface to his "Ancient Empires of the East," and Tolman and Stevenson "Herodotus and the Empires of the East" which is based on Nikel, "Herodot und die Keilschriftforschung." WaESG has excellent material on Berosus, Ctesias, and Ptolemy (see index). TiBAG, 12-49, goes thoroughly into the sources. The Kings' List is translated in SchKB, II. 286 f., RP², I. 13 f. (compare the Introduction); the Assyrian Limu List (Eponym Canon) in SchKB, I. 204 ff., III. ii. 143 ff., RP², II. 110 ff.

PART I. — THE CITY STATES OF BABYLONIA AND THEIR UNIFICATION UNDER BABYLON

I

THE DAWN OF HISTORY
See the histories: MaDC, 560-564; HoGBA, 195-263 (the cities), 269-280 (the surrounding peoples); TiBAG, 81-90 (the cities); McHPM, I. 77-95. The fragments of Berosus are found in Cory, "Ancient Fragments," London 1876. A readable article is Sayce, "The Antiquity of Civilized Man," in Am. Jour. of Theology, V. 4; DeIP gathers material on the early sites and districts; Lenormant, "The Beginnings of History," New York 1893, discusses the problems of early traditions. Map for period of beginnings down to 1100 B. C. in HeWG, III. 10.

II

MOVEMENTS TOWARD EXPANSION AND UNIFICATION
MaDC, 595-620; TiBAG, 100-124; HoGBA, 281-374; McHPM, I. 96-132; WiGBA, 18-49; MDelGBA, 72-84; RoHBA, 349-385. The texts are gathered in SchKB, III. i. Those found at Nippur are in Hilprecht, "Old Babylonian Inscriptions," vol. I. pts. 1 and 2, with valuable introductions. The chief Gudea texts have been published by Price, "The Great Cylinder Inscriptions (A and B) of Gudea," I., and English translations of these and other inscriptions of early rulers are made by Amiaud in RP², I. and II., "The Inscriptions of Telloh." The original publication of the Tello material was made by De Sarzec-Heuzey, "Découvertes en Chaldée." Compare EvNL, ch. V.; HiRR, "Explorations in Babylonia," 43 ff. Radau, "Early Babylonian History," New York 1900, collects and discusses thoroughly, though in a confused and difficult fashion, all this early material, and is indispensable for detailed study. On Gen. xiv.

there are discussions in the works mentioned under VII. "Babylonio-Assyrian Monuments and the Bible" in the Bibliography. Compare King, "Letters and Inscriptions of Hammurabi," I. xlix f. and EBi, art. "Chedorlaomer." The chronological problems of this chapter, revolving about the date of Sargon, have been recently attacked by Lehmann, "Zwei Hauptprobleme d. altorient. Chronologie," 1898. See Wi, "Die altmesopotamischen Reiche," in UAG, 65-90, and "Die politische Entwickelung Altmesopotamiens," in AOF, I.i.

III AND IV

CIVILIZATION OF OLD BABYLONIA
Besides the works mentioned in Bibliography VI. "Manners and Customs" and V. "Religion," compare chapters on the Babylonio-Assyrian civilization in DuHA, I. ii. chs. ii. and iii.; MaDC, 535-546, 623-700, 703-784; TiBAG, II. 485 ff. (summarizes the whole subject under "Die babylonisch-assyrische Kultur"); HoGBA, 375-406; McHPM, I.27-76; WiGBA, 5056; RawlGM, I. 61 ff.; LenHA, V. livre vi. (summarizes the whole as Tiele); MeyGA, I. 172-193; HeWG, 31-42, Simcox, "Primitive Civilizations," I. bk. ii. Texts of business documents with translations in SchKB, IV. and Meissner, "Beiträge zum Altbabylonischen Privatrecht," Leipzig 1893. On ancient Babylonian science compare the standard work of Jensen, "Die Kosmologie der Babylonier," Strassburg 1890; HBD, art. "Cosmogony" and EncyBrit. under same head.

On art, besides the great work of Perrot and Chipiez (see Bibl. VI.), compare Reber, "Ueber altchaldische Kunst," ZA, I. and II.

On the literature strictly so called, see Sayce, "Babylonian Literature," London, n. d.; Id., "The Literary Works of Ancient Babylonia" in ZK, I.; brief summaries of the Epics, etc., in HoHBD, I. 220-222; Geo. Smith, "The Chaldean Account of Genesis," N. Y. n. d. (full accounts of the legends, etc.); KiBRM, chs. iii.-v. An excellent discussion of the forms of the clay tablets, etc. in KiEBi, I. cols. 428 f.

V

THE TIMES OF KHAMMURABI OF BABYLON
MaSN, 19-50; TiBAG, 124-127; HoGBA, 407-417; McHPM, I. 132-142; WiGBA, 57-68; MDelGBA, 84-89; RoHBA, I. 386-397. The standard edition of the texts is King, "The Letters and Inscriptions of Hammurabi," 3 vols., London 1898-1900 (translations in vol. III.), introductions especially valuable. On the changes in civilization and religion, see WiGBA, 69-76, and JaRBA, ch. viii. An important article on chronology is Lindl, "Die Datenlist der ersten Dynastie von Babylon," BA, IV. 3.

PART II — THE RISE OF ASSYRIA AND ITS STRUGGLES WITH KASSITE BABYLONIA

I AND II

THE KASSITE CONQUEST AND ASSYRIAN WARS
MaSN, 111-120, 588-612; TiBAG, 127-149; HoGBA, 418513; McHPM, I. 142-151, 206-218; WiGBA, 77-100, 169171; MDelGBA, 89-94, 142-150; RoHBA, I. 398-429, II. 1-20. Delitzsch has written especially on the Kassites in his "Die Sprache der Kossäer," Leipzig

1884; see also Wi., "Die babylonische Kassitendynastie" in AOF, I. 2. The texts are in SchKB, III. i., ABL, 3 ff. (Agumkakrime), 217 ff. (Tel-el-Amarna), Winckler, "The Tel-el-Amarna Letters," London 1896 (English trans. of entire collection). HiOBI, I. i. has a valuable discussion of the Kassite kings. The "Synchronistic History" is translated in ABL, 196 ff., RP², IV. 24 ff. The early texts of the "Babylonian Chronicle" are in RP², V. 106 ff. For the other chronological documents, see "References" to Int. ch. IV.

The literature on the Tel-el-Amarna letters is large. Compare EvNL, chs. vi.-viii.; Tiele, "Western Asia according to the Most Recent Discoveries," London; Ball, "Light from the East," 86 ff.; Sayce in RP², II.-III., V. with translations. For the early patesis of Assyria, see Johns, "A new Patesi of Ashur," in AJSL, XVIII. 3.

III

CIVILIZATION AND CULTURE IN THE KASSITE PERIOD
On the Kassite civilization and early Assyrian conditions, see WiGBA, 101-110,140-151, 163-168; MaSN, 617-642; MeyGA, I. 334-336; KiEBi, cols. 351 f., 363 f., 446 f.; HoHBD, 180 f., 227. For the special interest of the Kassite kings in Nippur, see HiOBI, I. i. 30 f., and PeN, index s. v. "Kossean."

IV

THE TIMES OF TIGLATHPILESER I
MaSN, 642-670; TiBAG, 147-166; HoGBA, 514-537; McHPM, I. 219-223; WiGBA, 171-176; KrGAG, 104-107; MDelGBA, 150-156; RoHBA, II. 21-34. Texts and trans. are found in SchKB, II. 14-49 and in Lotz, "Die Inschr. Tiglath Pileser I.," Leipzig 1880. Trans. in RP², I. 86 ff.; ABL, 11 ff. On the dynasty of Pashe, see HiOBI, I. i. 38 ff. The Neb. deed of gift is trans. in ABL, 8 ff. The relations of Assyr. and Bab. are given in the Syn. Hist., col. ii. See EncyBrit. arts. "Armenia" and "Kurdistan" for geography. See also Meissner, "Der elamitische Feldzug Tiglathpileser I." in ZA, X. 101 f. Map for period 1100-745 B. C. in HeWG, III. 55.

PART III. — THE ASCENDANCY OF ASSYRIA.

I

THE ANCIENT WORLD AT THE BEGINNING OF THE FIRST MILLENNIUM
WiGBA, 176-181; RoHBA, IL 35-45; McHPM, I. 243-245; PaEHSP, 181-198; KAT³, I. 38 f.

II

ASHURNAÇIRPAL III. AND THE CONQUEST OF MESOPOTAMIA

MaPE, 3-51; TiBAG, 166-186; HoGBA, 538-588; WiGBA, 181-190; McHPM, I. 261-266; KrGAG, 125-131; RoHBA, II. 46-71; KAT³, I. 39-41. Texts, etc.: SchKB, I. L 50-129; ABL, 28-30; RP², II. 128-177, IV. 80. On the campaigns in the north, see the important papers of Streck, "Das Gebiet der heutigen Landschaften Armenien, Kurdistan und Westpersien nach den babylonisch-assyrischen Keilinschriften" beginning in ZA, XIII. 57. On the Syrian campaign, see PaEHSP, 199-202. For the Nabupaliddin inscription, see ABL, 30-33, and

BMG, 128. On Assyrian officials, see WiGBA, 209 f., and Delitzsch, "Assyrische Studien," 129-135. On the palace at Kalkhi, see LayNR, I. ch. iii.

III

THE ADVANCE INTO SYRIA AND THE RISE OF URARTU. FROM SHALMANESER II. TO THE FALL OF HIS HOUSE

MaPE, 52-114; TiBAG, 186-216; HoGBA, 589-647; WiGBA, 191-220; McHPM, I. 267-306; KrGAG, 131-141; RoHBA II. 47-103; KAT³, I. 41-49; arts. "Shalmaneser" in EBi and DB. Texts, etc.: Amiaud and Scheil: "Les Inscriptions de Salmanasar II.," Paris 1890; KB, I. i. 128-193; RP², IV. 38-79, 86-89; Hebraica, II. 140-146, III. 201-231; ABL, 33-52. on the Black Obelisk, see LayNR, I. 282 f.; on Imgur-bel gates, see PSBA, VII. 89-111. For the Babylonian Chronicle, see ABL, 200; RP², I. 22 ff. On the civilization of the time, see MeyGA,1. 420-424. On the western campaigns, see PaEHSP, 205-224. On the kingdom of Urartu, see the inscriptions trans. by Sayce, JRAS, new ser., XIV. 388 ff., RP² I. 163 f., IV. 114 f., and the epoch-making discoveries and investigations of Belck and Lehmann, Zeitschr. f, Ethnol., 1892, 131 f.; Verhand. d. Ber. anthrop. Gesellsch., 1892-1896; ZA, IX. 83 ff., XI. 197 ff., and Streck, articles cited, ZA, XIV. 103 ff. (an excellent collection of materials).

IV

THE ASSYRIAN REVIVAL. TIGLATHPILESER III. AND SHALMANESER 1V.
MaPE, 117-218; TiBAG, 217-238; HoGBA, 648-678 WiGBA, 221-235; McHPM, I. 323-338, 347-358, 372-395; KrGAG, 141-146; RoHBA, II. 104-147; KAT1, I. 49-63; arts. Tp. III, and Shal. IV. in EBi and DB. Texts, etc.; Rost, "Keilschrifttexte Tiglath Pileser III." Leipzig 1893; ABL, 52-58; RP², V, 115 ff.; KB, I. ii. 2-33; SmAD, ch. xiv, For the north-Syrian campaigns, see the inscriptions from Samal in MaOS, XI., Berlin 1893, and PaEHSP, 229-244; Jeremias, "Tyrus," Leipzig 1891, 27 ff.; Wi, "Das Syrische Land Jaudi," usw. in AOF, I, i.; Wi, Assyrien u, Tyrus seit Tp. III., AOF, II. i. 65-70.

V

THE ASSYRIAN EMPIRE AT ITS HEIGHT. SARGON II.
MaPE, 221-273; TiBAG, 238-282; HoGBA, 678-741 (here the house of Sargon is treated as a whole); WiGBA, 236-249; McHPM, I. 395-401, II. 237-247, 266-271; KrGAG, 146-152; RoHBA, II, 148-182; MeyGA, I. 460-463; KAT³, I. 63-75; arts. "Sargon" in EBi and DB. Texts, etc.: Winckler, "Die Keilschrifttexte Sargon's," Leipzig 1889; Lyon, "Keilschrifttexte Sargon's," Leipzig 1883; KB, I. ii. 34-81; ABL, 59-64; SmAD, ch. XV. For the Mardukbaliddin inscr., see ABL, 64-68. On the civilization of the Sargonid age, see WiGBA, 293-302, and a brilliant sketch in Maspero, "Life in anc. Egypt and Assyria," London 1892. On the Sargon palace, see the great illustrated works of Botta and Place; KaAuB, ch. iv., and PCHACA, On the western expeditions, see PaEHSP, 244-251; Jeremias, "Tyrus," 30; Wi, "Die Sargoniden und Egypten," usw., in UAG, 91-108; "Samal unter Sargon," AOF, H. i. 71-73. On the Elamite wars, see BiS, 77-82. On Muçri, see Wi, "Musri, Melukha, Main," in MVAG, III. i. and iv.; and in AOF, .I i.; AT, Untersuchungen, 168-174; also KATE, I. 136-153.

VI

THE STRUGGLE FOR IMPERIAL UNITY. SENNACHERIB
MaPE, 273-346; TiBAG, 285-325; WiGBA, 249-259; McHPM, II. 272-302, 322-332;
KrGAG, 152-157; RoHBA, IL 183-215; KATE, I. 75-86; arts, "Senn." in EBi and DB. Texts,
etc.: Smith (G), "History of Sennacherib," London 1878; SchKB, I. ii. 80-119; Pognon,
"L'inscr. de Bavian," Paris 1879; RP², VI, 80-101; ABL, 68-80; SmAD, ch. xvi. Meissner u.
Rost, "Bauinschriften Sanheribs."

On the western campaigns, see PaEHSP, 251-262; Jeremias, "Tyrus," 31 ff. On the Elamite
campaigns, see BiS, 82-92; and for the Battle of Khalule, Haupt, in Andover Review, May,
1886. On topography of Nineveh, see SmAD, ch. vi., and Billerbeck u. Jeremias, "Der
Untergang Nineveh's," in BA, III. 87-188.

VII

IMPERIAL EXPANSION AND DIVISION, ESARHADDON
MaPE, 346-381; TiBAG, 325-351; WiGBA, 259-272; McHPM, II. 333-350; KrGAG, 157-
159; RoHBA, II. 216-245; KATE, I. 86-92; arts, "Esarh." in EBi and DB. Texts, etc.: Budge,
"History of Esarhaddon," London 1880; Harper, "Esarhaddon Inscr," (cyl. A and B), New
Haven 1888; SchKB, I. ii. 120-153; ABL, 80-94; Meissner u. Rost, "Bauinschr. Asarh.," in
BA, III. 189-362; the Samal inscription in MaOS, Ausgr. in Sendschr. i. 36-41; SmAD, ch.
xvii. For the western campaigns, see PaEHSP, 262-265; Jer., "Tyrus," 35 f.; AOF, II. i. 11 ff.
For the northern campaigns and the oracles thereupon, see Knudtzson, Gebete (Bibliog. III.).

VIII

THE LAST DAYS OF SPLENDOR. ASHURBANIPAL
MaPE, 381-442, 459-464; TiBAG, 351-400; WiGBA, 272-302; McHPM, II. 351-390;
KrGAG, 159-164; RoHBA, II. 246-282; MeyGA, I. 480-482,483-496; KAT ³, I. 92-98; arts.
"Ashurb." in EBi and DB. Texts, etc.: Smith (G.), "History of Ashurbanipal," London 1871;
Smith (S. A.), "Keilschrifttexte Asurbanipals," Leipzig 1887-1889; SchKB, I. ii. 152-269;
ABL, 94-130; Sm AD, ch. xviii.

For the Babylonian campaigns, see Lehmann, "Shamashshumukin," Leipzig 1892; BiS, 96-
120; ABL, 130f. On the Western campaigns, see PaEHSP, 265-270; Jer., "Tyrus," 37 ff.;
Haupt, "Wateh-ben-Hazael," in Hebraica, I. 4. On the art and literature of the time, see
PCHACA, DuHA, III. iv. ch. ix., and for the library, Rassam, "Asshur," etc., 31; Menant, "La
Bibliothek du Palais de Ninevé."

IX

THE FALL OF ASSYRIA
MaPE, 445-458; TiBAG, 400-415; HoGBA, II. 742-746; McHPM, II. 391-414; WiGBA, 290-
292; KrGAG, 165-169; RoHBA, II. 283-295; KAT³, I. 104 f.; Billerbeck and Jeremias, "Der
Untergang Nineveh's," usw. in BA, III. 87-188; Johnston, "The Fall of the Assyrian Empire"
in Studies in honor of B. L. Gildersleeve, Balt. 1902. Texts, etc.: SchKB, I. ii. 268-273; for the
Nabuna'id inscriptions, see ABL, 158-168; Messerschmidt, "Die Stele Nabuna'id's" in MVAG,
I. i.; for the Greek fragments, see Cory, "Ancient Fragments," etc., London 1876, 83-90. See

Wi, "Zur Medischen u. altpersischen Gesch." in UAG, 109-132, and "Kimmerier, Ashguzäer, Skythen," in AOF, I. vi.; KAT1, I. 100-103.

PART IV. —THE NEW BABYLONIAN (OR KALDEAN) EMPIRE

I

THE HEIRS OF ASSYRIA
MaPE, 486-518; TiBAG, 416-424; WiGBA, 303-310; Ro HBA, II. 297-315. Texts, etc.: SchKB, III. ii. 2-9; ABL, 131- 134. On the Kaldi, see Wi, "Die Stellung der Chaldäer in der Gesch.," in UAG, 47-64.

II

NEBUCHADREZZAR AND HIS SUCCESSORS
MaPE, 518-567; TiBAG, 424-441, 454-458; HoGBA, 749-777; WiGBA, 311-314; McHPM, III. 143-171, 220-244, 268-305; KrGAG, 170-182; RoHBA, II. 316-358; MeyGA, I. 587-592; KAT³, I. 106-110; arts. "Nebuchadrezzar " in EBi and DB; Harper, "Nebuchadnezzar, King of Babylon," in Bib. World, XIV. 1. Texts, etc.: SchKB, III. ii. 10-79, 140 f.; ABL, 134-157; RP², III. 102-123.

For the western campaigns, see PaEHSP, 271-278; Jer, "Tyrus," 40-48. For the religion of Neb. see JaRBA, chs. xiv., xvii. 295-299. For the fortifications of Bab., see Billerbeck, "Nebuchadnezzar's Befestigung," usw. MVAG, III. ii. For Wi's theory of Bab. politics, see "Zur inneren Politik," usw. AOF, II. ii. 1, and KAT³, I. 108-112.

III

BABYLONIA UNDER THE KALDEANS
TiBAG, 441454; McHPM, III. 152-159, 321-393; WiGBA, 320-325; RawlGM, II, 497-580, III. 1-33. See also SaBaA (passim); PeiSBG, in MVAG, I. iii. (passim); Marx, "Die Stellung der Frauen," usw. BA, IV. 1-77; EvNL, chs. x., xi., xvi. For the religion, see JaRBA, ch. xiv.

Texts of business documents in SchKB, IV. 176 ff,; Kohler u, Peiser, "Aus dem Babylonischen Rechtsleben," Leipzig 1891; RP², III. 124 f., IV. 96 ff., V. 141 f. On Babylon, see a popular sketch of recent discoveries by Jastrow, "The Palace and Temple of Nebuchadnezzar," Harper's Mag. Apr. 1902, and the official reports in Mitteilungen d. Deu. Orient-Gesellschaft, 6 ff.; also McGee, "Zur Topographie Babylons," usw. in BA, III. 520-560.

IV

THE FALL OF BABYLON.
MaPE, 567f.; TiBAG, 459-484; HoGBA, 777-790; WiGBA, 315-319; McHPM, III. 393-414; KrGAG, 182-184; RoHBA, II. 359-381; KATE. I. 110-115. Texts, etc.: SchKB, III., ii. 80-139; ABL, 157-174; RP², V. 144-176. See Hagen "Keilschrifturkunden zur Gesch. d, k. Cyrus," in BA, II. 1, and the Bibliography under VII. "Bab. Assyr. Mon. and the Bible."